The Sangreal Tarot

The Sangreal Tarot

*A Magical Ritual System
of Personal Evolution*

William G. Gray

SAMUEL WEISER, INC.
York Beach, Maine

First published in 1988 by
Samuel Weiser, Inc.
Box 612
York Beach, Maine 03910

Library of Congress Cataloging-in-Publication Data

Gray, William G.
    The Sangreal tarot.

    1. Tarot.   I. Title.
BF1879.T2G714   1988   133.3'2424   88-17118
ISBN 0-87728-665-5

Typeset in 11 point Goudy
Printed in the United States of America

Contents

Preface

This is not a book for students who are looking for a beginning book on the tarot. Nor is this a book for those who are only interested in the tarot for fortune-telling purposes. It is meant as a guide for sincere followers of our Western Inner Way who are looking for methods of *using* the tarot cards as a practical means of gaining what might be termed a Sangreal-state of spiritual awareness. It is intended for those who are seriously seeking a deeper and more mystical significance behind the tarot, which has become so much a part and parcel of our modern Western esotericism. The Sangreal Tarot is the latest investigative step along the line of inner light leading to the strange spiritual truths presented symbolically by the tarot itself. Some people may find this work difficult to follow. My best advice is that you should read only a little at a time—say perhaps a single chapter at a time—then put the book aside to allow your subconscious mind time to digest the concepts. Commence study again only when you feel ready to do so.

It has been my aim in writing this book to take a single spiritual ideal (in this case the Sangreal) and relate it to the tarot so that the tarot can amplify and explain the Sangreal from a different perspective. This has already been done with the Qabbalistic Holy Tree of Life, but in this work I have drawn on another base-pattern, the Cosmic Circle-Cross, sometimes called the Solar Cross since it aligns with our usual concepts of cosmos from a seasonal standpoint. Both are dealt with in this book, the former rather briefly since it is covered more fully elsewhere. The pattern of the Circle-Cross is treated in depth in this work—this is the first time a Sangreal arrangement of the tarot has ever appeared in print.

So what may you expect to gain from a study of this work? First and foremost, a spiritual experience which could well change the course of a lifetime if applied as indicated by the tarot system outlined herein. Secondly, an opportunity to see the tarot as something more than a mere pack of Gypsy fortune-telling cards. Instead, you will be meeting them as an extremely careful arrangement of principles and precepts intentionally designed to lead human beings toward their divine destiny. Thirdly, this is a chance to study the tarots seriously according to the latest light shed upon them from an unusually recondite source.

Perhaps you may have heard cards called the "Devil's Bible" by puritanical people? This book shows that the tarot cards are exactly the opposite. A good guide to God for all those students who are able to follow the secret patterns portrayed by their single or associated meanings. In fact the tarot might be fairly called our contemporary Urim and Thummim which the old high priests of Israel once consulted when confronted with what seemed like insoluble problems demanding special help and advice from their God to cope with. With the sincere intention that this book will help solve at least some of the same problems disguised in modern dress, it is hopefully offered to all fellow Wesoterics.

Wm. G. Gray

CHAPTER ONE

An Introduction to the Sangreal Tarot

T HIS IS NOT just another book about tarot. We are going to look at the tarot from the Sangreal viewpoint to see the spiritual significance of the tarot in terms of today's values and tomorrow's possibilities. In this first chapter, we will consider what the Sangreal means and then review the concepts represented by the Ten Spheres on the Tree of Life. We will then discuss the Four Ways, and finally, present a methodology for integrating the tarot with ourselves. Armed with these basics, we will then delve into the cards and learn how the Sangreal tarot system provides us with a workable way of dealing with our Western Esoteric tradition.

For our purposes, any tarot deck will do. The real tarot are not pieces of printed cardboard at all but are only a visual representation of their concepts as understood by their designers. The true tarot are symbols of our collective consciousness, collated with each other so as to make spiritual sense out of our every experience. There are very many tarot decks to choose from, but you will probably want to stick with the "classics" – the Marseilles Deck or the Rider-Waite Deck.

The tarot can certainly answer our self-searching questions; but they will not answer so much by the spread of the cards as by the direct communication they make with our inner beings. So we will be looking at the "language" of the tarot—how it speaks to us. Looking at the tarot through a Sangreal "lens" will make that language clear to us. But before we can get into the tarot in any detail, it is best to briefly describe some of the major concepts concerning the Sangreal itself.

What Is the Sangreal?

The general idea is that at some uncertain point of our very remote prehistory, an entirely new type of consciousness came to this planet and commenced a breeding program among the then animalistic humanoids, which has since completely changed them into the beings we have now become. That was the beginning of our civilization, accounting for all our evolutionary trends, and is still impelling our species towards some unknown ultimate and obviously very superior state of spiritual existence quite apart from this particular planet. For the sake of identification, this influence has been called the *Sangreal*, which is synonymous with Blood-Royal, and later the fabulous "Holy Grail."[1]

This might raise suppositions about a spaceship coming from some dying planet in a remote galaxy, searching for somewhere to colonize so their species would continue elsewhere in favorable conditions. That could have been possible, but on the other hand there might have been no necessity for a physical spaceship of any sort. Suppose such postulated beings did not inhabit bodies, but were pure energy held together by concentrated consciousness? We know nothing of the details behind their visit and only inherited intuition tells us anything of its happenings whatever. All we have to rely on are the uncertain

---

[1]For further information on the Sangreal, interested readers should see the section entitled A Sangreal Catechism, from my book *Sangreal Ceremonies and Rituals*, Volume 4 in the Sangreal Sodality Series, published in 1986 by Samuel Weiser, York Beach, Maine.

factors of race-remembrance in our genetics, which are only as true as the trust we place in them.

Those early visitors may not have looked anything like us at all, although the chances are there was a faint resemblance at least between the different orders of being. They could even have been a *virus* which worked its way into human systems until it was strongly enough established to identify with humanity and continue its species through biological reproduction. Many types of virus can live in space conditions and travel through incalculable dimensions of time and distance. There is nothing to suggest that every type of virus is something evil and destructive to living creatures. The sort of beings we are talking about now were plainly just the reverse.

All indications are that these visitors were very far in advance of the humanoid races they found inhabiting this planet. Their intelligence was greatly beyond anything we know today, and their consciousness was certainly capable of abilities far beyond what we can imagine. So what made them take the slightest interest in human animals or start their close contact with our earliest ancestors? We may only presume that the species were somehow suitable and necessary for the survival of the visitants, or that their motives were entirely altruistic and derived from high spiritual sources. Both alternatives could have been true, but it makes no difference to us now which was the most probable. We are what we have become at present because of that initial impulse at the commencement of human history. Such are the bare bones of the Sangreal story.

It might well be said that if our primal progenitors were as wonderful as that, why did they not leave some memorial of themselves on earth to mark the event? Something solid in stone maybe, or an enduring artifact that might make mankind wonder at the strange inscriptions millions of years later—some permanent record of their presence among us. This they did, but not in stone, metal, or anything of an outwardly evident nature whatever. They "wrote" in and on nature itself. Their records are written forever in our genetics and inscribed in characters formed from our very blood. They perpetrated themselves in patterns—made not only by combinations of every living cell in our physical bodies, but also by those made in our minds out of constructed consciousness. We, their living descendents, *are* the characters they wrote their identity-names with all over the face of this world and possibly many others also.

Out of such deep "divine designs" at the rock bottom of our human natures there occasionally floats to the surface of our very limited consciousness some recognizable pattern, or symbol, which stirs or awakens a vague awareness of something important at the back of our beings, something we feel we ought to think about—or do something with—for the sake of our welfare as evolving entities. That may be all we know on the surface, so we call it an instinct; but factually it is our genetics talking to us through the medium of whatever the surface-encounter symbols were. They are usually simple enough, and in this work we are going to look at two symbolic systems that connect the very deepest life-layer of our spiritual subconsciousness with the most modern concentration of consciousness we can manage. The first is the familiar Tree of Life pattern, and the second is the Circle-Cross symbolizing the Sangreal and displaying the same fundamentals in a different type of design.

The Tree of Life pattern and the Circle-Cross symbol are very closely connected with the tarot, which has so recently become peculiarly popular among Wesoterics.[2] Why should this be so? Prior to the world wars at the beginning of this century neither tarots nor the Tree of Life were known to any wide extent at all. The former were associated with gypsy fortune tellers mainly on the European continent, and the latter was more or less confined to students of Hebraic folklore and those relatively few people interested in esoterica of various kinds. Within less than a human life span, both have become topics of almost worldwide study and endless books have been written about them. The point is whether we are trying to reach them with our consciousness or they are trying to reach us with theirs.

---

[2]Wesoterics is a term I coined to describe Western people who are pursuing an esoteric tradition.

Maybe it is mutual, but if so, why the hurry and apparent intensity? Could it be that they are trying to catch up with our consciousness on ordinary surface levels of life while there is yet time and opportunity to do so? Those are surely fair questions calling for some considered answers.

The first query arising is whether designs like the Tree of Life, the Circle-Cross, the tarot deck, and many other collections of symbols are not actually arrangements of Archetypes printed, as it were, into our genes long ago by those responsible for our becoming more than mere animals. Are they now almost desperately trying to attract our attention through the only relics of their language left with us? If so, then why so, and are the answers to be found through the signs set before us linking us with a consciousness so close that we cannot stand back and view it objectively? This book is being written from a feeling that such could very well be the case.

After all, the main concern of cosmic creatures like those sometimes called the Lords of Life would be to continue their species throughout cosmos as evenly as possible and according to the evolution rate applying to every area in question. Therefore their earth-mission might be to find a compatible life-form, develop it to the utmost, and then either move it along to another area of existence or abandon the experiment altogether and begin again elsewhere. After millions of earth years their inner pushings have propelled us along our paths of progression until we have reached our present point of planetary peril. Humanity has now come to a crux in its so-called civilization and culture. We are at the position of either rising to the heights of amazing developments ahead, or plunging into the depths of our destruction. Small wonder then that the consciousness which dragged us out of a dim past should display some signs of concern regarding our activities. Their problem is whether or not humanity as a life-species is worth salvaging.

This is not greatly different than the problems faced by an ordinary banking corporation in the normal course of earth-events. Is a crumbling business worth saving or not? There are endless factors to take into consideration. It would have a structure of some kind, however shaky that might seem, and it would also have some assets, connections, and possibly a workforce – even if all these are unsatisfactory. To close everything down and dispose of assets is certainly going to cost *something*. The potential backers either have to make a profit out of their investment, or simply close the business, cut the losses, and look for more likely prospects. This is common commerical procedure which everyone takes for granted. How many realize that this applies to life in other than earth-economy terms?

If the human race was backed by developers in the far past of our history, perhaps now they are calculating whether it will be worth continuing that spiritual support considering the condition humans have come to in contemporary circumstances. Their investment took the form of energy poured into this planet as pure consciousness to be processed by human beings. Has our humanity not only proved a loss but also incurred debts it is very unlikely to pay off in the foreseeable future? Bluntly, has this planet enough time left for human beings to prove profitable?

Money is only being used here as an analogy to be considered metaphorically in relation to method. The simple facts are that the evolution of the human race took incredible amounts of energy which had to come from somewhere, and that "somewhere" was what humans have come to call "God," or whatever else they choose to name their life-source. The agency that applied such energy to our species has a special sort of intelligence which we have termed the "Sangreal." This was intended to structure a spiritual scheme of evolution to make humanity into something very special, which might eventually entitle our human species to earn its own seat at the Council of Cosmos, later symbolized by the Round Table. How far are we falling from that mark, and shall we ever be fit to sweep the floor of that imaginary chamber?

On the other hand, we have no right to assume ourselves unfit for service anywhere. Given enough time and application, we could yet come very close to a satisfactory state for working this world into a much better shape than it is at present. Everything depends on how we think and act, and our thinking depends on how closely we can make and keep contact with the fundamental forms of consciousness responsible for humanizing us in the first place. These are with us still—underneath everything we have piled on top of them through the ages. All that is needed is clearer communication between the top and bottom of our beings coupled with the firm intention of following out the initial instructions of what we may as well call our Divine Designer.

Under ordinary circumstances, this channel of communication is not clear at all, and in many cases there is no such channel observable. Most of us can only partially clear it with considerable trouble and rearrangement of our thinking processes. At best, only a "watered down" and very much distorted version of those inner instructions ever reach the point in our normal consciousness that would convert them into action or store them for information. That is certainly better than no communication whatever, and even that much depends on our efforts to establish and improve its workings. Methodology is another matter. Some use prayer, others meditation, some combine these in ritual practice, and most humans find some system of approach that seems to suit them best. One of the most primitive was the practice of counting or numeration.

How often has it been said, "Count to ten before you answer"? In other words take time to think first. Very sound advice, but who considers how the ability to count developed human mentality in the early stages of our evolution? The action of counting cannot be done without expenditure of effort and calculated employment of consciousness. You can observe and react almost automatically, but that is not thinking in the sense of deliberately applying awareness for specific purposes. All animals react a lot faster than we do and we once acted with the same instinctual ability. When we developed the art of thinking however, we became capable of counting, or assessing amounts in terms of relationship with each other and ourselves. Thinking and counting became a process of consciousness, separating one thought from another while connecting them together like a chain. Very slow and laborious to begin with, then subsequently speeding up to keep pace with progress. Putting one with one to make two became a procedure of volitional intelligent thought.

The chances are that counting began with the fingers, which is still an instinctual habit. Since fingers are limited to ten, ten was the pattern first laid as a foundation stone for human constructive consciousness. Even now in the computer age we still rely on the decimal system and it seems to work for us with unabated usefulness. The decade, or tenfold pattern, has followed us for untold centuries instructing, informing, and inspiring the human mind to greater and greater abilities of awareness. Possibly the greatest ten point construction of consciousness produced from our underlying patterns of genetic arrangement is the Tree of Life, as set forth for our consideration by the Holy Qabbalah, or inner tradition of Israel, handed down through the centuries and enhanced by many Gentile hands.

This Tree of Life should be well enough known to Wesoterics not to need any elaborate or exhaustive explanations here, but a fairly rapid recapitulation could be of practical use in relation to the tarot. The fundamental idea behind both was to associate an idea with a number so that when one was counted, its attached ideology would be automatically called into consciousness, even if only to a slight extent. Prayer counting, too, is a most ancient practice, and by combining prayers with numbers all sorts of ideas come to mind. Rosaries are still with us and they began as counting beads put to religious uses. They are still in bunches of ten with the Christian versions.

The ten points of the Tree of Life are connected by a system of lines known as the Paths or Channels. We can imagine ourselves as plodding from one life-concept to another, or as a force flowing freely from the Godhead connecting all the Ten God-aspects together as a whole. Since there were twenty-two of these Paths, they became aligned with the letters of the Hebrew alphabet. The Tree as a whole was brought into being by the sheer energy of the Infinite expressed by the power of numbers and letters making words, and the Master Word was believed to be the Divine Name IHVH (Yahweh). That again explained the creative process in four stages of consciousness: believing, conceiving, formatting, and expressing. So there we have a correspondence too close to be coincidental between the tarot and the Tree of Life. Ten concepts for the Tree, twenty-two channels for the trumps, and a quarternity connecting the four suits with the "Great Name of God," which was described as a tetragrammaton, or four-letter word.

Because the Tree idea is older than the tarot we will consider it first, and then transfer the entire ideology over to the more recent Sangreal system. The Tree has already been considered in detail in *The Talking Tree*,[3] and any careful study of the subject in other works will prove of great value. We will begin here with a résumé of the ten concepts or Spheres of the Tree from apex — in the very highest imaginable type of life — to base — at the very bottom as we know it in this everyday world on earth.

[3]William G. Gray, *The Talking Tree* (York Beach, ME: Samuel Weiser, Inc. 1977)

CHAPTER TWO

The Tree of Life

THE QABBALISTIC TREE of Life and the tarot are inseparable. The ten spheres of the Tree, each approachable from four angles, relate to the Minor Arcana. The twenty-two connections between the spheres—the paths—align neatly with the twenty-two cards of the Major Arcana, usually called the trumps. The "people cards"—or Kings, Queens, Knights and Pages—can be associated with the paths as well. In the version of the Tree of Life portrayed in figure 1 on page 12, we see that each path is aligned with a letter of the Hebrew alphabet, as well as with the 22 letters of the Latin alphabet. Why 22 letters and not 26? Because in this system we subtract the vowels, and then add in an old English character, *Th*. This character is used to indicate the final path joining the body of the Tree with Concept Ten—the world as we experience it in our ordinary lives.

Just as letters can be associated with each other to form word meanings, so can cards representing life meanings be linked together in patterns that will make "sense." Each separate tarot card is like one "lump of life," which, when put together with other cards, offers a comprehensive view of the entire life. The tarot is like a jigsaw puzzle—each piece, when viewed with the whole, presents a picture that makes sense. Before we go into detail drawing associations between each piece (or card) in the

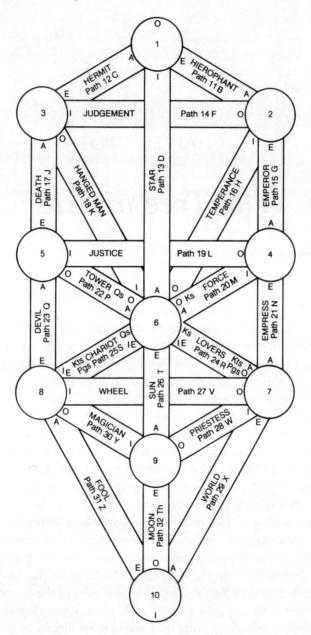

Figure 1. The Tarot on the Tree of Life.

puzzle, let's first look at the individual cards to comprehend their own particular significance. The logical thing to do is to grasp their concepts as ascribed to the Holy Tree of Life. This has already been covered exhaustively in previous publications, so we will only review them fairly rapidly here.

The Ten Concepts

Initially we have Concept Zero, or "pre-life." The nil-factor of Negative Existence. All we have not yet become, which we mean to become, and everything we have no intention of ever becoming. The unexplored universe. Apparent emptiness. In the original Hebrew, the word "ain," usually translated as "nothing," actually derives from two small interjections "eh na?" signifying where or what now. In modern colloquial speech this would be said as, "And so?" That makes all the difference in the world as to how the zero-concept should be approached. It is the eternal enigma of life which we never solve on this earth, yet without it our lives are nothing indeed. Take it away from us and we have nothing really worth living for; alter the letters to make "ani," and that in Hebrew means "I," the "Me who is." The self in the process of selection from nil. Wesoterics have made the mistake of fearing and undervaluing their concepts of Nothing, equating this with unimportance, total insignificance, and even something evil, whereas in reality it is the supreme meaning behind every possibility of being. The saying "Nothing is greater than God," indicates Infinity beyond Divinity. A law larger than life. We can really do nothing with NOTHING except wonder and worship while awaiting it. We cannot think of nothing. The most we can do is search for suitable symbology which might inspire us to become living question marks aiming ourselves at an indefinitely receding reply from the "Voice of the Void." In arriving Nowhere, we shall encounter everything else on the way. No matter how we connect ourselves with this preconcept of the Holy Tree of Life, our entire train of con-

sciousness has to be focused through the mathematical value of
the cypher or zero.

Concept One

Concept One of the Tree is the Apex, the Crown, or Summit.
Here we connect with the highest angle life can reach short of
disappearing into the Nothing, and its first appearance as any
kind of existence. It stands for the Single Spirit which contains
all consciousness throughout creation so that its incalculable
individual lives amount to only One. At the end of everything
there is but One of us, and this is IT. Here is every idea of
uniquity, our slightest suspicions of a controlling consciousness
behind all cosmos, and our beliefs in the possibility of a Supreme
Being. The mere suggestion of a single purpose within our lifestream, which is steadily leading us towards some inscrutable
state of perfection, and all such intimations, point unhesitatingly to Concept One of the Tree. Whether we will ever arrive at
this pinnacle, or alternately be broken up for fuel to supply its
energy expenditures, it will employ us one way or the other since
we are part and parcel of its economy. The Tree teaches us that
we shall have a chance of deciding our ultimate fate if we really
intend to individuate through our incarnationary experiences
and evolve beyond animal-body types of human housing. It
further indicates that such is the reason why our "Gods" are
ready to talk with us if we become capable of listening to them
intelligently. They, like us, are linked to the single Life-Spirit
evoked in our ordinary awareness by Tree – Concept One. They
have specific functions and obligations to fulfill within the
Great Life analogous to our miscrocosmic organisms. It is all
part of the serial story they are trying to tell us for the sake of
our eventual education and possible inclusion in the "intelligence network" which amounts to a nervous system distributed
throughout the Cosmic Corpus. Like them, the complete cycle
of our existence begins and ends with Concept One.

Concept Two

Concept Two is Wisdom: Here we come to a special category of consciousness, sometimes considered male because of its analytical characteristics, as contrasted with its complementary stream of intuitive or feminine awareness. It is really one side of a polarized power which cannot exist without the other. This duo-division of life is the primary pattern of its initial activity. Life cells multiply and commence making themselves into complex constructions by the simple process of splitting (mitosis), and subsequently recombining in another fashion. The Tree does exactly the same, and did so long before biology ever became an exact science. Here we have the essence of masculinity per se, its old title being Wisdom, which puzzles a few people who associate that word with feminity in the scriptures due to the bivalancy of gender. It could be used either way, like the Greek Sophos or Sophia. Wisdom as a pure principle is common to both sexes and either can use it as their polarity determines. In this case, we are considering the male half of humanity and its equivalent cycle of energy in the Creative Consciousness. An ideal human being may be a perfectly balanced combination of both sexes in one individual, but we have not yet evolved to that point on this planet, and we ought to take the facts of our lives as we come to them. We should never forget that the Tree of Life is a perfection pattern, and therefore we must think about its Spheres and system only in the light of whatever helps humanity develop and grow towards a condition of "divinity" relative to our present position on the scale of existence. So in using Concept Two types of consciousness we are specifically directing ourselves into relationship with divinity as a polarized power from a masculinized angle of approach.

Concept Three

Concept Three is Understanding: This is the equal and opposite complementary of Two, and neither could exist without the other—like halves of the same body. We usually think of this as feminine because its awareness is of the intuitive and comprehensive type. One might say this is the gestative sort which creatively develops and produces what Concept Two has implanted embryonically. If Two is the seed, then Three is the soil and its nutriment. Two may be the inspiration of an idea, but Three is its germination until it is ready to emerge as an independent unit of intelligence. Theologically, if Concept One was the Holy Spirit, then Concept Two would be God the Father, and Three God the Mother. God the Child does not appear until Six—the apex of another Trinity. The sequence may be logically One, Two, Three, and Four, but with the Tree design Spheres Four and Five are essential life-adaptive factors assuring the mutual relationship of Six with Two and Three. Considered for itself, Concept Three is the matrix of our consciousness, carrying it into constructive continuity and keeping it going from one generation to another until the end of time. Birth and Death alike are equal events here. This is the Mother from whose womb we emerge into this earth and whose mouth eats us up at the end of each incarnation. We cycle our living through her. She is nature on a very high level of life indeed, and we are only one species of her cosmic children inhabiting this temporary home. Our happier habitat is the depths of her subconscious mind where we may dream securely in her welcoming womb awaiting projection into whatever objective world she may send us. When we are eventually worn out she will run us through her regenerating process and think us out again so long as our little lives contribute something of value to the whole idea behind everything. To summon all contacts with such kinds of thinking by a single concentration point in Concept Three may seem an unlikely proposition, yet it does prove practical.

Concept Four

Concept Four is Mercy: This might perhaps be thought of as the *ne plus ultra* of the "live and let live" principle. Mercy on a scale akin to madness almost, and only method saves it from exploding itself into extinction. Here we have the analogy of the human male sperm pouring out by the millions, with apparent abandon, when only one will complete its journey to conception. Their cheery Creator seems to cry, "Let them all have a chance and may the best one win," and sporting bets are placed on likely winners. We might even imagine a genial Father-God holding a human race meeting for his own entertainment. Some old wit claimed that God invented man with a shout of laughter. May we hope not to be disinvented one day with a sigh of regret from the same source. Laughter is actually a very high form of worship, and here is its origin in the release of "rightness" as a flood of fulfillment. Providence with a capital P. All the resources of cosmos assured to anyone willing to accept them, regardless of payment, price, or responsibility. The benefits of Jupiter with their built-in banes. Every expansive (and expensive) idea of improvement and enhancement of life. Blessings, beneficences, and all kinds of wonder worked on our behalf through alignment with this class of consciousness. Virtually no end to the liberality and compassion of a Creative Consciousness anxious to build its human play-people into the best specimens they are capable of becoming. Put in childlike terms, the better we make ourselves, the happier God would be for his own sake. Though common sense ought to curtail our impressions of euphoria, it is still pleasant to think we may establish contact with Concept Four of the Tree by concentrating on that figure.

Concept Five

Concept Five is Severity: We now come to a salutary stop with this injunction of Severity, which is the law of strict selection for the sake of survival. One sperm out of millions is saved. Only one individual will reach puberty out of many. Few of those will make old bones. Spiritual survival works on the same principle. Unless this control factor limited the largesse of Concept Four, our lives on this earth (and elsewhere) would have been impossible long ago. Both Concepts Four and Five are indispensable to each other for the economy of existence. We may be reminded of the Good Fairy Godmother who wished the Pampered Princess a little trouble to balance her colleague's idiotic plethora of presents, but she knew exactly what she was doing. It may be often true that Concept Five seems to over-control our lives, but while we swing them around so wildly in this world, it has little option. The cosmic laws of compensation are exact in the end even if they take many of our little lifetimes to work out. There is no question whatever of "divine punishment" in the sense of an offended God retaliating like an annoyed child on misbehaving humans. There never was. It is simply that cosmos can only keep functioning correctly by balancing its condition continually. We have to do the same in our smaller state of being. If our bodies cannot correct their unbalances adequately, we die. Literally they have to wipe out millions of viral and microscopic lives every day so that we may go on living. To save what we need we must eliminate what threatens its integrity. Insofar as we ourselves are involved with the lifestream of cosmic consciousness, the laws by which it lives compel it to take equivalent measures with us. If we become incompatible with that consciousness, it must ultimately and automatically either neutralize us, or convert us into absorbable energies. Nothing more complicated than that. There are very wide issues concerned with Concept Five, and they will all come under that heading once we learn how to use it as a call-sign.

Concept Six

Concept Six is Beauty: This is the point of balance and harmony in the entire plan. Consciousness originates at One, separates at Two, gestates at Three, expands at Four, contracts at Five, and now settles to its regular life-rate at Six. All life systems have rhythms which are regulated by some special center, and this is it on the Tree—which is why it aligns with the human heart, and also the sun of our solar system. Every idea linking concepts of centralization, harmonious relationships among groups, beautiful arrangements of associated units, and similar connections, has a natural affinity with Concept Six. In fact, without it life as we know it could not continue here at all. Four and Five would cancel each other out on their level and short-circuit back to origin – just what happens to a still-born baby. Birth and Death canceling each other out. When focused from Concept Six, the life-force can continue to project itself closer to this world by its normal procedure of going from one extremity to the other and then coming to a compromise between both. That is the way life works, which is why Concept Six is connected with the "redeeming principle" of humanity and associated with the Christ spirit. If we can once get past Five and reach Six we have a chance of continuity in consciousness, and so long as we keep contact with Six somehow, we are unlikely to be eliminated from existence down the Abyss of the Abandoned. All thinking along such lines is called into focus by Concept Six of the Tree.

Concept Seven

Concept Seven is Victory: This is a life-quality which amounts to the triumph of our best emotions over our worst predilections. Here are all the ego-expanding experiences which help develop us into sensitive and appreciative souls, realizing the loveliness there can be to life for those able to live it with even a fraction of divinity conditioning their consciousness. Here the rhythms of Six are translated into dancing, music, movement, and singing. This is a consciousness which enables us to keep improving our aesthetic and artistic standards of living, making us want finer and fuller lives along such lines for every human being. It governs the civilized and cultural side of our natures from every angle of emotional and empathic approach. This is what gives real depth to sex relationships between people and makes them of spiritual importance and significance. Consciousness throughout this sphere is one of our most wonderful achievements in this world. Without it we should lead very dreary and colorless lives with no vivid and heartening experiences to bring us any confidence that there might be more to life than mere survival from one body to another. Concept Seven is where we gain some incentive to look above the lowest levels of mortality and see something joyous and gladsome behind the surface of everyday existence. It may be that relatively few humans ever experience this concept to any intense degree per incarnation. In fact it can be unbearable to an almost killing point for those unable to mediate its influence properly. Nevertheless, even an average assurance of its inner reality from time to time will help most people through otherwise desperate periods of life. Concept Seven of the Tree holds out more than welcome lifelines to hopeless humans struggling with waves of depression in this frustrating world. It is a remarkable feat to be able to summon this Concept at will when it is most needed.

Concept Eight

Concept Eight is Glory: Glory is the complement of Seven along purely intellectual lines. This is where we develop our technology and science from, together with literature, and all the skills connected with inventive applications of awareness. As Seven was concerned with music, so Eight is concerned with mathematics. Our modern electronics and other techniques for dealing with the finer forces of nature derive from Concept Eight type of consciousness. So far, it has led us along a line of intelligent inquiries into the working of our universe until we have mastered one secret after another, producing our present civilization. Small wonder it is called the Glory of our Life-Tree. Admittedly, its uncompensated energies could quite well destroy us, and we need to learn how to regulate a flow of consciousness that is beyond our power to handle adequately. Undiluted intellect is too raw a spirit for humans to stomach comfortably. Concept Eight is needed to control the overabundance of Seven just as Five works with Four, but likewise its constraints and simplifications should act as conditioners which will channel consciousness along living lines aimed at the perfection of our species as a whole. Intellect is useful for rationalizing emotion compatibly with our advancing spiritual status, but unless it is tempered with the warmth and kindness of human feelings, it can shrivel our souls to a frightening extent.

Concept Nine

Concept Nine is the Foundation: This is the "collecting in" of consciousness, and is used to make a foundation in order to construct lives which have coherency and continuity of meaning. We could call it a pool of thought or reservoir of basic beliefs. It is full of dreams, ideals, ancestral memories, and indeed all the items of inner awareness we need to make ourselves into whatever we aim to become in each incarnation. Concept Nine holds our immediate source of supply behind the workings of our everyday consciousness. Perhaps we could think of it as a wholesale warehouse from which we stock the retail shop where we transact business with other humans like ourselves. We could also see it in reverse, as a collecting point where we hand in quantities of consciousness we have processed with our own living so that this can be sent back to source along a line of life linking with our particular origins. Here we have a consciousness which speaks with us in symbols, representations, and impressions. Because of its reflective characteristics, Concept Nine was connected with the moon. It actually forms an adaptive filter allowing humans to deal safely with modified intensities of awareness which might otherwise drive them insane. This is something like the way our atmosphere screens us from radiations which could be fatal in their pure condition. We need this Concept to protect us from potencies we could not cope with unshielded. In one sense we have to rely on our dreams to save us from realities until we make those dreams come true enough to handle things harmlessly. Once we can appreciate the function and value of Concept Nine, we might have more respect for the so-called illusions of life and realize why it is often wrapped in so many protective layers which we rip off wantonly at our peril. How many of us can remember the shock of our births as we were suddenly stripped defenseless and shot wet, naked, and wailing into this alarming world? Concept

Nine has an analogous function to the placenta while we are yet spiritually enwombed waiting our wakening into higher life levels. It does that for us and a lot more besides if we invoke its number clearly.

Concept Ten

Concept Ten is the Kingdom: We should all know quite a lot about this concept since it is this very world around us and the consciousness we normally employ to cope with its problems. It is particularly the type of awareness which is concerned with the improvement and development of humanity as a species of life, and our prospects of living in better conditions elsewhere – whether physical or otherwise. That is to say it is really the consciousness of the "Gods" working through us. Humans who have no wider views on life than those confined to single incarnation limitations, are not likely to appreciate this aspect of Concept Ten awareness however much they may be influenced by its subtle action on themselves. Why anyone should suppose all their intelligent thinking originates only in their own minds encouraged by what other humans have previously thought is a mystery. In old days most people believed that their Gods talked to them through nature. Nowadays some might imagine telepathic communications reaching them from other dimensions, or from Outer Space, or originating from Life forms outside our solar system. Whatever happens, the end effect is that the reach of human consciousness is undoubtedly extending in range and quality over the centuries, and we have witnessed a great leap forwards during the last space of a single incarnation. Concept Ten is now making its most impressive movement for many millennia.

• • •

So there we are, the ten fundamental types of consciousness which have the Godlike properties of raising humans from purely animal levels of living, and have evolved us into higher and finer specimens of sentient beings. It should be particularly understood that these concepts deal exclusively with conscious-ness of this perfecting kind. If we choose to disregard its prompt-ings in ourselves, and deliberately follow counter-currents for one incarnation after another, there would be none to blame but ourselves for our eventual reduction to non-entity. It does not speak through the Tree of Life alone, of course, but in every way capable of reaching the human heart and inner awareness. The Tree system is but one way devised by humans and Gods for communicating with each other to some intelligent degree of mutual recognition. Like other systems, it is limited by the indi-vidual ability of humans to align their inner sensoria with its arrangement of integrals, and their willingness to work at this until able to apply the art to their actual living.

The first completed stage of this ability is gaining such famil-iarity with the ten concepts that they can easily be called to mind with a single numerical summons. For normal minds this means a lot of thinking—concentrating on each concept day after day until it becomes possible to hold them all as separate items of actual inner experience for long enough to realize them as spiritual states while they are in view. In other words, we have to make relationships with them and realize their significance as we live them. They have to be as real for our minds and souls as a physical contact would be with our bodies. There is no deny-ing this takes a lot of effort to achieve.

To take in the concepts from outside so to speak, we have to absorb them like any other esoteric lesson is learned, particu-larly through psychodramatic methods. In these days with the aid of tapes, colored lights, musical effects, film projectors and videos, there should be some quite powerful arrangements con-trived by people of even modest incomes. Imagine, say, a small modern temple set up to convey a Concept Four experience. Lighting would be of the correct blue, possibly flashing at four-fold intervals or in groups of four together. Alternatively, you could use a full detail Tree of Life design with only Concept Four illuminated. There would be endless lighting possibilities. Cedar or some equivalent scent would fill the air and the music would match—maybe Holtz's "Jupiter." There would be velvet or similar rich fabric to touch. Nor should taste be forgotten. A sweetshop seems the obvious place to look for something with a Concept Four flavor, or for real enthusiasts, an entire meal could be concocted to suit each Concept. Additionally, a projector might show changing scenes, symbols, or whole episodes entirely connected with Concept Four topics. Anything whatsoever is in order providing it links directly with Concept Four through a human sensorium. For those with means and ability, it could be a delightful pastime to plan and perform a whole series of appropriate experiences from the top to the bottom of the Tree.

Maybe needless to say, yet advisable to remember always, is that no amount of elaborate and expensive equipment will be of the slightest use unless conscious attention is concentrated and held within the framework of the concept in question. The mind especially must not be allowed to wander from the fundamental frequency of whichever concept is being worked. Nor is that enough. The soul also has to coincide in its feelings with what the mind may be thinking. Everything has to be a whole experience integrated by the individual conducting it. In point of fact, there is really no need for any of the costly and decorative ritual gear at all. That may be of great help to those who cannot keep their minds focused easily, and would probably be of benefit during the first experimental runs with this system. Sooner or later cumbersome exercises have to be superseded by neater, faster, and increasingly improving techniques. After all, adult humans do not normally continue communicating with picture books for the whole of their grown up lives.

The very simplest equipment will serve perfectly well. A handmade and detailed chart of the Tree is an essential to start with, and if a copy of *The Office of the Holy Tree of Life*[4] can be obtained it could be of considerable help. It is a collection of

---

[4]*The Office of the Holy Tree of Life* was once published by Helios Books, England, but it is now out of print. However, it is part of *Sangreal Ceremonies and Rituals*, Volume 4 of the Sangreal Sodality Series, by William Gray, published in 1986 by Samuel Weiser, York Beach, Maine.

statement-invocations dealing with the traditional characteristics of each concept and path where two concepts are joined. Reading the Office at the rate of a path a day is a very practical way of commencing work with the Tree-alphabet. No real progress will be made, however, until each concept or path can be called to consciousness, banished, and replaced by another in the matter of a moment. Nor is this a matter of flicking over them with no depth of contact. Everything depends on the penetration of awareness rather than its duration. At first we have to work slowly in order to ensure this depth of perception, but as progress improves, perception should be reached with increasing rapidity. Then moves may be made from concept to concept, forming one relationship after another, so that these will spell out letters, syllables, and then whole sentences of "God-talk." In that way you could soon build up an inner vocabulary of spiritual speech.

What we should be doing, in fact, is learning to talk all over again—but this time in terms of "God-language." Intentionally associating items of consciousness together which are specifically connected with the divine perfection plan behind our ordinary lives. Each collection of items to be taken as one component of a single letter formed by a combination of two concepts constituting a path. In this case you would use consonants only, like the Hebrew alphabet. The five vowels associate with the elements of life symbolized by earth, air, fire, water, and truth. The consonants are taken as the bodies of words, while the vowels signify their enlivening spirit, without which words by themselves would be dead. Thus each word is really a concentration of consciousness and comes from a vast source of supply concerned with our survival and status as individual integers of the One Great Life comprising our whole cosmos. In other words, we shall be learning how to speak intelligently with our own immortal identities and recognize the reality of our spiritual selves with our ordinary waking consciousness.

How long it might take to get a good grip on the ten concepts of the Tree—and their interrelationships—is a matter for all to discover by their maximum efforts. Parrot-learning and superficial skimming will be useless. The only sensible thing to do is continue working away until the Tree starts "talking back" of its own accord. For example, something might have happened which necessitated a swift and stringent countermeasure of disciplined action. If this automatically suggests a Concept Five situation, then the Tree is relating itself to life through the consciousness of the individual concerned. In other words, it would be "coming alive" or making itself felt from inside someone in connection with ordinary worldly experiences. When we start measuring the conduct of our lives by the scale and standards of the Holy Tree, then we shall be able to make more elaborate use of its more esoteric facilities.

There are endless opportunities for practice, and inventing exercises is an interesting exercise in itself. For instance, we could look for concepts wherever numbers are encountered in ordinary ways. Try looking at the number of a book page and then thinking mentally, "That is Concept Number such-and-such," while making a flash-contact with it at the same time. Try that with car numbers, telephone numbers, *any* numbers until they start suggesting the concepts by themselves, yet always keep control of the decision to see them as ordinary or Tree values. Develop the knack of seeing figures from either viewpoint at will. Look at a watch dial and think, "It's half past Harmony," or whatever. At eleven, the Abyss might be thought of, and at twelve Zero, so the whole Tree scheme could be considered over the course of a day. For those who like using prayer-beads, the qabbalistic rosary is rather a lovely procedure, and there is a Sangreal version also.

It could be a good plan to include life-element work with that done on the sphere concepts before any path workings with letters are seriously begun. What this amounts to is a comprehension of life under four main headings grouped around a central concept of truth and poised between the extremities of God and humanity. This Cosmic Cross arrangement has been exhaustively dealt with elsewhere, but here we are principally concerned with its communicative function via its assorted vowels. This is of sufficient importance to think of in some detail since it outlines the principles invoked when tackling the consonants. In particular, it indicates the way to work with the tarot in a methodical and orderly manner which may make its meaning a lot plainer when we try to connect it with anything conveying really solid sense for us in this world.

The tarot cards are Qabbalah on cardboard so to speak, and they are only moveable versions of the same values and concepts that comprise the Tree of Life. Therefore they should not be thought of as entirely separate systems, but as alternative methods of expressing identical ideology in another light. The main difference is the framework of presentation, being the Tree of Life in the case of the Qabbalah and the Quartered Cross with the Sangreal. The same story of relationships between God and humanity is told from somewhat varied angles, but the tale is fundamentally the same however it is put to people. So now let us have a look at a fourfold view of life looked at through tarot and Tree alike, with a vision of the Sangreal appearing through them all.

CHAPTER THREE

The Four Ways

A N OLD SAYING IS: "There's more ways than one for looking at things." From both qabbalistic and tarot viewpoints there are four ways. The reason for this is simple—if we encounter anything fixed, we have to walk (or move) all around it in order to get a complete idea of its nature, and to learn all the information about it that our visual senses can tell us. On earth this means viewing it from the east, south, west and north as the sun moves. Only when something had been completely covered from all four angles would anyone have felt entitled to pass an opinion concerning it, or feel entitled to comment about it to another person.

Now these four ways from the qabbalistic angle of approach are the Four Worlds, from the magical angle the Four Instruments (or weapons), and from the tarot angle the Four Suits or Grail Hallows of the Cup, the Dish, the Staff, and the Sword.[5] All these amount to exactly the same principle. A quarternity of questing. From the Sangreal standpoint they symbolize the four ways of working towards truth. Truth shown as a central concept with an infinity sign attached. For purposes of reference, the four tarot suits will be termed Cups, Shields, Rods, and Swords. Shields are synonymous with the old term

---

[5] The Grail "Hallows" are the cup, platter, staff and sword.

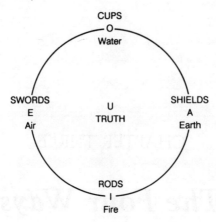

Figure 2. The Four Ways. The four suits of the tarot are aligned with a vowel and an element. Together as a circle, they form a cord around Truth in the middle.

Coins or Pentacles, and Rods with Staffs or Wands. The underlying symbology is the same. Alphabetically these four ideas align with the four vowels grouped around the central fifth as shown in figure 2. It should be noted that the central letter of the word "Truth"—the *U*—coincides with the central concept.

This idea of allotting a vowel value to each suit is purely for a convenience of consciousness, so that in thinking the letter *A* strongly enough, all its other associations should spring up around it and form themselves into an appreciative attitude capable of comprehending the chosen concept from an entirely earthly viewpoint. For instance, in this case an interpreter should be very conscious of his or her body and all its abilities. Everything here is physical and very "down to earth." Now all we need is the ability to identify with any of the four angles at will. Otherwise how could the nature of any card be determined in relation to the subject it was supposed to be either explaining or approaching?

Perhaps it would be helpful to see the suits aligned with their elemental attributes. Most people have at least some idea of the traditional life elements as distinct categories of consciousness.

We generally know what would be meant by someone thinking in a watery, earthy, fiery or airy way about anything, and that is more or less what we have to do with the tarot cards through their suits. With Cups we make a watery approach; with Shields, an earthy one; Rods supply a fiery view; and Swords, an airy outlook. The reason Swords represent an airy angle is because the symbol was originally an arrow. Arrows could be considered as flying swords, or swords as hand-held arrows by those who like their symbology straightforward.

Therefore it is fairly reasonable to imagine yourself going around any central concept, examining it from all sides with four changes of consciousness to suit each quarter. If it would help to imagine a view seen through colored glasses—blue for morning, yellow for midday, red for sunset and deep indigo for midnight—east, south, west and north angles respectively. It is best not to try to work in too many visual effects. What is of primal importance is the ideological significance of the theme or subject in question. Following this, the attitude, angle, or nature of approach to it. Always in that order. Just like the rules of grammar—subject first, predicate afterwards.

You could also imagine yourself encircling a concept with the four weapons, one after another. The Cup would cheer it, the Shield protect it, the Rod rule it and the Sword wound it. Or, the Cups pleasure it, Shields preserve it, Rods provoke it and Swords pain it. Or, Cups for joy, Shields for work, Rods for will, and Swords for sorrow. Always a quarternity of connected and progressive ideology describing a circle around the concept being considered.

This visualization means that if you intend to enter the "tarot spirit," you will have to learn how to assume the characteristics of each suit as required. In olden times this was called "assuming the God-form," and that means arranging yourself in the same way that an actor would who appears in character to play some particular part. There is no need to do all the elaborate dressing up and alteration of voice and appearance. Simply an inner alteration of attitude to match the suit in question. This can be done very swiftly and efficiently with a certain amount of practice, which will be well spent for the sake of the exercise alone. Let us run through these four attitudes in turn to see how this should be done.

Cup Attitude (Water)

Here we can really let ourselves go and experience the wonderful things of life, even if most of them don't materialize in this world. This is the creative world of flowing ideas and everything that pours out of the plentitude of a beneficence known as Providence – a happy, laughing and lovely world of dreams come true and whatever makes life worth living. A Cup is the Christian symbol of the Grail. It can be the vision of a heaven far beyond the bestiality of humans. Perhaps it is species of humanity with all the hate, viciousness, and nastiness of human nature bred out of it, so that only a state of refinement would be left. A state in which everyone would be noble by nature, regardless of social status or occupation. The sort of people we might all become in a few more million years of earth experience. Imagine living permanently in such a condition of consciousness. This might suggest a Cup attitude to adopt. In purely sensual terms, this could be conveyed by the following:

Touch:

Anything of a lovely and kindly description; soft fabrics, like warm water caressing the skin: smooth and delicate materials, or most intimate and satisfying sex.

Sight:

Whatever brings out the best feelings in a viewer – maybe a beautiful ballet or lovely picture; splendid scenery of a lush and encouraging sort; everything suggested by water; sunsets and glorious sky colors.

Hearing:

Orchestral music with emphasis on bell-like notes and liquid tones; kindly and loving voices whispering intimacies; gentle rain falling; thrilling and friendly sounds.

Smell:

Flower fragrances of the richest kind – especially deep red roses – but all satisfying and pleasing smells may be included, such as a well-cooked meal or any welcome and appreciated odor.

Taste:

Again whatever causes contentment and feelings of well-being – maybe rich red wine, or some particularly succulent fruit. The Grail always provided everyone's favorite food.

It should not be very difficult to construct an inner scenario to fit the suit of Cups. Simply sitting back and sensing the richness and satisfaction of it all, as it rolls past your mental screen, should be sufficient, though it is preferable to put in a bit more meditative work than that. Cups really mean a lot more than satisfying greeds or needs. They mean offering benefits to others from your own supply; generosity and pouring out blessings in the direction of those who seem to deserve them, sharing the good things of life with others who lack them just for the joy of causing happiness. Sometimes the Cup may be one of consolation as well as of celebration, always a sign and symbol of cheerfulness and optimism even though that may be only a good wish and a hope.

Adopting a Cup attitude ought to be a very welcome inner experience. All the Cup cards have happy if sometimes ambiguous meanings. They may only sugar the pill or soften the impact of an unavoidable blow, but at least they ameliorate the worst things which can happen to dwellers in this world. Even if the Cup may not be the first prize in life, it can still be a very pleasing consolation prize for taking part in the competition. All these ideas have to be summoned up by the single vowel letter O, sounded as if it were meant for an exclamation of happy wonder and surprise that something so pleasing had happened. Imagine a gasp of amazement at some outstandingly delightful event, like winning a colossal amount of money, or being chosen for the job that you really wanted, or maybe being accepted as a mate for life by the one person dearest to your heart. The "Oh" vowel attributed to the Cup symbol of the tarot should have all those implications and many more of the same nature attached to it.

Shield Attitude (Earth)

This tarot symbol concerns the affairs of the material world in particular—money, position, social values, physical possessions, bodily conditions of health or sickness, property, inheritances, marital affairs—everything dependent on being incarnate in a human body. Associations connected with this attitude in terms of sensual experience would include:

Touch:

Anything giving a sense of weight or solidity. Solid earth or stone, roughness, coolness, physical sexual contacts.

Hearing:

Silence; slow, dragging, or thudding sounds; cavernous echoes; heavy breathing; deep drumbeats; very low notes; clinking of money or the rustling of banknotes.

Sight:

Darkness or very dim light; caves or vaults; underground railways or shelters, tunnels, graves; the globe of the world; masses of humanity or hordes of herd animals.

Smell:

Fresh earth; manure; farms, thick heavy incense such as dittany or poppy; sexual smells.

Taste:

Raw mushrooms, root vegetables, meat, dry wholemeal bread.

Encounters with the Shield symbol also connect with its form as a Coin or Denier, showing its financial associations – both good and bad. A pentacle was only the five-point Star of Man displayed on a shield or coin, both of which connect with the principle of coverage or protection. We often say we are "covered" by an insurance policy which is purchased for money against loss of property or health. Also we may be protected against poverty by the coin we may have collected. Any or all of these factors should be made up into a meditative scenario which can be entered and experienced imaginatively, then summed up and headed by the Shield, Coin, or Pentacle, and given the call-sign of A. Whatever is associated with this world in terms of earth value should be put together as a picture which can be called to consciousness by the symbology of a Shield or the sound of the letter A, which can be sounded "Ay" or "Ah" depending on circumstances.

It should not be difficult to elaborate the symbolism and make up an inner script involving the practical use of a Shield to protect yourself, or Coins for buying some desired item. It is the principle which is important. For instance, the Shield would apply to protective clothing, such as a raincoat or overalls, and so would a welder's helmet or a catcher's glove. If Coin is being imagined, it must be visualized as purchasing some physical thing rather than services or intangibles. Nothing away from or out of this world should come into conscious focus when the Shield symbol is being worked. It is perfectly in order to make up or adopt prayers and invocations dealing exclusively with this earth attitude, or devise any form of psychodrama which appears to concern it clearly and conveniently. The main thing is to categorize consciousness in an earth direction and bring this under control so that it can be summoned or dismissed in less than seconds.

Rod Attitude (Fire)

Here the Rod or Staff, sometimes inaccurately called a Wand, is to be taken as a sign of rulership in relation to your own or another's conduct. It can be compared to a ruler's scepter or a conductor's baton and is supposed to control the actions of a whole realm of people or an entire concert orchestra. It directs the attention of observers to whichever point they should be considering in the opinion of an overruling intelligence. Thus consciousness is led from one point to another of its complete course by the indications of a director's Rod. It also represents the support it offers as a Staff to feet that may be faltering somewhat along the spiritual path they are trying to follow as faithfully as they may, yet because of human fallabilities are stumbling and slipping in places where they would welcome a good grip with firmness and surety.

The Rod as a weapon can be considered as the cane of correction, which is really a minor chastisement compared with the terrible Sword. It may prevent the employment of a Sword in all cases of conduct it has managed to correct with its curbing influence. Its connection with the fire element is best described as a burning desire for knowledge, the illumination sought for enlightening ignorance and darkness, and even the consuming fires of curiosity which impel us along our paths of life. Here the

Rod becomes both a prod and a probe in our investigative Quest of the hidden and Holy Grail. From a sensory viewpoint it becomes an instigator of:

Touch:

Feeling the fingers palpating anything to discover its nature; being touched for the same reason; feeling a lover's warm body inquisitively and being felt in return.

Hearing:

Crackle of flames; all types of fire music; the action of fingers doing anything energetically – such as typing or clapping hands; brisk voices explaining something or just calling to attract attention.

Sight:

Anything being pointed out in books, maps, or solid scenery. Index fingers in action; finger gestures indicating intentions; straight lines being drawn with rulers; people walking with sticks, canes, or staffs; flickering flames.

Smell:

Any odor arousing interest or curiosity. Whatever cannot be instantly identified and consequently demands a further follow-up or investigation.

Taste:

Whatever is commonly described as "piquant," especially with a hot or spicy flavor.

These are some of the things you can use to visualize Rod ideas. They may be combined in order to present approach methods used from a purely Rod viewpoint. Everything has to be summonable by an "I" code call. This is not to be seen as a long drawn out sound, but a connected series of "I" sonics, each so clear that it makes a distinct sound of its own, yet is part of a larger sound picture which makes up the whole idea. Perhaps if a big bundle of "I's" could be imagined as being crammed together and then turned endwise–on so they presented a mass of individual dots of varying shades which in their totality showed a complete scene, this might convey something of the concept behind the whole notion. They would still be "I's", yet from such an angle would offer another view altogether of something quite different to themselves.

Sword Attitude (Air)

This is also the arrow viewpoint. Both Swords and arrows are meant for wounding or slaying, and life can be very hurtful as well as sometimes happy. This is the wind which is keen rather than kind, cutting with the cold of steel and biting with all the bitterness of heartbreaks caused by sorrow and separation. However, this is all part and parcel of being human on this earth, and a life without sorrow or trouble at all would not belong here. Here are all the unhappy and troublesome experiences we encounter because we are human. Most of these we make for ourselves since we are still stupid and silly enough to do this for no other reason than our humanity itself. At the same time those who can face and surmount these experiences are bound to become better people in the end by making such changes in their own characters. So the Sword signifies our determined battles with life, and all the alterations we have to make with ourselves and our environment by efforts against opposition and oppression. Translated into sensual terms, this might mean:

Touch:

Anything sharp and cutting; cold winds; steely surfaces; armored clothing; uncomfortable skin sensations; unsatisfied sex.

Hearing:

Wind whistling sharply; cutting voices; birds screaming; screech of shells approaching—war sounds of zipping bullets and whining rockets; crying and sobbing. Any sound connected with sadness; perhaps the "Funeral March."

Sight:

Enemies approaching; storm damage; war wreckage; hurt and harmed people; cold colors; shivering souls trying to shelter. Bleak and bitter conditions of being; an execution shed, or an operating theater.

Smell:

Pungent and sharp odors like ammonia, bleach, vinegar, urine, acids, disinfectants or scouring chemicals; also smells of sweat and death.

Taste:

Bitter tastes like aloes or wormwood, also vinegar and sharp dry wines.

It should be borne in mind that the Sword symbol not only signifies experiencing all these feelings in yourself, but inflicting them on others as well. Preferably this should not be felt from any vicious viewpoint whatever, but purely defensively in justifiably retaliating for injuries received, or in defense of beliefs and "causes" which are considered fully called for. It has to be remembered that Questers of the Grail were symbolized as fighting knights whose swords were employed for combatting wrongs and wickedness—not only in others, but mostly in their own natures. So a Sword can signify determination to fight against evil in your own soul and nature. Perhaps the injunction, "If thy right hand offend thee—cut it off," may come to mind with the Sword symbol, remembering that this was the literal punishment for stealing valuable property in old times and is still practiced in some countries today. Dishonesty brought disgrace, and the word meant someone who had dishonored himself by such actions.

All this scenario and anything associated with it has to be summoned clearly into consciousness by the vowel *E*, usually sounded as being long and drawn out, but it could also be sharp and piercing like a whistle, often written as "Wheeew." Our world can be very hard and hurtful sometimes, and we humans are only too apt to wound others as we try to carve niches in it for ourselves. Swords are two-edged as a rule, and while poking a hole in somebody else, it is possible to cut yourself very badly in the process. Christians may feel a need to question why their reputedly peace loving leader should have said: "I come not to bring peace, but a Sword."

This is the sort of ideology to deal with in assembling the mental attitude of a tarot Sword, which should never be thought of as evil in itself. It symbolizes nothing more than what is regrettably necessary for establishing a workable economy in our own natures. Swords can also be scalpels or pruning knives, and the symbol can be seen in the light of saving lives or trimming trees so they will bear better fruit. All cutting-tools come under the Sword symbol and without them we could never have reached our present pitch of civilization. So the Sword should never be seen as a totally adverse emblem. Consider the amazing advances in surgery due to terrible wars. Good can eventuate from evil in the end, even though the cost of the lesson may be considered a bitter price to pay.

• • •

Getting all these thoughts together will take a lot of time and trouble, but the work will have to be done if an airy Sword attitude is ever to be invoked with a single reference to the vowel *E*, or one glance at a pictured Sword. It can be considered as a sort of inner attunement in which the whole of your being will resonate or vibrate with a specific key-note. It might help to practice this while calling up these inward experiences. The earth-attitude should be on a very low and thrumming note, the Air on a sharp and high one, while the Cup would be thrilling and vibrant, with the Rod stirring and interesting. Anyone with musical talents might conceive this as a string being tightened or slackened to required pitch, or as the tones of four different instruments – drumbeat for earth, a whistle for air, a plucked string for fire and a tintinnabulation for water. Imagining the distinctive sound types combined with their spoken vowels can be helpful with setting up the tarot suits.

We are not trying to arrive at end-concepts in any of the suits by these imaginative practices. We are trying to construct frames, or special glasses, through which objectives may be seen in that special light for the attainment of increasingly clearer comprehension. In effect, we are making a telescope with four object-glasses for viewing whatever we direct it towards, or a projector which will throw a picture on our screens from four entirely different angles which will appear solid and substantial when examined for truth. To some extent this exercise is rather like making a hologram rather than a flat photograph, or quad-raphonic sound instead of a single speaker badly placed and consequently distorted. This all begins with the art of aligning yourself according to the tarot suit selected.

Combined together, the four suits center around the myste-rious truth factor in the middle represented by the vowel *U*, or oo oo oo. This is the most ancient of God Names – Hu, IEU, or IEW. The symbol is appropriately a cord that circles down to a noose with which truth – the ultimate quarry of humanity – can be caught and, if possible, hung on to. The Indian God of

Death, Yama (pronounced Yaum), is armed with a noose in which he catches the souls of the dead. In the symbolism of the tarot, it might be noted that the Hanged Man is caught by a noose round his foot instead of his neck. Trapped by truth, he has to depend on it for help and is evidently content to do so. Some day maybe someone will design a tarot deck with five suits, the extra one being that of the Cord, symbolizing the Truth in everything. We certainly have not reached a stage of development where this is likely to be possible.

CHAPTER FOUR

The First Step

THE INITIAL STEP on the Sangreal tarot journey is
integrating the ten spheres and the four ways, or suits.
What matters most is the methodology rather than the
results obtained. Applied to the Tree of Life, each concept has
to be considered in turn and examined through the four suits in
sequence so that a total comprehension can be reached when
the circuit is complete. This means encircling each concept with
an intentional act of consciousness and then arriving at an
understanding which could hopefully be related to ultimate
truth—so far as this may be seen by any human type of
comprehension!

First Concept (The Crown)

Take the First Concept—the Crown, Summit, or Apex. Exam-
ine it through the Cup symbol and we arrive at an impression of
the purest pleasure possible in union with God—the greatest
good imaginable, the height of Holiness, and everything else of
wonder and amazement in the absolute. This is the Mystic Marriage consummated, the Grail gained, and the Cup or Cosmos
full to the brim and running over to fill up all the rivers of life
flowing to lower levels.

From the Shield angle, the First Concept is seen as the origin and end of everything that life on this earth would mean if it ever reached its proper degree of perfection—the most that we could ever become at the absolute apex of our capabilites and potentials. This may be unimaginable, but it is not beyond striving for while we are incarnate creatures. Maybe it is best described as a divine drive in humanity making for its highest aim.

From the Rod angle, the First Concept is viewed as the supreme source of our attentive interest in life and all that constantly directs us toward divinity. It provides us with a purpose higher than anything else we are liable to encounter, and is the maximum meaning behind the whole of our lives, which would otherwise be quite pointless.

From the Sword-angle, the First Concept shows the necessity for sorrow, because our imperfect and faulty natures need reconstruction and reconstitution before they can be considered fit for any divine duties. Here we see the purpose of pain for changing our characters, altering us to accord with the original intention behind our beings. This is the divinity which shapes our ends however we may rough-hew them.

Everyone must arrive at their own truth conclusions by their own efforts, so no ultimates will be suggested here. If the meditative contemplation has been carried out properly along the lines suggested, and no kind of combined estimate of the First Tree Concept can be made after all that work has been done, then it is extremely unlikely that the tarot will ever talk to you and you had best look for an alternative means of Questing. But for those of you who found this visualization process fruitful, let's consider Concept Two in the same way.

Second Concept (Wisdom)

This is Wisdom in the true sense of the term. Here wisdom is an actual faculty, rather than just a collection of information stored in the physical brain which will also die with it. Adopting the Cup attitude, we find a plenitude of perception and perspicacity.

Concept Two deals with the sheer joy and pleasure in being wise for its own sake, and for what it enables us to do for our fellow creatures. Wisdom is a lot more than mere knowledge, for it is the ability to apply that properly in all circumstances. Without wisdom, we shall never be able to enjoy life fully, and this is the point where humans find their cups filled with the wine of wisdom at its most mature condition of consciousness.

Studying the wisdom concept through the Shield (or coin) we come to realize how only genuine wisdom can tell us how to protect ourselves from all the perils of life prevailing on this planet, and also how we can come out of them with the best profit. Wisdom is something that has to be earned after experience and an expenditure of effort. We pay for it at the cost of our own comfort a great deal of the time. Those who are not born with wisdom must buy it very dearly. Its price, we are told, is beyond the value of every pearl in the sea.

Changing to the Rod attitude for viewing the wisdom-concept, we get the impression that something at the back of life is trying to point out the lessons we ought to have learned as we went through it. There are rules for living which we either observe for the sake of all concerned, or we break at the risk of having life itself break its rods on our bent backs. We will never learn to be wise if we ignore what is pointed out to us for our own good, and if we really mean to reach wisdom, we shall have to pay more attention to what life is trying to teach us. Only attentive scholars pass eventual examinations, and the first prize is the Grail itself—the only Cup worth winning with wisdom.

Shifting at last to a Sword attitude, we should be reminded of the old saying, "A sadder but wiser man." It is probably sad that sadness should bring wisdom with it. Eventually even a Fool can acquire wisdom with enough sad experience behind him. It is also said that the fear of the Lord is the beginning of wisdom, and Sword experiences are apt to teach the value of wisdom if they cut deeply enough to reach our souls. All these four outlooks should do something to teach us what truth means in life—the wellspring of wisdom as a concept of consciousness.

Third Concept (Understanding)

Let's move to the third Concept, Understanding, and consider it carefully from the Cup angle. We should see at a glance that this degree of intuition is on a divine level of life, though we can claim our proper proportion of it in ours. It is a comprehension of gladness and joy that such an ideal state of being can be shared by all the souls who celebrate it together, because they truly understand each other and are happy together for that very reason. This is the sort of understanding which has to be reached before we can come to a common communication of consciousness with each other, and one that would surely be something to celebrate with the cup of kindness amongst such close companions.

The Shield (coin) attitude tells us that understanding, like wisdom, has to be earned and paid for before it will protect us under its hospitable roof of reasonable relationships. Using the currency of consciousness we can purchase all sorts of well-being in life at this position. Once we truly understand not only each other, but the reasons why everything is put together in the way it is, we can deal with each other as we deserve.

Taking up a Rod attitude, understanding becomes more clearly defined as a kind of super-instinct indicating anything we ask about. Understanding brings tolerance and co-operation. It also tells us that if we refuse to understand what life is all about, it is liable to correct us with a sharp rap from its ruler. Then too, it tells us that we should understand the reason for all the rules in the Game of Life, because until we do we shall never play it properly.

Striking a Sword attitude should show us that lack of under-standing is the cause of most trials and troubles we are likely to meet with in this world or any other. Unless and until we fully understand the necessity for striving to secure an amiable under-standing between all contending parties in any quarrel, there will never be a proper state of peace among people. Moreover if we have to fight for the sake of upholding such an understand-ing, then fight we must and agree to terms of an armistice afterwards. Very often this is a bitter experience, yet if it results in a better understanding among ex-combatants, then we shall surely become better people.

Fourth Concept (Mercy)

Coming to Concept Four, Mercy, we first view it with Cup–conditioned consciousness. It seems majestic and magnanimous, a true Cup of kindness and kingliness combined. It brings beneficence and blessings with it, and as the bard truly says, it blesses he that gives and him that takes. Mercy does indeed seem to become a throned monarch better than his crown, and it is a prerogative of those with real power at their command. Mercy should never be confused with weakness or lack of resolution. Mercy should flow like a healing balm from the Cup of compassion and companionship.

From a Shield (coin) attitude, we realize it seems only right that if offenders are to be requited, well-doers should certainly be rewarded with mercy and magnanimity. Generosity goes with both these characteristics, and this is where purse strings should be untied for those deserving such consideration. Moreover, those who do the right things need to be protected from predators who would take unfair advantage of them, and they are entitled to pray for this from the power regarded as the greatest protector in creation. It is hoped they will be heard from this point.

A Rod-attitude shows that it is better to be given a gentle reminder in time than a sharp stroke later on. Also a quiet prod in time is often more effective than a fierce cut later. Careful probings often reveal more truths than violent jabbings, and kings ruling with kindliness and mercy have a much happier realm than those who try the rod of iron treatment. Perhaps the psalmist might be remembered when he sang, "Thy rod and thy staff they comfort me." Then of course there was the reminder

that the Lord would chastise the ones he loved. The Rod attitude has a great deal to reveal here.

Lastly, the Sword-attitude might seem out of place at this
point, but it is not. A Sword is also a scalpel that can save a life,
or cut the bonds of captives struggling to free themselves from a
dangerous situation. This may bring to mind a rather famous
picture of a Grail knight in heavy armor cutting free a damsel
from a tree where she is tied to await some dreadful dragon. It
may be tempting to wonder if they are simply indulging in sex-
fantasies, but the huge sword wielded by the knight does have a
Freudian tale to tell, and so does the eagerness in the eyes of the
damsel. Apart from this, are there not mercy killings when
death is brought as a kindness to those suffering more agony
than any human being should bear? Do we not offer it to our
animal friends out of the mercy and compassion with which we
love them?

Fifth Concept (Severity)

The Fifth Concept of Severity is just the opposite. Here the Cup
seems out of place, and yet it can be fitted in after some thought
has been taken. When wrongdoers get what they justly deserve,
does that not give a sense of satisfaction to the wronged? Do
they not get a feeling that there must be some justice in the
Universe? No one would call for vengeance, yet all would expect
an exact requital of wrongs and injustices inflicted on innocent
parties. When Heaven seems to intervene on behalf of the
beleaguered and deals out some deserved compensation as a
retributory reply, shall we not lift the Cup to our lips with a
pledge of support and as a thankful gesture to a Just God? If we
were asked to sacrifice some surplus happiness in order to secure
some loved-one's safety, would we not offer it instantly and

gladly? Let the Cup be raised in honor of a deity with a sense of cosmic discipline.

The Shield (coin) attitude shows a Mrs Be-Done-By-As-You-Did viewpoint altogether. Here is nothing but deserved retribution for previous offences against the laws of life, seeming to consist of heavy fines. Also consider poverty and deprival so common on earth, a condition that would be meaningless in a plentiful condition of cosmos. There is, however, a certain amount of protection in poverty from the wickedness and waste of those who exploit wretchedness for the sake of their own profit. Those who have nothing to steal need fear no thieves. Occasionally a state of deprival is needed to start a struggle against it that brings out character qualities which could cause outstanding changes in society. That applies especially here.

The Rod angle points out an exact and absolutely fair return for what we may have done with our lives. Nothing more or less than the most scrupulously correct compensation for relatively minor things which may yet have disturbed the equilibrium of existence. A rulership which can scarcely question or deny its own justice—the eye for the eye, and the tooth for the tooth principle. Not exactly nice, yet entirely necessary. A correction of bad behavior and an appropriate punishment for naughty children of cosmos.

The Sword attitude sets forth the worst of anything that can happen when this concept is being considered. Those who do not willingly submit to the control of the Rod must meet the "Sword of the Lord" in retribution, yet they encounter no more than they have called upon their own heads. This may sound old-fashioned in our times, yet it is true. We may suppose such effects are not more than natural calamities, but they happen because we have not yet learned how to control their causes, and ignorance of the law has never been taken as an excuse in any earthly court of justice. Neither will it serve to excuse us in cosmic courts which administer the highest justice under the eyes of heaven.

Sixth Concept (Harmony & Beauty)

Reaching the Sixth Concept of Harmony and Beauty, wherein the whole universe seems to balance on this point of powerful poise, the attitude of the Cup can scarcely be anything other than cheerful and beautifully brilliant. It should make for a real celebration to know that we have reached this place at last. Though we cannot expect to live permanently in a state of perfect poise, the momentary attainment of such a state should be enough to make us joyous. This is where the phrase "joie de vivre," seems so appropriate, for that is what the Cup seems to indicate in the sixth position of the Tree, the tarot, and the Sangreal.

Coming to the Shield (coin) approach, we encounter all that we earn or are entitled to hold under the aegis of this concept. Perhaps the use of solar power is a contemporary sign of this. Here is where patience and perseverance pay off and protect investments we made so long ago when we started turning our attention to the beauty of balance and heavenly harmony. Apollo, the sun God, is the patron of music, and here he is at his best when protected by the celestial canopy of heaven itself under the singing stars. Perhaps we sometimes need to screen delicate things from the fiercest blaze of our sun until they are strong enough to stand these rays, but that should not present a very serious problem in our time. This may also mean that we ourselves are usually not strong enough to withstand the full glare of internal illumination, and we need to have this screened down for our benefit until our souls grow accustomed to dealing with it.

From the Rod-Staff attitude, we discover that the best way to get through life is by maintaining as perfect a balance as possible. Who is not familiar with the principles of balancing on a tightrope with the aid of an extended Rod in the form of a pole? A tightrope is probably about the straightest and narrowest path in this world, and the pole provides the best hope of walking it safely. The same principle applies to staffs which help people negotiate perilous paths in mountain ascents. Also, the ancient instrument of navigation known as a backstaff was pointed at the sun to measure angular positions, and early calculations of time were made by shadows cast by a staff stuck into the ground. Staffs of one kind or another gave us guidance and support since humans first tried to stand upright. Assistants in any enterprise are still called "staff" to this day because of their supporting function. Rods are regulators of conduct to much the same extent as the sun regulates the seasons of the year and the time of day. This is where we have to learn that the rules of life are made as much for the convenience as the control of humanity.

At the Sword-Arrow approach to this concept, we find that it may sometimes be necessary to fence ourselves around with swords in order to protect the peace held precariously in such a circle. Tranquility in trouble can be a welcome respite. Probably only those who have lived through such an experience would appreciate what this means in terms of its actuality, but the contrast of conditions is only possible at swordpoint—which is holding the enemy off just long enough to obtain the needed breather—which enables the defender to fight on until victory at the next concept.

Seventh Concept (Victory)

The Seventh Concept of Victory may sound like a happy one, yet not be so at all, since any kind of victory in life is often paid for with considerable cost. Nevertheless, the Cup symbol shows a satisfactory state of things, possibly because of a victory inside the self where some serious fault may be conquered, or defect of character put right. There may have been a conflict of conscience where good triumphed over evil—something that might be called a "soul-war," in which angels beat devils for once. Here the Cup is called for to celebrate a victory of virtue against vice, light against darkness, and cosmos over chaos, something worth pledging fresh faith in the forces of heaven against all the horrors of hell. Maybe the Cup symbol shows the prize for only an occasional victory, yet well worth winning for the sake of the encouragement it offers to others still engaged in individual conflicts.

The Shield (coin) angle informs us of the inevitable price we have to pay for a victory in life at any level. Nothing is ever won at no cost at all, and the only serious question is whether that cost will be worth paying. Nowadays the economics of war are the immediate concern of the combatant commanders and planning politicians. This principle extends in terms of every kind into the fields of morality and behavior. Here we have to ask ourselves whether it will be worth curbing our activities in one way at the expense of increasing them in others. Such as: if there are only so many hours in a day and you want to become efficient at one ability, then you will have to spend more time at that and less on watching TV or lying in bed. Also cosmos runs its own brand of protection racket. If we expect shielding or protection from evil influences, we shall have to pay a price for this by offering our services on behalf of others, or some equivalent sacrifice. What will it be worth to safeguard ourselves and our victories from risks of failure and loss? This is where we have to ask ourselves questions of that nature and calculate very carefully whether some of the battles in life are really worth winning.

Reaching a Rod-Staff viewpoint of Victory, it might help to remember that even in modern times the ensignia of a field marshal is a baton, which in earlier days was wielded literally as a pointer for indicating the marshal's estimation of wherever he wanted his troops to attack. Sub–commanders were responsible for moving the soldiers wherever the marshal's baton pointed, since visual signals were better than vocal ones amid the din of battle. The marshal, usually sitting on horseback atop of a convenient hill, had the best view of a battlefield, and so a better chance of directing a victory. That is the position here on parallel fields of inner conflict. If victories are to be obtained, get a commanding view of the situation and direct all available energies into the most advantageous areas of attack. The Rod here represents our inner instincts and intentions, clearly indicating what we should do in any given life situation so as to come out of it – not only with credit – but with some claim to success as well.

Lastly the Sword (arrow) angle shows us that not every victory is a happy or cheerful one. Its price may be have been too great, or what we supposed was a victory may not have been one at all. Nobody wins wars these days, they only survive them. Swords do not guarantee victory in the least, they only offer a means of battle. Besides, how is a victory to be defined? Only by determining which of two courses gains temporary ascendancy over the other. Victory is a relative and ambiguous term. It could be that the metaphorical Sword will have to be turned against your own faults and failings. There is such a thing as spiritual surgery in the sense that some propensity must be cut out of your soul, or connections with undesirable contacts be severed completely. The Sword is the proper instrument for use here, and only good degrees of skill can determine how to employ it effectively.

Eighth Concept (Honor & Glory)

After the battle comes the Eighth Concept of Honor and Glory. The celebratory Cup here shows how our concepts of honor are glorified and glory is honored so the two are almost synonymous. Definitions may differ very widely depending on codes of conduct, but there are distinctions recognized by most of humanity. The original Hebrew word for glory also meant brilliance, and we use the term to describe an extremely intelligent or able individual. That is a usage especially implied at this point. An honest man meant one whose behavior was honorable because he followed an approved code of conduct, and whose health could be pledged because long life was wished for him. The Cup thus represents here all the respect and good wishes from fellow humans offered to those who live honorably.

It also indicates that the roots of such behavior stem from this life-principle in particular. The expression "Glory be to God," signifies that the cause of any human being's altruistic behavior should be credited to God alone. The implication is that we would not be able to act that way on our own initiative. The Cup here stands for honesty and truth, and the Quest in search of it would start with a "stirrup-cup" (or a Farewell cup of wine) offered to those who ride forth to find it instead of waiting, like Diogenes in his tub, for the truth to visit them.

The Shield (coin) attitude shows that honor has to be earned and protected by any means. An honorable reputation is something to be shielded with the greatest care, because once broken it can never be restored to a pristine condition, no matter how often it is patched. To a great extent such a reputation is a shield in itself, protecting people from slander and scandal to a considerable point—though by no means an impenetrable one. Enough weight of evidence will always smash its way past the stoutest shield, and the point of truth will penetrate the thickest protection if that protection is only composed of pretence. So there is need for the Shield to be a good solid one, and the coin has to be earned honestly if there is any real glory to be gained at this position.

With the Rod (staff) attitude regarding honor, this has its own rules which have to be observed if honor is to be satisfied, as they used to say. Maybe old fashioned honor was full of rules we would totally disregard in our times, but the principle of the concept was sound enough. Without some kind of standards what would human behavior amount to in any century? One of our major modern troubles is that we have no such generally recognized contemporary code, so the whole of our culture and civilization is suffering for it. Lying, cheating, stealing, and other dishonesties have become quite socially permissible if practiced under other descriptions of conduct. In becoming a society without honor we have made ourselves inglorious. The Rod here stands for regulable codes of conduct in conformity with the principle of honor—not necessarily inflexible—yet certainly capable of affording support to our shaky social structure. There is no substitute for the Rod of Honor for we need it in ourselves and everyone else.

The Sword (arrow) attitude for honor reminds us that the admonitory motto on old swords often read "Draw me not without good cause and sheathe me not without honor." This meant, of course, not to commence any conflict without the most solid and substantial reasons and never to cease it without an honorable conclusion one way or another. This did not mean the battle must necessarily be won, but that agreement must be reached which would ensure that the terms of cessation would be satisfactory to both contenders. The principle consideration was to satisfy the rules of honor under which the battle was fought to a finish. An agreeable armistice on both sides according to the rules would be an acceptable reason for stopping the fight. There never has been any glory in war, despite opinions of previous centuries. Bitter experience in this century has exploded the glory of war myth forever. The glory, if that is the correct term, is due to those who suffered its horrors with quiet heroism while attempting to ease its inflictions on others. Not the wielders of swords, but those who bore the blows with fortitude because nothing else was possible for them. The silent survivors.

Ninth Concept (Foundation)

The Ninth Concept of Foundation begins with the Cup being raised in honor of the ancestors who founded the families we spring from. If we care to push this idea back far enough, we shall come to the "Grail" itself, which could be said to have been the blood which it is hoped will eventually civilize and culture humanity as a whole on this planet. Surely that is something to celebrate. This particular card has always been regarded as particularly fortunate, or lucky, among professional fortune tellers. The nine of hearts in an ordinary pack is known as the "wish card" and means the granting of a wish. The nine of Cups has the same significance, plus indicating great happiness and joy.

The Shield (coin) attitude shows "foundation" in the light of what it means in terms of being a protected life-species on any planet, and how we shall have to earn our keep as conceivers of not only other human beings, but of ideas, inventions, and all imaginative constructions of consciousness. Many of our best ideas come first in dreams when our awareness comes closest to the deep underlying subconsciousness we share with the Sangreal. We dreamed of how to live, but our dreams have taken millions of years to come true and are still very much in the making. Our earliest dreams must have been concerned with how to protect and shield ourselves on this planet so full of perils, most of them from fellow–creatures. Eventually money was used for this shielding purpose by providing arms and other defenses like castles, and more recently, atomic shelters. Insurance is another form of shielding the foundation we base our lives on. We cannot do without protection no matter how much it costs us. Protection of our ideals, as well as our ideas, can be an expensive process, yet it is not a luxury anymore.

The Rod (staff) attitude indicates how closely we should follow the pointing finger of inquiry which endeavors to trace the outline of our foundation on earth. Why should we concern ourselves in the slightest with past affairs? What makes us so interested in the dead and gone of long ago? Think of what we spend on archaeology, historical research, and every other science connected with expanding or enhancing our consciousness in that direction. For heaven's sake why? There should surely be no doubt that we are instinctively seeking our roots with the Sangreal through every trace of this divine design. Scientists deny God under any name they choose, yet a lot spend their lives searching for "something" that will prove how we got here, although they disguise it under whatever description they please. The further they probe into the structure of our universe, the more they discover that what they formerly thought was "nothing" is really an increasingly subtle "something" which they have to invent elaborate names for to justify their own existence. Have you managed to probe your own being to its spiritual basis yet?

The Sword (arrow) attitude regarding foundation brings us to the depths of sorrow humans may experience when hearts have been pierced by grief and emotional suffering. Only the highest orders of animals are capable of this most moving happening—the loss of a loved companion, the break up of a love life, separation from those we love and value because they were the earthly bases on which we built our hopes and happiness. What can be worse than having our foundation cut away from under our feet, for that is what this card indicates in the tarot. With fortune tellers the nine of spades is usually dreaded as the "death-card" if it comes up with the feared Ace of the same suit. In tarot, this card always stands for serious loss of happiness for some basic reason or another, usually because of the emotional effects involved. In the case of death among close relatives or friends, the normal sense of grief is not on their account, but mainly because of the gap this will leave in your life. Though this may sound selfish, it is perfectly natural. Sword experiences may be bad enough from the emotional angle, but what if they were concerned with being cut off from our spiritual foundation rooted in the Sangreal? That is a fundamental fear which no thinking human can contemplate without risking insanity. Indeed it may well be behind many types of insanity regardless of what many psychiatrists might think or say. Even though our spiritual roots may not be anywhere near severed, they can still be wounded (to slight or severe degrees) enough to cause Sword sorrows at this point of our life-tree. Fortunately there are healing agents available for the asking. Otherwise our earth experiences would have been so unbearable we would probably have been extinct by now.

Tenth Concept (Kingdom)

The Tenth Concept of the Kingdom brings us right down here to this world around us. The Cup symbol signifies the joys of earth life, whatever these may mean to us. A cup of plain water for someone dying of thirst in a desert will bring more joy than a glass of the most expensive champagne to a satiated gourmet. Joys are always relative to people and circumstances. As yet we have not discovered any scale for measuring degrees of joy. The Cup covers them all so far as the tarot is concerned. At this point they are specifically concerned with the happenings of this world because we are humans here. This means hearts delight — such as love affairs, friendships, or close relationships of any kind. Good news or rejoicing, as well as entertainment and pleasure arising from artistic activities and appreciation. The purely physical pleasure of sex comes in here, too, as apart from the spiritual side to it. However, since so many earthly pleasures are brief and ephemeral, this factor must always be taken into account. Time is the most difficult thing to assess with the tarot and only approximations may be made as a rule. The safest assumption is that joys will be brief and sorrows long.

With the Shield (coin) attitude we come to our commercial and financial interests, as well as our need for protection against the adversities we are likely to encounter in this area. This could be good, bad, or indifferent, according to the circumstances or people. The card also indicates social status, appointments, promotions, and the side of life where money or its influence is involved. It applies to protection, too, where this may be purchaseable, but might also mean escapes from accidents, muggings, bad health or the like. In a way, it is insurance coverage of the highest kind, being a fateful non-event that alters life by avoidance of hostile occurrences. Screening from adversity may not always be in keeping with the will of God, but such is certainly welcome in case of trouble.

The Rod-Staff approach to the kingdom will point out all we have to learn in this world for making it livable, and it indicates the means and methodology of obtaining all such learning. It represents anything investigative in every physical field this world has to offer. It speaks of all we should do in our efforts to rule over this material world, and it explains why the

Sangreal strain in us should be considered as Royal Blood. If we are supposed to be the Lords of Creation we shall have to behave as if we were kings and royalty in the true sense of those words, and realize our responsibility toward ourselves and fellow mankind. We must never forget our duties towards all living creatures that share this kingdom with us. Above all, the ruling Rod points out the obligations of royalty, and indicates that the real mark of a king lies in the willingness to sacrifice ourselves on behalf of the people we rule. Those who are unwilling to offer themselves for such an oblation have no real claims to the crown of this kingdom. Only people who obey the rules of life have the right to extend any claim toward a higher form of living in a more advanced state of being.

The Sword (arrow) approach to the kingdom gives the gloomiest view possible of happenings amongst humanity as the kingdom relates to our affairs on and in this planet. Complete ruin of commercial prospects, serious sickness, doom, disasters, unhappiness, adversity—all the very worst things which can happen in a lifetime—are presented here as a prospect. Only the most dedicated masochist might find encouragement from this approach. The question is the degree of seriousness it might indicate. Something that would crush one person completely might only be a set-back which could be surmounted with some expenditure of effort and ingenuity by another. The positive certainty is that this tarot card offers some very definite and significant obstacle to the smooth running of life from an earthly viewpoint. Enmity and malice are indicated, as well as opposition from some source which might be shown by adjacent cards. This will manifest as a material and tangible eventuation rather than in any subtle or spiritual form. The only good point about this card is that it leaves the interpreter in no doubt that something nasty is coming round the corner, and it should alert the inquirer to stand alarmed and armed, ready to take on whatever it may be with as much fortitude as may be mustered.

● ● ●

Such are the ten concepts of the Tree of Life seen through all the angles of approach available in the tarot. They cover every eventuality likely to happen in the course of a human lifetime, though, of course, they were designed before the days of nuclear energy. Interpreting their meanings in the light of modern happenings and focusing their fundamental ideology is mainly a matter of practice coupled with intuition and insight. These concepts have been discussed to demonstrate the methodology which you will apply to the Sangreal system. The tarot doesn't have a definite meaning in itself. What it does have is a distinct system that can be used for viewing the objective the cards are directed toward. The Minor Arcana can be regarded as forty ways of looking at the same thing, each revealing another characteristic of its nature and the relationship with who or whatever may be in question. The numeral value and suit symbol provide all the factors needed for using the tarot as their designers intended. The present pictorial arrangements are mostly a distraction and no more than individual artist's impressions of what any card should signify—which could be right, wrong, or merely misleading.

What is meant here is that absolutely any deck will serve the Sangreal purpose, because the deep significance has very little or nothing to do with the fundamental concept advanced for attention. The meanings of the cards are hidden in their names, and their characteristics are enhanced by their relationships as I will explain later. This is to say that an end-interpretation is not to be made according to the nature of any card, but in the light of what that nature reveals when directed toward a specific object. There is a considerable difference between those two aspects of approach. One is using the tarot to look *at*, and the other is using them to look *through*. This is actually a reversible process in which the tarot can be employed as a means for an *inner intelligence* to communicate with those who have the ability to allow the tarot to convey consciousness *through* the meanings of the cards rather than *by* them.

This entails developing the knack of "looking past the last meaning" in the same direction to discover (if possible) what lies just beyond in direct line. To get the idea of this, select any six or seven cards, and, after lining them up, direct attention to the first. After translating it, go to the next in turn until the end of the line. When the final card is reached, your attention should be moved ahead in the same fashion and fixed questioningly just outside the spread. To emphasize this action somewhat more, the last card can be made a blank one (blanks are supplied with most decks). If you do this with a physical deck, some suggestion of a card should appear when the blank is reached. Pay particular attention to what this is. The image is a mental one, of course, but the significance of this simple little exercise is that when known factors are assembled and followed to their end the next to appear will be the sought-for, unknown connection — providing the probing process is maintained and not switched off because the apparent end had been reached. It is only a matter of continuing pressure a little longer along the same path.

I am not suggesting that you practice this exercise more than a few times. You only need to do it to get the fundamental principle behind it. After that it can be included as general practice, and it can be done with one card quite as effectively as with several. This is the idea: use the tarot for pushing consciousness past a sticking point to contact what lies in that area and to bring it within the bounds of ordinary awareness. It is in that part of the conscious spectrum where most of the answers we seek in life lie — or at least the vital clues leading to their discovery.

CHAPTER FIVE

The Tarot on the Tree of Life

O BVIOUSLY, THE BEST plan for putting the tarot together is by classifying all the cards according to a master plan, and the most practical of these seems to be the Holy Tree of Life. With an understanding of the ten spheres of the Tree, it now becomes possible to classify the ten cards of each suit in the Minor Arcana. Integrating the card with the Tree of Life becomes a simple matter of:

1) the card number, which determines the Tree of Life Concept or archetypal idea of the card; and

2) its suit, which shows the angle from which the concept should be approached.

All the rest is a matter of judgment and experience, which will depend on the amount of time and effort you are willing to spend.

On the Tree of Life, the Major Arcana are normally attached one to each of the 22 paths, according to whatever system of attribution may seem best suitable. There has never been any argument about the Minor Arcana because these so clearly belong with their clearly numerated spheres. The Minor

Arcana values are more or less fixed, while the Major Arcana are mobile. A cross is a fixed symbol, while a circle always gives the impression of mobility. The two combined produce a "wheel of life" design. In Chapter 6 we will further delve into the wheel of the Major Arcana, which we will call the Sangreal Trump Cycle. The trumps are arranged in a circle so as to make meaning, and the circle tells the story of the Sangreal from one end of the cycle to the other in relation to humanity on this earth.

But that still leaves the lesser cards with their same fundamental meanings. Nothing in the circle-cross is altered except the relationship of the placement of the Major Arcana to the Minor Arcana on the cross. In this first section, we will look at the meanings of the court cards and the meanings of the Minor Arcana. Because the suit is so important to an understanding of the Sangreal, let's first consider how the four suits should be approached from a Sangreal point of view.

The overall conceptual ideal to bear in mind is that of a Priest King, or an idealized, semi-divine human who sacrifices his life for his kinsfolk. This concept must be understood correctly since it applies to the Cycle of Life it shares with us for as long as we exist. The quaternities of life are considered as Cups for joy, Swords for sorrow, Shields for protection, and Rods for progression. So the King aspect of the master figure would be symbolized by the Cup and Shield, while the Priest aspect would be indicated by the Rod and Sword. Since we are grouping the suits according to the Sangreal system, let's call the Cups its satisfactions, the Shields its secularities, the Rods its sacerdotalisms, and the Swords its sorrows. We may further classify those quarters as:

> Cups: the quadrant of *entering earth*;
> Shields: the quadrant of *learning life*;
> Rods: the quadrant of *overcoming obstacles*;
> Swords: the quadrant of *anguishing adventures*.

The idea of the *quadrants* is an important one, and will be elaborated on in our discussion of the Sangreal Tarot Cycle in Chapter 6. For now, it's best for you to grasp the concepts behind each of the suits. So, to determine the ideological value of any Minor Arcana card, it is only necessary to know that Rods are concerned with the *origination* of ideas; Cups with their *creation*; Swords with their *formation*; and Shields with their *expression*. In the Sangreal Tarot Cycle, the first quadrant is concerned with the life that brought the Sangreal to this world; the second quadrant relates to the laws we have to observe in order to stay here; the third, to the lessons we shall have to learn if we are to evolve; and the last quadrant to the liberation we shall earn at the cost of suffering and sorrow. We could take almost any four suitably related concepts to describe the four suits. For instance: Cups are the nice things in life; Shields are the normal ones; Rods are the necessary things; and Swords are the nasty happenings of and to humanity. The instrument symbols themselves are supposed to suggest appropriate attributes. A Cup suggests rewards and rejoicings; a Shield protects and preserves; a Rod supports and signifies; and a Sword shows sorrows and strife.

Or, you could call the Cups the best happenings in life; the Shields, the usual sort of things; Rods, the difficult ones; and Swords, the absolute worst. Again, if we can accept an imaginary "lifemeter," with a scale marked from one extreme of experience to the other, commencing with the worst and ending with the best, Swords would start and Cups complete the calibration, with Shields at about one-third and Rods about two-thirds between them. It's a useful way of considering the suits in relation to life. At least there can be little argument about what we think are the best and worst experiences that people encounter in this world! And anything else is bound to fall somewhere between them.

The entire symbology of the suits needs to be very well known at the beginning of serious tarot work, or nothing worthwhile will ever be possible. Everything about them ought to be read, studied and meditated on in order to bring the tarot alive in your hands.

As you'll recall, the suits are further coded by the vowels A, E, I, O and U. It will further help your understanding if you study Table 1 on page 67. Here each card in the Minor Arcana is shown with its appropriate keyword by suit. Note that it's an alliterative system — in other words, the vowel A represents Shield. So our keywords here all begin with the letter A. The "people" of the court cards have special identities of their own, so these keywords don't apply to them. Let's start by taking a look at the meanings of the court cards.

The Court Cards

It is generally thought that the court cards were added late in the evolution of the tarot, since they are a somewhat awkward addition and nobody seems quite certain where to place them. They were obviously meant to cover all categories of average humanity likely to be encountered in the course of a lifetime. Which they will, as a rule, if you do not insist on too detailed a description! In principle, they consist of four senior males, four senior females, four junior males, and four juniors who could be of either sex. The court cards are supposed to represent the various classes which more or less controlled the conduct of the world, and on whom the fate of the people depended. In a general way, they included people as a whole, classified by character. It was customary for a client to identify with an appropriate court card so that he or she could be placed correctly in relation to the rest of the spread.

It should be particularly noted that none of the court cards represent clerics of any kind. All are connected with the strata of secular society. The Kings and Queens naturally represent the men and women who make and propagate the laws and customs of human association, the Knights signify the enforcement agencies of the Kings and Queens (or the power people) and the

Table 1. Codes for the cards.

	A – Shields	E – Swords	I – Rods	O – Cups	U – Truth
1	Absolute	Eternal	Infinite	Omnipotent	Unity
2	Acumen	Elucidation	Intelligence	Omniscience	Utterance
3	Awareness	Encompassment	Inspiration	Omnipresence	Understanding
4	Affability	Eagerness	Integrity	Outgiving	Ubiquity
5	Admonition	Economy	Inevitability	Opposition	Uncomfortable
6	Admirable	Energy	Illustrious	Organization	Universal
7	Affection	Emotion	Invincible	Optimism	Upliftment
8	Adaptable	Education	Ingenuity	Oratory	Urbanity
9	Acquiescence	Elusive	Imagination	Oblivion	Unconsciousness
10	Assiduous	Experience	Impetus	Obligation	Utility

Pages portray the oncoming generations charged with the obligations of continuing the structure of an ordered and regularized society. The court cards also indicate all the functions applying for that same purpose to be carried out in any single soul. The Kings show our overall control by reason, the Queens our emotional systems, the Knights our constant striving to come to terms with ourselves, and the Pages our yet undeveloped natures which are full of potential and only need proper disciplined attention for raising them to an adult stage of ability. The court cards are a kind of chain of command of our characters from top to bottom.

The suits again divide human nature into four parts or attitudes. Cups symbolize the soft, kindly, comfortable and generous side of it. Shields show the practical, protective, acquisitive, and commercial side. The Rods portray the rule-conscious investigative and curious part of ourselves, while the Swords represent the hard, severe, and sternly disciplined attitudes we sometimes have little option but to adopt. Not a bad division if very generalized. Any individual could have all these characteristics, each liable to predominate at any given instant. As we all know, a fully grown adult male is perfectly capable of exhibiting the character of the most petulant Page for perhaps considerable periods. Therefore the court cards have to be interpreted very flexibly.

Although it is possible to attach classified meanings to the court cards, it is still important that this be done solely for the sake of having something to look *through* rather than at. The cards are ways for looking at people, and they present the way people appear to observers, or the pictures they make of themselves in the minds of others. It could be that the same individual might appear in two totally different and perhaps opposing ways to two different observers. Rather as in the political scene an armed and active warrior is either an heroic freedom fighter or a cowardly and filthy terrorist depending which side an observer favors. Therefore it does not do to take any of the court cards as more than general guides of which way to look while trying to identify anyone concerned with the queries. Let us commence with typical King characteristics.

The King of Cups

He is a kindly lovable male, generous, good hearted, outgoing, and very friendly. He does, however, have the usual weaknesses normally associated with this type of person—being easily imposed upon, taken advantage of, and too permissive of poor behavior in himself and others. It is important to realize that none of the court cards are either good or bad in themselves, for they simply show human characteristics per se. People are usually good along some lines and bad along others, so the court cards have to be understood as showing both in complement to each other. It just depends which side comes uppermost at any instant. The court cards do not define the profession of anyone, but it might be expected that men of this nature would be drawn to the sorts of occupation which would serve humanity as doctors, ministers of religion, welfare workers, teachers, or even entertainers. This type loves to be loved and wants to be on the very best terms with his companions, but he can be capable of attracting such attention by moral bribery and possibly a bit of gentle graft as well.

The King of Shields

He is very common in this world. He may be met in any trading or commercial capacity whatever. Only his social status distinguishes what he does. He is concerned with making a presentable appearance and a standard set of values. He has the virtues and vices of a very ordinary human being since he is neither outstandingly good or evil but just average. He is not greatly concerned with much outside the field of social activities, though he may pay lip service to any orthodox or approved religion for the sake of their social advantages or prestige. He can be completely dishonest once he has managed to disguise or mask his conduct by naming it differently or presenting it in some way acceptable to gullible victims. He would regard this as entirely justifiable under the heading of "business is business." His position and possessions are the most important things in the world to him, and that includes his wife and family insofar as they enhance his status. There must be many millions like him alive in every generation.

The King of Rods

He is an instinctive ruler and regulator who can also be an investigator in any field, such as a scientific worker or a criminologist. He pokes and prods into everything, turning it all over with the point of his Rod which represents the mental finger of inquiry and exploration. He is naturally curious and inquisitive, seldom able to leave anything alone for very long. He can either be quite patient or irritable and quick tempered according to circumstances. His mind may be very rapid and restless or slow and deliberate in following trends of thought. He can be a creature of extreme contrasts. He is relatively honest by comparison with many mortals, but he does like everything explained and clearly comprehensible. He may be precise and pedantic in character. If involved in crime, he would favor intellectual frauds and despise violence because he would consider it crude. The mind is his field rather than the body. He could be a lecturer or instructor, a vivisectionist or a virologist, and he would tend to work by any rules, preferably those he made himself.

The King Swords

He is a severe, serious, and dedicated to duty type who is either a magnificent example or an absolute menace. Keenly conscientious with a propensity for inflicting his idealism on others. Since this is liable to be Spartan, it is seldom popular. Proper and puritanical, his commitments and convictions compel his course of action. He is a type that is respected yet never loved. He can be terribly cruel and vindictive, and is seldom very forgiving or tolerant of behavior he believes should be punished. He usually looks for the worst in human nature and can be certain of finding this very widely distributed. Usually ruthless in outlook, he can be a killer in suitable circumstances. Humorless and often dour, he does not smile easily, and even if he does, his smile will have an element of bitterness about it. There is nothing negative about this man. He is a most determined and forceful individual, though frequently undemonstrative. He is liable to be a legal official, a soldier, statesman, terrorist, or almost anything of a demanding nature calling for the utmost resolution and unswerving dedication to whatever cause he has adopted. Extremist fanatics are often this type of man.

• • •

Now we come to the Queens, who tend to mirror the Kings, though from a feminine angle, which alters or modifies a great many of the characteristics, some for the better and others for the worse!

The Queen of Cups

She is an affectionate, demonstrative, kindly, and also motherly woman whose sweet nature can be cloying (and even smothering) to those of an independent disposition. She can seldom see any faults in her husband or children however badly they may behave. She loves animals and is at her best with her dependents, caring for them constantly even without knowledge or proper skills. Apt to kill with kindness, but at least her victims have a very comfortable death. She is very much the Mrs. Do-as-you-would-be-done-by type of person, often muddling along with the best of meanings and the worst of methods. She can be a bit of a dreamer but her dreams are beautiful. Practicality is not her strong suit, though pleasantness and affability definitely are. She may not be intellectually brilliant, but she can cope with situations which would drive a more demanding woman into desperation. She loves smiling and feeling that all around her are happy and satisfied. Good at gardening and games that are not too strenuous, but apt to be a bit slapdash with household duties. She could be a successful actress, hostess, entertainer, dress designer, any occupation having to do with display arts.

The Queen of Shields

Here we have the typical businesswoman at her best. She is good at most things of a material nature, including sex in which she sometimes specializes—for some of these women are prostitutes who protect clients' reputations and their own with admirable discretion. She knows the value of money and would make a good mate for a poor man, probably adding considerably herself to the family fortune. She can be competent in most occupations and is very adaptable to the majority of social situations. Generally reliable and honest. More dependable than most. No nonsense about this woman. She usually offers a fair deal in all areas of action, is not overly sentimental, and is capable of coping with life's problems from a practical and commonsense angle. If she has a family, she will treat them well without spoiling them. She can, however, be miserly with both money and her affections, tending to regard both in the light of economical expenditures to be rationed with reason and accounted for afterwards. She very seldom does anything impulsively or without calculation. Would make an ideal farmer's wife though she does not seem to specialize in the marriage market because she is such a good all rounder at management. She is a very common type in this world and will fit in most of its frames.

Queen of Rods

This woman is a dominant type and apt to be bossy or incisively overbearing. She knows quite well what she wants and will get it if she possibly can. She is usually intelligent though she could be short on affection and emotion. Ruled by reason, but has a strongly inquisitive streak which accounts for far-out trips now and again. She can be loyal, but if she feels she has been betrayed she makes a Rod for her own back and for those of others. She is not likely to suffer fools very gladly and can be intolerant, though she is always open to argument and can be convinced that she is in the wrong. She enjoys discussions and often joins groups for that purpose, mostly to push her views on others. She is often quite intriguing and companionable, and being a bit outstanding, never lacks for friends who are fascinated by her character and who respect her rulings on most matters. By occupation she may be an academic, researcher, policewoman, or schoolteacher. She may not be fond of domestic duties but will do them with method and efficiency. She often rises in rank and is quite capable of reaching the top of her chosen profession.

Queen of Swords

Usually has a serious and often sad aspect frequently due to personal misfortune. She is sometimes widowed in early life or else loses her lover in some strange way. Is often one of those women who seem to bring ill luck in their wake and would have been accused of witchcraft a few centuries ago. Is sometimes attracted to the darker side of magic and what were once called the Black Arts. She always seems to be "overshadowed" by something a little uncanny. Not a comfortable woman to associate with. She has an enormously compelling character. She need never be lonely unless she wants to be, which is often the case when she prefers her own company to that of other people who irritate her with their cheerful chatter. She can be quite cruel and sadistic as she enjoys making her victims suffer in peculiar ways which please her inventiveness. She sometimes stays unmarried and may be homosexual. Her occupations can be concerned with politics, legal positions, management, accountancy, pathology, surgery, or highly technical work—such as electronics.

• • •

Now we come to the Knights, sometimes called Princes, or young militant males. They are all troublemakers in the sense of stirring things up and disturbing tranquil but static situations, often with the best of intentions, yet seldom with anything more than enthusiasm and zeal for whatever they believe to be their "cause." They could be classed as activists who are prepared to face persecution and unpopularity if they can call public attention to whatever they support with their service. They are often exploited by unscrupulous politicians and commercialists who make a profit out of their activities. Yet the Knights are idealists whose youth is directed rightly or wrongly towards a vague Divinity they instinctively feel must live somewhere at the other end of their ideals. Their inner instincts are awakening them enough to urge them on energetically, but they have insufficient experience for guiding them either wisely or expertly. This they are learning as they quest along.

Knights can refer either to males or females in our times, but the convention of knighthood puts forward the concept of a young, dedicated, enthusiastic, and especially well-bred person of courage, self-confidence and ability who is prepared to risk life and limb in such service, expecting no more reward than the privilege of inclusion among the company they choose to fight in. They are opposed to wrongs, injustices, barbarities, ill behavior, and all that may be contrary to their best beliefs. Their cause is more important to them than anything else, and sex would have to take second place if they were ever faced with the choice of loyalties. Nearly all worthwhile souls go through this initiatory stage of knighthood during the early part of their lives, and it is part of the essential program which prepares our souls for the most difficult duties ahead. The four classes of knighthood are these:

Knight of Cups

He is sometimes called the Grail Knight because of the cup symbol he bears, though this only refers to his nature. He is very much of an idealist but not in a warlike way. His contribution to any conflict would be an inspirational one. It is he who writes the songs, composes the music, and arranges the backgrounds against which later battles will be fought. This young man is a hopeless romantic, and is apt to see things through the rosiest of spectacles which may turn red with blood later on. He is the dreamer who incites the doers, the painter who depicts his dream so that he may share it with others. He sometimes craves martyrdom for the sake of its crown, yet rarely risks it for fear that fate may take him at his word. His feelings uplift him, yet fear of failure holds him back from actual encounters with open enmity. It is really he who puts the concepts that he and others believe in with all their hearts into words they can understand, formulae they can follow, and clear ideologies they can share with the strongest sense of companionship among them all. He is certainly their leader in the spiritual sense of the term. The others will rally round his call, and if he falls they will fail in their mission. He cheers and gets them going with the cup of comradeship, consoles them for any temporary set-back, and in general encourages the morale without which all troops would be useless. If he has a fault, it is trusting the wrong people or misplacing confidence in those who are likely to collapse without warning at the vital moment.

The Knight of Shields

This youngster is much more practical and believes in as sound a defense as possible. He knows the necessity for money and a firm financial backing for every enterprise. What is more, he will obtain it if he has to wring it out of the hardest heart and loosen the tightest purse strings. That is his specialty and he is not afraid to carry it out by fair means or foul. He is honest insofar as the cause is concerned, but he may be a Robin Hood type who would gladly rob the rich in order to give the poor their share of ill-gotten gains. He feels protective toward the poor and under-privileged, and enjoys fighting with those he regards as oppressors of the helpless and hopeless. He knows quite well that if the poor are to be fed somebody has to take the food from the tables of the rich and that is his mission. He is obsessed with the unfair economics which allow honest and hardworking people to starve while speculators and politicians prosper. He is upset about cruelty to animals also, and defends all the SPCA's and other organizations of that nature he can join. He will carry their collection boxes everywhere and crusade as hard as he can on behalf of battered babies and their mistreated mothers. He will even rescue a damsel in distress occasionally, demanding no more than the girl is willing to give him. A down to earth lad this one, who would grudge him his petty percentage?

The Knight of Rods

Here is an equally enthusiastic fighter but for quite a different reason. This young man is a stickler for the rules of the game and correct conduct of conflict. Though he can on occasion be unscrupulous, he prefers a fair fight, but will bend the rules if he has to. He is more concerned with the intellectual ideology of the cause but may involve himself with the activism as much as anyone and more than most. He will volunteer for special missions that call for courage, initiative and leadership. He is happiest when leading a group and is a good disciplinarian who is not afraid to take risks. Could be overbold sometimes. Likes to analyze the reasons for failure and see them all logically. For him, battle can be an exact science, and he will fight with a computer as much as with a sword. He is the one who invents new weapons and designs the special tools of his trade. He is good at logistics and all the purely technical aspects of conflict. He is also likely to be a good theoretical strategist and may be brilliant when working out elaborate schemes for winning his wars. He is a soldier of the sand-table who plans the details of every assault. Possibly a keen chess player or good at anything involving mathematics or calculations. No real battle could be fought without his type. He may become a general.

The Knight of Swords

This is the deadly killer and ruthless warrior in every company of knights. Though he can see the cause as plainly as the next person, he cannot see the point of fighting unless it leads to extermination of the opposition. For him, warfare and conflict are very much black and white affairs and he can see no value in arguments or intellectualism. "Kill or be killed" is his motto. Not for him the conference tables and negotiating platforms of any political kind. He will remain unswerving in his determination to hit his enemy wherever it may hurt most. In fact, gaining the Grail would be a disappointment if that finished his fighting. He does not envisage dying, but finding some heaven where he will be allowed to continue the conflict forever. Perhaps he has been a Viking in a previous life. He is actually the most vulnerable of them all, since the impetuosity of his devastating charge carries him right through the enemy who cleverly part before him and allow him to run straight on to their minefield which blows him away like thistledown in the wind. Still, he may have done a little damage on his way to Valhalla, and his erstwhile comrades mourn him for a moment before summoning his replacement from the eagerly waiting ranks of enlisted esquires.

• • •

Here follow the Pages, sometimes called Princesses, applying equally to females as males. They are possibly the most difficult of the lot to assess on account of their youth and inexperience. Their full characters have not yet completely formed, being still very mutable with room for dramatic changes in any direction. Although there may be many indications and likelihoods, who can ever be certain how any average youngster is going to turn out? That has to be borne in mind when dealing with any of the Pages. There is a tendency to underestimate them, which might be unwise, since they represent a potential which could develop at a later period. It is therefore useful to consider them in forecasting future possibilities. It is important to remember that the Pages are people at the commencement of their careers as Questers of the Grail, and they may be a lot older, in fact, than the ideology of a Page would suggest.

Pages were and always will be trainee-Knights, as the Knights are trainee-Kings and Queens who again are trainees for a higher form of life altogether. Who can tell where this train of trainees might end? Wherever that may be, the Grail will be there to welcome them all. A Page has a lot more latitude than a King or Queen since he or she is in a state of spiritual flux which is in the process of settling down to its definite level for a lifetime. Allowances have to be made for this factor when trying to calculate any spread with a Page in it.

The Page of Cups

This lad or lass is gentle, compassionate, and full of feeling for friends, animals, and the lovely things of life. Perhaps more mystical than practical, introspective and very sensitive. Religious and interested in everything connected with beliefs and ideals. Possibly poetic. A very pleasing youngster to deal with, yet not very reliable nor entirely truthful. Apt to be somewhat indolent and not very methodical in manner, yet with a charm which attracts quite a number of friends. This one is too easily imposed on and is liable to lose a great many chances through neglecting opportunities and not following up advantages. Normally affectionate and companionable, with a beautiful smile and a willingness to caress and be caressed. Associates sex with love and will only do it with those coming very close in relationship. Takes everything to heart and makes personal contacts the main thing in life. Often has great difficulty in deciding on an occupation because the things loved most are outside commercial areas or paid appointments.

The Page of Shields

This page is quite different from the last. Here is a practical and no-nonsense type of young person, very capable of coping with the ordinary affairs of this world. Perhaps inclined to be a little dogmatic and opinionated. Willing to work and fast to learn. More materialistic than mystic. Good ideas about the values of anything and how to look after it. Takes a lot of care with clothing and possessions. Good at mending things and likes caring for sick animals and people. Generally reliable and honest and straightforward. Very mature about sex and not inclined to treat it as anything romantic or spiritual – just plain enjoyable or abhorrent according to circumstances. Makes a useful mate for the average individual. Mostly looks on causes as good things to follow providing they do not interfere too much with the business of life. Nevertheless, these people can make most valuable contributions toward causes of any description even if only on a temporary basis.

The Page of Rod

These types are the intellectuals of the bunch. Their fascination is facts and figures, statistics and logical deductions. Sometimes they are apt to be a bit of a pest on this point. They want to know the reason for everything, and are constantly asking "why?" usually of everyone without an answer. This Page seems never satisfied and always seeks alternative explanations. Inclined to be pushy. Insists on some rational story to cover any new concept encountered. Refuses to fight without adequate reasons. Not completely reliable, since they can invent plausible reasons for not keeping their given word, yet by no means are they untrustworthy or lacking in loyalty. Nevertheless, this is the Page most likely to betray any cause at a later date on account of a liability to change loyalties after being convinced of some greater need for their services. Susceptible to flattery concerning ability and intelligence. Should always be encouraged along those lines and particularly praised for any good efforts made. Thrives on adulation and places high values on favorable opinions from others. Is both inventive and ingenious in sexual affairs which may make these quite novel encounters.

Page of Swords

Here we have born fanatics in the process of dedicating themselves to any cause they feel may be worth killing for. These are the Pages to watch with great attention because they are likely to be made or marred for a very long time. Given due care and guidance they may become very valuable, but if they fall into the wrong hands they may turn into a danger, threatening everyone including themselves. They present a very serious problem in all organizations. They may be noted for deadly seriousness, lack of genuine humor, and a conviction that they have some definite mission in life which has to be fulfilled at all costs. Their character is very hard and usually unloving; impressive maybe, but never truly loving. Dislike being touched or caressed, and may be indifferent to sex, or they can be cruel partners. Otherwise, they have sterling qualities of unquestionable value to any cause, and are entirely reliable to the extent of their power. Unfortunately they are not very original and are largely dependent on taking orders from those regarded as superiors. Literally everything hangs on their being directed into useful channels at as early an age as possible. It is a tragedy when youngsters of this kind are misdirected.

The Minor Arcana

It would be a great mistake to underestimate the importance of this tarot section because of its name. It is neither minor nor lesser in terms of meaning and significance when applied to peoples lives. We should never forget that each card represents one particular aspect of a single sphere on the Holy Tree of Life. There are ten Spheres, and four cards to each—thus forty cards to relate with every sphere from four distinct angles. That is the master-key to unlock the main meanings of the so-called Minor Arcana. First you must align the card number with its associated sphere, and then consider the subject of that sphere in the light of whichever suit the card belongs to. That should afford a useful interpretation of what the card in question means, although you must use your own intuition to make the sequential linkage of all cards concerned. With this in mind let us look at each card of the "minor" deck and see what may be learned from them.

Ace of Cups

The Grail itself. The absolute root and fount of Grail faith. The highest happiness possible in the closest companionship with the power we call God. So far as the Sangreal is concerned, this card signifies the *ne plus ultra* of the quest, the having and holding of heavenly bliss in the blood. It indicates the selfstate of utmost union possible for people of this planet. So far as the average individual is concerned, this card implies the presence of a strong spiritual principle under some guise or other, and may indicate the action of that principle behind quite a commonplace presentation. It certainly calls the attention of the querant to the Grail-ends of our existence and symbolizes the influence of these on whatever is being queried. It stands for the love of God that passes all understanding. Maybe it is best thought of as the Supreme Serenity of Life.

Ace of Shields

This is the seed of secularity and the root of royalty in every human being. The centerpoint around which a whole kingdom collects and expands. It is the matrix meaning of our material manifestation and the reason why we are roaming this Earth. It signifies the original essence of our physical existence and symbolizes our primal purpose on this planet. Namely that we must learn to live in accordance with a planned and organizable pattern in such a manner that we shall eventually perfect ourselves. On this shield should be set forth the pattern we adopt and follow so as to gain the Grail, which will mean that we have fulfilled our purpose on earth and are fit for finer forms of living other than in mortal bodies. This will obviously need the very best form of rulership we can find and since it has to start somewhere, this card stands for the central principle of "royalty," or the Supreme Spirit that raises the secular self to the height of its attainment on earth.

Ace of Rods

The root of priestliness in people. It amounts to the spirit of self-sacrifice in its truest sense – The rule of life that continually offers itself for the sake of its own continuity. The kind of instinct which makes a mother sacrifice herself for her child, or impels anyone to lay down a lesser life for a larger one. The spirit of service in the most sincere sense. A Staff is a support or guide, and the ace signifies an impulse in people to help, guide, and support others towards the same divine destination we all need to find. It can indicate that we should hold out our hands in support of our weaker brethren and defend them in their difficulties. The priest-instinct should prompt us to mediate between powers and people on behalf of the latter, and this ace is a symbolic card suggesting a necessity for that function.

Ace of Swords

The root of sorrow itself, which lies in the sense of separation from God. Sometimes called "Self," but meaning that each individual feels "lost and alone" albeit in company with millions adrift on this earth, each working out its unique purpose. The greater the sense of separation, the greater degree of sorrow is experienced. Most ordinary folk would not interpret sorrow in such definite terms, but would recognize it by associated pain and suffering in physical or mental areas of intensity. Nevertheless, the common root symbolized by the ace of Swords is the cutting off or disconnection of individuals from their life-source at any level. All sorrows, whether physical, mental or spiritual, stem from this single factor, and everything depends on the degree and nature of such separation. At birth it becomes expulsion from the womb mythologized by the Fall and Garden of Eden legend. At death it becomes reabsorption into the Eternal where consciousness encounters whatever fate it has formed during its material manifestation.

Obviously such separation is not total while any soul still retains its instinctive grip on life itself. This may be done without any kind of religious awareness, for what a religious person calls God and invests with imaginative ideology, an ordinary mortal thinks of as "life" to be taken as experienced. All these people would know is that the closer they feel to life, the happier they are, and the more they feel alienated from it, the more miserable they become. The same experience is seen from two different viewpoints in the Ace of Swords. Thus we should really consider it an attenuator of the vital life-sense rather than a complete severance from our maker. It is the Root of Sorrow in any language.

Two of Cups

The Serenity of Knowing, or Sapience. It was once said: "Blessed are the pure in heart for they shall *know* God," and this is what this card stands for. Knowledge was used in a sexual sense, and this is indeed connected with the ideology of a mystical marriage where a human soul of either physical sex "married" God by absorption into that energy. Wisdom is the faculty (or ability) which makes knowledge possible, and the possession or capability of true wisdom is a Grail-gift beyond all price. This card means either a need to gain or increase wisdom, or an opportunity of doing so. It certainly signifies the happiest of encounters.

Two of Shields

Two is a 100% increase of one, and this is the card of increasing wisdom which improves experience of life. Those who are wise increase their wisdom by comparing one thing with another and learning right relationships. Everything has to be weighed against something else and calculated to the right conclusion. No wise king would judge any subject without affording equal attention to the opposite viewpoint. Just as an increase of wealth and material possessions begins by turning one into two, so should a king make additions to his kingdom, whether physical, mental or spiritual. This card shows that the constructive qualities of kingship in human beings should be correctly augmented and expanded so that the guardianship of the Grail becomes increasingly effective and intelligent.

Two of Rods

This clearly indicates the wisdom of making a right choice between alternative methods or procedures. The card may not show the actual making of such a choice, but stresses the necessity for asking inner wisdom for help in making a wise decision. From a Grail viewpoint it signifies a need to mediate between divine wisdom and a human seeking its directive influence. It may indicate the presentation of a problem calling for care and attention in coming to a wise conclusion about anything, or the encountering of an enigma which cannot be solved without the application of wisdom (as distinct from either knowledge or information). Rods are pointers, and this card shows a promise that the right way will be pointed out by providence.

Two of Swords

The Sorrow of Stupidity. This indicates being severed from the wisdom-principle. Bewilderment, indecision, lack of enlightenment. Whatever prevents clarity of consciousness. This card stands for the sorrow of being unable to reach required wisdom, a lack of self-confidence, sense of insufficiency, or the realization of not being wise enough to cope with problems presented. The card can, however, act as a timely reminder of inadequacy and if it cuts deeply enough, sting the recipient into action against ignorance and inanity. Again it may mean hurts received due to non-knowledge and willful refusal to listen to reason. Or it could indicate a risk of wounding others through ignorance of likely effects.

Three of Cups

The serenity of certainty through comprehension. Who can shake the serenity of a consciousness that completely comprehends what everything signifies? This card shows the confidence common to experts in their own fields. In this instance, it indicates the confidence which comes of understanding both the veracity and validity of the Sangreal. It may be an assurance of this, or an admonition to seek such spiritual support, and it could suggest an approach to follow, or an ideal to adopt, so as to gain satisfaction and serenity while questing for the Grail. In lesser ways it signifies agreement and amity among those who understand each other in respect of a common cause or objective. There can be no conflict among such people, and this is a card of faith and friendship celebrated comprehendingly among good companions of the blessed blood.

Three of Shields

The main problem of life is choosing a correct course between alternatives, and this card shows that this can or will be made possible. Understanding and intuition are the guiding principles involved, and it could mean that a woman would know best what to say or do in the circumstances being queried. It signifies a truly royal sense of judgement due to comprehension of all factors involved. It shows how puzzles and problems should be dealt with, since what humans do not understand in themselves, the great consciousness of God comprehends completely. It is therefore rational to ask the God within oneself for guidance in all matters of doubt. Old time kings were advised to pray for this assistance. Hence this card could be cautionary, advising inquirers to pray for protection in whatever undertaking might be in question.

Three of Rods

Here the three positively points out the need for comprehension concerning the subject of inquiry. Bearing in mind that we are concerned with the sacerdotal side of human nature, it is obvious that the faculty of understanding is vital when trying to deal with spiritual problems. How can anyone counsel another who cannot comprehend the factors involved. This card could be a reproach for not trying hard enough to understand whatever is being queried. It may also point straight to the solution if studied closely enough. Contiguous cards should be carefully examined for any signs of likely solution.

Three of Swords

This is the sorrow of misunderstanding which is inclusive of being misunderstood. One of the most hurtful happenings to humans. The card indicates misunderstandings and mistakes on any level of life, or an inability to understand whatever the problem may be. It has nothing to do with mere lack of information or intellectual ignorance, but indicates a character deficiency of comprehension calling for rectification. Again and again lives can be wrecked by this single factor. How often do people say ruefully: "I didn't know," when they should have said: "I could not comprehend"? This card speaks of such a disability and the circumstances arising therefrom.

Four of Cups

The Serenity of Kind Compassion. This card suggests the calm and contentment accompanying all acts of compassion activated by magnanimity or mercy. This has nothing to do with futile forgiveness of puerile permissiveness, but refers specifically to intelligent intervention with the purpose of preventing needless and unprofitable suffering. Compassion for its own sake is pointless, but when directed with purpose and intention it accomplishes its highest aim. Here the card is calling for the application of compassion or indicating its presence in particular problems. It may signify the reception of generosity and benefaction from some source or other, but might indicate that this should be extended in specific cases.

Four of Shields

Monarchial mercy means mitigation or suspension of punishment, augmentation of insufficiencies, or alteration of afflictions which lie in the power of a human ruler to effect. This card signifies that such benefits may or should be applicable in the case of the query. The keyword is magnanimity which means greatness or kingly kindness. It is sometimes said: "None but the generous shall gain the Grail," and here such an outpouring type of generosity is needed. Distribution of largesse was regarded as a royal privilege rather than a duty. Giving was the privilege of kings, and with it was supposed to come the gift of giving gracefully, often a rare ability. The card here calls for the cultivation and application of that regal faculty.

Four of Rods

From a priestly viewpoint, this card points out the necessity for exercising merciful compassion in the area of consultation. Not sentimental weakness, but that feeling where one human identifies with another because of common capabilities and so is sympathetic to whatever may be in question. Thoughts to remember here are: "God hates the sin yet loves the sinner," and, "There but for the grace of God go I." Mercy derives from great spiritual strength and the sort of kind care that curbs bad behavior either in oneself or in one's charges. Mercy goes under many guises, and this card is an indication that its applicable form should be sought for and applied.

Four of Swords

The Sorrow of Suffering. This card is indicative of suffering endured to a point of surfeit, the respite that sets in, and the temporary remission that results. Human capacity for both joy and sorrow is limited by the capacity to endure either. Here a merciless and unkind fate brings us to the point where death or unconsciousness would be a mercy in itself. It could indicate that a lack of compassion is causing trouble, and it could be construed that suffering might be a sign of divine mercy because of some misfortune that has been sent, so we will struggle against it and so improve ourselves spiritually in consequence. In order for this to be effective however, sufferings would have to be exactly of the right kind in each case.

Five of Cups

The Serenity of Self-discipline. This is the contentment and quiet confidence that comes from reliance on self-control and perhaps long and exhaustive training in the art. While being not exactly a gift, it is recognized by all Grail gainers as a primal requisite before committing oneself to the Quest unreservedly. This can be a bitter cup which has to be swallowed uncomplainingly by those called upon to take their medicine as Deity demands. It signifies dedication to duty and the pledge made for the performance of it in the service of the Sangreal.

Five of Shields

This card is indicative of many things pertaining to restrictions and rational economics. It can mean "cutting the cloth in keeping with one's station," making rulings for preventing waste and extravagance, being sensibly sober in serious situations, and generally living well within one's means. Both king and commoner are bound by such secular sense, and more kingdoms have been lost by bankruptcy than by battle. The card may mean an approaching crisis from a socio-economic standpoint which might curb cultural activities connected with the Grail on earth. It could indicate a need to be very careful in material matters, or it may generally call attention to restrictions which need loosening.

Five of Rods

This card shows struggle and strife, very much a sacerdotal concern. Constant struggle with adversity and contention with opponents. Struggle may strengthen or weaken anyone according to circumstances, and has always to be estimated in context with other factors. This card can call for corrective discipline and indicate the chastisement dealt out by divinity to those loved. This could be a need for self-discipline and character corrections which are pointed out for attentive action.

Five of Swords

The Sorrow of Severity. This could indicate the "Wrath of God" extended because of misdeeds or misbehavior, or might mean alienation from life due to ill-treatment of it or disregard for its rightful demands. Painful punishment of rulebreakers defying divinity in themselves. Perhaps "just deserts" could be interpretive here. The card should be seen as a needed corrective applied before the spiritual situation worsens. Possibly humiliation may be experienced to lessen overweening pride, or sickness sent to induce the comprehension of infirmity in others. It could also indicate cruelty or unkindness in the inquirer which calls for cosmic compensation. It also may indicate brutality, needing a beating, or viciousness demanding vengeance.

Six of Cups

The Serenity of Sweetness. Seldom does life feel exactly right — when everything seems in harmony and all appears to balance perfectly. Here we have at least a semblance of a state which appears to be a sample of heaven. The card indicates the temporary tranquility symbolized by the "Cup running over" of the psalm. All the indications are "set fair" for the Sun of righteousness to shine on those who call upon it for illumination. God seems to be in his heaven and all is right with the world. Perhaps this indicates that the time has come to take things at their flood while the tide lasts. It signifies an abatement of ill and the augmentation of good. The only limiting factor is time, and there are strong hints here to seize opportunities.

Six of Shields

Prosperity and good health are indicated by this card. Affairs of this world go well for guardians of the Grail. It could be that this card gives a vision of what things might be like here if everything were run on Grail principles. It may be remembered that the Grail was supposed to provide whatever each individual liked best, and this is perhaps the single card which offers possibilities of such a promise being fulfilled. It is at least an assurance that the Grail is by no means an entirely out of this world affair, but is concerned with the well-being and prosperity of all its people. There is a reminder, however, that the Grail is never given gratis and always has to be earned.

Six of Rods

The priestly function of mediation has the central concept of harmony being radiated to all in communication with it through the officiating priest. This card points out the indescribable qualities of the influence being applied to whatever may be in question. It signifies that a balanced condition is being, (or will be) brought to bear on the affair. Perhaps this may indicate the stabilization of a shaky state or the centralization of an unclear situation. Illumination of it maybe, or harmony restored to a discordant condition. Remember the connection here with Apollo, God of medicine and music. This card can mean good physical and spiritual health. It always points to hope during difficulties.

Six of Swords

The Sorrow of Spoilation. This indicates blighted beauty, harmony disturbed, happiness reduced to misery and disappointment, or a threat to balance of mind, body, or soul. On the other hand, it could be a counterbalance to indolence induced by idyllic tranquility, or shaking up to induce vigilance in an overconfident individual or group. A provocative prod as it were. This card could mean an inability to appreciate either beauty or harmony, signifying a sort of spiritual tone-deafness which might lead to physical sickness or disability.

Seven of Cups

The Serenity of Success. To succeed at anything does bring contentment, although this is only transient and temporary. This card shows promise of success in undertakings, but gives no assurance that this is lasting or in the least permanent. Nevertheless, it should be welcome as an event within a wider field of questing. At least it is something encouraging to look for and makes a good memory of some pleasant interlude when looking back on life.

Seven of Shields

This emphasizes the necessity for earning the Grail, which is always spoken of as being gained, attained, or achieved, thus indicating its ultimate value as a rightful recompense in return for effort expended. The greatest thing any king can give is his life for his people, and that is what the card indicates. The Shield symbology specifies that the terms of the physical world apply here, and whoever would become a Grail king in secular style must learn how to arrange life accordingly, whether it be that of a beggar or a prince. The methodology counts, not the magnitude. Here advice is given to learn and study such a system, whatever your actual life-position may be.

Seven of Rods

This card points to success with priestly potentials. These are character qualities connecting us with God in the most direct and convenient manner. Strictly speaking those most suitable for individual cases. It could be more simply put by saying that the best in ourselves triumphs over the worst, and the angels are on the winning side for once. This card should always be interpreted as an encouragement or a congratulation for active efforts directed to an improvement of character and the rectification of faults in ourselves or others.

Seven of Swords

The Sorrow of Submission. This card shows the natural sadness deriving from a sense of defeat or lack of success in life. Efforts that apparently fail or are frustrated, careful calculations proving wrong, and everything coming to a sticky and inglorious ending. Yet it would not do for humans to win all the time, and sharp sword-like lessons are often the best to learn from in order to discover how to do better next time. Here we do not find irrevocable defeats, but temporary setbacks that we will live to fight about again. In fact, the card may indicate that a show of submission could be tactically advisable if you need a respite before continuing the conflict on improved chances.

Eight of Cups

The Serenity of Satisfaction. Here we have a card signifying the natural satisfaction derived from feelings of glory and pride in something well done. Though this may happen seldom enough in this world or anywhere else, we definitely need this sensation from time to time in order to inspire fresh efforts in other directions. Sometimes efforts may seem small and successes relatively unimportant, yet they all contribute toward the glories of the Grail, and every single one of them is an encouragement.

Eight of Shields

This particular card implies that honorable dealings in all matters are expected of a Sangreal aspirant. It might signify the glorious company of the Grail in this world, or indicate a particular need for something to be honored. It could even signify that an honor will be granted to some worthy servitor. The importance of honor in connection with the Sangreal is something that only those with genuine qualities of kingship in their souls can understand. If necessary, it has to be upheld with life itself.

Eight of Rods

This points out what used to be called the "Honor and Glory of God." In other words a sense of splendor and privilege in serving so high a cause as cosmos itself. This should never suggest superiority, but always indicate genuine humility (not self-depreciation) and an accurate and dispassionate assessment of our potential value. This gives a sense of "doing the right thing" and an assurance of correct conduct. It may also mean that a question of honor is involved, or call for what once was termed "propriety."

Eight of Swords

The Sorrow of Shame. This card signifies ignominy and inglorious grief due to disgrace or dishonor. An oriental person might call it "loss of face." It may show a loss of self-confidence due to the lowered opinion of abilities on account of being discredited or distrusted. It could also indicate exposure of a shameful or embarrassing secret. Maybe loss of reputation or damaging influences acting on individual integrity. Perhaps slander and character defamation.

Nine of Cups

The Serenity of Stability. A stabilized and steady life may not be the most thrilling one, but it can be secure and reliable, affording a sound basis on which to build whatever is wanted. The card indicates this in a number of directions. Stability in oneself is a first and foremost requirement, closely followed by that of family, friends, work, current circumstances, and life situations in general. Stability signifies safety or minimum risk, and that is implied here especially. Often this is called the "wish card" because so many human wishes depend on this one factor. It always has the most fortunate meanings.

Nine of Shields

This is the basis of the Grail's spiritual structure in this world, and the card stands for strengthening and supporting of all its best beliefs by every possible means. It calls for protection and preservation of Grail-principles at all costs, and the provision for upholding these principles wherever they are weakest. Here is a reminder that the ideology of the Grail was founded and based on this necessity. It can mean an incentive in the direction of any scheme to enhance the earthly establishment of the Grail Kingdom, or inspiration regarding "foundation ideas" which contribute toward building it.

Nine of Rods

This points out the basis of faith itself, and the need to deal with the deepest dreams of humanity accurately and clearly. It indicates visions and revelations reached by psychic means. Hints and suggestions rather than certainties, providing fascinating interest which entices the enquirer. Teaching obscure traditions, mysteries and mysticism, the necessary element of magic in all religions. The passage of power into people, yet providing puzzles which impel us to seek solutions. This card indicates the priestly function of giving guidance to those in doubt and bringing light to dark places in the human mind or soul.

Nine of Swords

The Sorrow of Shattering. Here we have sorrow to a degree which can shatter the stability of mind or soul. The instability of insanity and all diseased imagination. This is a "dark night of the soul" type of card which most mystics undergo at least once in their lives. It brings a sense of desertion by divinity, betrayal of beliefs, and plunges people into the depths of depression. Here are the horrors of upset ideology, worries, fears, and agitations about everything. The Sangreal offers no immunity from it, since it is an experience which everyone must undergo in their own way as part of the purgatory preceding eventual enlightenment.

Ten of Cups

The Serenity of the Sangreal. We must have all wondered what life would be like without any of the horrors humanity has cause to dread on Earth. No wars, no waste, no wickedness, no sickness, or sorrow of any kind—that would certainly be a Sangreal sort of world resembling the kingdom of heaven on Earth so frequently prayed for. This card indicates something connected with this possibility and indicates at least a hint of such a happening through human experiences. This is always a very good card and augurs well in any consultation. It is most certainly a cup of consolation kindness and companionship.

Ten of Shields

This indicates the kingdom of the Sangreal in this world and all that means as a material manifestation. All the obligations and responsibilities appertaining to kingship represented by those who are agents of the Grail on Earth. A timely reminder that such would involve the sacrifice of life if need be in the cause of cosmic companionship. A true king must be the servant of his people in the highest sense and the two titles must be accepted together or not at all. A king should be the protector of his people, and this card is a reminder that such an obligation may be imminent. It is a most important card from the material aspect of the Grail-ideal, though it has to be estimated in context with contiguous cards for any accurate assessment.

Ten of Rods

This is the onus of priesthood or bearing the burdens of others. Responsibilities for making rulings that may control the conduct of other humans by appealing to their religious beliefs. The card may indicate an opportunity for this practice, or indicate a need for sacrifices on behalf of those who are entitled to claim them. This card is always concerned with the affairs of this world, so it would specifically refer to what happens in this sphere in regard to the ideology and religious implications of the Sangreal.

Ten of Swords

The Sorrow of Subjection. This is the very worst human sorrow-card in the whole pack, and it means the maximum that humans can suffer in this world because they are mortal. Anything varying between death and disease, to degradation and deprival of everything cherished. Something very serious at any rate. Proximal cards may mitigate or reduce it to a risk, but the card is indicative of adversity encountered on Earth in material terms. It may not be altogether bad from a spiritual standpoint, since its end-experience may actually enhance the soul who is able to contain and cope with it. That, however, can seldom be considered a consoling side-effect.

• • •

Such are the general attributions of the Minor Arcana seen purely from a Sangreal standpoint. The cards can be expanded almost indefinitely, though this leads to a lot of difficulties when trying to assess their exact meanings in relation to whatever is being queried. No two people are likely to interpret a tarot spread in an absolutely identical manner, yet both could be correct.

Reversed Cards

Very divided opinions exist on the question of "reversed" cards. Some would have it that a reversed card means exactly the opposite of what its face value shows. Thus a fundamentally favorable card could signify the opposite if upside down in relation to the reader. This seems quite untenable, since a number remains its own value from whatever angle it may be viewed, and the significance of a card depends entirely on the suit and numerical value therein. The actual ideology is thus a constant, however extensible or improvable its interpretation may be.

While bearing all this in mind, the principle could be adopted if a "reversed" card might be taken to signify an "in" directive rather than an "out" one. After all, we relate to life by two main methods: 1.) how life affects us by pressing in upon us from outside, with all its influences and energies, and 2.) how we affect life by our reactions and intentions that are directed from inside ourselves back into the main lifestream for further circulation. Our entire lives are reciprocal combinations of these two general directions of energy classifiable as either "in" or "out." Things may be more complicated than that in actuality, yet this concept is a convenient way to look at them. So it could be postulated that part of life is having its effects pushed into us from a variety of angles, and the other part consists of bouncing back at these with energies coming from self-sources which are impelled by intention or will modified through consciousness.

It could be quite useful when seeking counsel from the tarot to discover whether some external influence or event is indicated, or if we are simply being advised to make contact with such a factor ourselves because some need for this seems evident. In this case a "reverse" possibility could prove very practical, indeed, without altering the meaning of the cards in the least. The card indicates a symbolic value relative to the query or person posing the question, but many possibilities arise instantly. Does the card indicate something that will happen, should happen, or ought to be avoided? A reversed card could signify an "out" so far as the questioner is concerned. This is to say the indications are not of some experiences about to be encountered, but are injunctions as to what the individual is being asked to find in him- or herself and forthwith put into the lifestream of consciousness for circulation. Cards facing the individual correctly of course will show "in" eventuations likely to be experienced in the course of oncoming life. In order to obtain such a result, the cards have to be turned round in the hands at irregular intervals (as shuffling proceeds) so that reversing will be distributed on a random factor. It is also advisable that if the cards are being interpreted for someone present, the querent should sit beside the interpreter so that no confusion concerning reversals can arise.

It is, or course, entirely optional whether or not to adopt reversal procedures as an aid to interpretation. If not, then the reader must rely entirely on intuition to decide how the cards connect together. As a general rule, if the tarot is being employed as an advisory oracle, it is best to use the reversal rule, but if it is used only for contemplative purposes or similar reasons, then the cards ought to be associated in their normal positions only.

Selecting the Cards

After being selected, the cards should be laid face down at first and turned up afterwards. If the reverse card method is employed, it is most important that the cards are turned up the correct way (which is by their sides and not by their ends—which would reverse the reversal and so spoil the calculation). Tarot cards should always be laid out face down and then turned up for consideration. This is advisable because premature knowledge of cards still in the process of selection can upset the spontaneity of judgement—which is so important for the intuitive faculty. Some readers find it best to turn the cards up with their eyes closed, keeping their eyes closed until all the cards have been upfaced. Failing that, they close their eyes while someone else turns the cards up and when they have set their minds so that everything feels right, they open eyes suddenly and let the tarot spread impact on their vision with maximum effect. Correct viewing distance will depend on individual eyesight and the lighting employed. Black velvet or a matte surface is best so the cards alone stir visual responses. It must be stressed that it is the ideology alone which is important rather than any method of presentation, though that should certainly be considered.

The methods of card selection are of primary importance, and most people pick cards singly from an outspread pack laid randomly on a table large enough to take them all in an extended way. The cards are first shuffled with two hands (with reversals if required) then spread out as largely and evenly as possible. If there are no opposing reasons, it would be permissible to frame the motivating reason for the consultation in as clear a manner as possible, then type or print it on paper where it can be seen by all concerned during the selection. Any device which helps concentrate attention upon the matter in hand is allowable, though there is no real substitute for the clear calm concentration of a human consciousness engaged on an esoteric investigative enquiry.

The thing to do next is to sensitize the hands and fingers by rubbing them together briskly, shaking them from the wrists, flicking the fingertips against each other, or adopting any preferred procedure which may seem appropriate. Different people have their own ideas on this subject, and it is for everyone to find their own favorites. Some people prefer to wash their hands under running water and let them damp-dry afterwards. Some ignore this preparation altogether, but this formality ought never to be omitted altogether, even if a quick flick and a casual rub are all that may be managed. At the same time, everything should be done to bring the entire consciousness into a condition of alert and attentive sensitivity.

This may be accomplished by controlled breathing with various rhythms, or any other esoteric exercises that suggest themselves, providing these do not take too long. A quickly learned breathing method consists of interrupted exhalations. A full breath is taken fairly fast and then expelled in a series of small regular jerks at any chosen speed. At first the intaken breath is expelled by four or five muscular movement at distinct intervals. Then the same procedure is speeded up until the expiration becomes a prolonged series of quite small and very rapid expulsions until the lungs empty when they are refilled for repetition. Once more, however, it is well to remind ourselves that we each find our own methods sooner or later, and those should be the ones employed.

Once a suitable self-state has been reached, allow both hands to range over the cards on the table quite slowly, and with only the very lightest finger contact. Some say there should not be actual physical contact, but only an approximation. After a preliminary exploration, only the right hand should be used for selection while the left one is kept palm down on the table top. (In the case of the left-handed person, of course, this would be reversed.) The eyes may be open or closed according to preference. The guiding principle is to let the card pick the person rather than a person pick the card. That is a highly important point and should be taken very seriously. Selection movements should be very slow, ranging from one end of the deck to the other, somewhat in the manner of a hand-held mine detector sweeping a field. Consciousness must be kept "tuned in" all the time. A very fine tremor may be imparted to the hand from the muscles and nerves of the arm, and the fingertips may be allowed to describe very small circling movements simultaneously.

It is very difficult to describe exactly how the selective movement is decided, but most sensitives find that a card seems to attach itself to their fingers almost of its own volition. Though this can scarcely be so in physical fact, there need be no doubt that some kind of strange affinity attracts the questing fingers to a responsive card and the choice is made. If the eyes are left open, the sight seems to play a part in the selection, and vision is drawn to the card as well as the fingers. For that reason it would appear best to select with closed eyes. Once the card is picked it is either handed over to the reader face down for placement or put straight in place for later revelation. The selector, of course, should always be the querant, but this need not be so if the query is being put on behalf of an absent person.

It is important that those present keep their minds on the subject of the tarot reading while selection of cards is in progress. There should be no trivial chatter for instance, nor should cards be selected while smoking or drinking. If a tarot reading cannot be taken seriously, it should not take place at all. Once the full selection has been made, it is permissible to relax the atmosphere while the reader or interpreter translates the cards to understandable terms. Also, it is advisable to make a brief note of the spread for later reference. Very often when thinking back to previous readings, a great deal may be learned by keeping notes.

There are other methods of card selection. One is with a pendulum where such an instrument is held between finger and thumb and slowly over the spread cards until a right reaction occurs which varies according to the dowser. Sometimes there is a circling and sometimes a back and forth swing. This is apt to be a very slow method, yet some prefer it to hand picking. The cards need to be separated somewhat widely to avoid confusion. Then there is the "black bag" method. This is no more than an appropriately sized bag containing seventy-eight counters marked with tarot designations for each card. To make the selection, it is only necessary to insert your hand and pull out a counter to see which card has been chosen. Alternatively a miniature deck could be employed in the same way.

However the cards may be selected, the primal importance of the Minor Arcana is that it represents the stages of life and experience which have to be undergone before we can become fit for "gaining the Grail." In other words, they represent an entire series of initiations put in their proper sequence in order to condition us from the beginning to end of its progress toward whatever ultimate truth we are likely to reach through the Sangreal. Some people may like to think of this as a production line from start to finish, with raw material going in one end and a finished product at the other. Later we shall consider just such a soul as it goes round its course questing for the Sangreal in itself, but here we are concerned with the more ordinary approach using the tarots as calculators of human conditions in this world as we know it.

What may seem very minor from a cosmic viewpoint is not minor at all to a consciousness experiencing it at first hand as personal pressure. Life is made up of a long series of such pressures varying all the time with rhythms and frequencies which mould the soul into what it becomes because of its incarnation. Each one of the Minor Arcana represents a specific type of pressure which can be calculated according to the number and nature of the card concerned. Generally speaking, the nearer the number is to one, the broader and more "spread out" it will be in the material sense. The closer it gets to ten, the more detailed and localized it becomes. There is usually an element of doubt as to whether aces should be regarded as high or low, but they actually have a bivalancy depending on the difference between body and soul.

On the whole, aces are high as regards soul and low as pertains to body. Aces indicate very deep soul-changes or alterations which are likely to have long-term effects. Although tens may seem very serious in connection with Earth events, they do not necessarily indicate an indefinite duration. It must also be considered whether the cards are being used for forecasting actualities, or as an oracular adviser. That is quite an important point, because it alters the approach entirely. If a spread is intended as a forecast, for instance, the nine of Swords would indicate ruin, but if it is being meant for an oracle, the same card would caution against thinking ruinous thoughts or perhaps offer advice against the ruin of someone's reputation. The element of ruin would still be there, but in an advisory, rather than a predictive, sense.

The real use of the tarot, of course, is for classifying consciousness into terms of value. In combinations the cards can produce other values with corresponding changes of consciousness. In that way, intelligence can be converted into an ordered process, instead of being like so many minds in a state of disordered mess and muddle. Thoughts can be made in a mathematical way to produce patterns that lead somewhere in the direction of eventual enlightenment instead of chaotic confusion. Such was the primal purpose of Qabbalah among the Hebrews. The tarot was designed for those with no aptitude for Hebrew symbology.

Association of numbers with ideas is as old as counting games taught to children so they could learn the rudiments of the calculation. The principles of tarot are as ancient as that. Most people had their own notions of lucky and unlucky numbers, or good and bad influences. The tarot simply extends this principle using specific and esoteric meanings. For instance, when suggestive of the Tree of Life Spheres, tarot figures become very clear and definite indeed. It all depends on what basis or frame of reference is being used to value the figures.

The best way to begin your study is by the old-fashioned way. Make up a personal "Book of Numbers," starting with ten blank pages in a loose leaf file. Write down everything suggested by numbers One to Ten. This may seem simplistic, but in fact it is not, because it is the methodology of the process which is important. It helps arrange ideas in association with figures and that is the vital part of the exercise. For example the first page might read something like:

One: Unit of anything. Me. "One is one and all alone and evermore shall be so." Essential essence of any substance or idea. First principle and final fundamental. Emergence from

Nothing into Something. The Monad. Primal purpose. Initial energy. Single cell. Seed. Self. Number containing all others within itself. The Idea behind Existence. I AM. One is He, the Lord of the Universe. All religions based on the One God principle. The single drop which the contents of the Magic Cauldron boil down to after one year and one day. The dot in the center of a circle drawn to show the saying "God is a circle, the center of which is everywhere and the circumference nowhere." The Yang principle. Kether on the Tree of Life. Etc., etc.

Such a list could be extended indefinitely without any attempt being made to classify it further until a sufficient quantity of material is collected. Everything should just be jotted down as it comes into the mind and eventually enlarged until it becomes quite a reasonable book. This will help computations of the tarot more than anything else. People have been accepting set formulae for the Minor Arcana for far too long. Apart from obvious generalizations which are needed to start discussing the tarots at all, you should have your own associations made by your efforts at extension and expansion of each number. The overall rule here, however, is that nothing should be written that is not fully comprehended. Every linkage must be quite clearly understood and seen as sensible. Never because "somebody said so" or "that's what it said in the book." Both might be quite accurate, but the genuine tarotist must know *why* he or she was right and fully agree with it in his or her own mind.

The first general glance at a tarot spread will reveal more than might be supposed. It should first be observed if any one suit predominates, or similar numbers repeat more than once. In other words, where does the main emphasis lie? Obviously a collection of Cups would indicate cheerfulness, while the same in Swords would indicate a gathering of gloom. Rods would underscore interests and activities, and Shields or Coins place their accent on financial or family matters. When similar numbers are present the interpretation depends on which number

Table 2.   Interpreting a Spread

Aces: If	4, favorable; 3 doubtful; 2 probable
Twos:	4 argument; 3 disagreement; 2 agreement
Threes:	4 progress; 3 hesitancy; 2 possibility
Fours:	4 benefits; 3 borrowings; 2 promises
Fives:	4 disturbances; 3 doubts; 2 difficulties
Sixes:	4 satisfaction; 3 strangeness; 2 sufficiency
Sevens:	4 success; 3 struggles; 2 depletions
Eights:	4 intelligence; 3 problems; 2 information
Nines:	4 favors; 3 gifts; 2 friendship
Tens:	4 responsibility; 3 changes; 2 rewards
Knights:	4 troubles; 3 quarrels; 2 annoyances
Pages:	4 childishness; 2 irritations; 2 trivialities
Queens:	4 female dominance; 3 female difficulties; 2 female friendship
Kings:	4 strongest support; 3 dissentions; 2 friendship

means what. For instance, Table 2 shows the overall meaning of several of the cards.

The list in Table 2 only indicates very general indications of what a spread might mean rather than what it actually conveys. However, first impressions should always be considered because they are frequently more accurate than opinions formed in the mind from thoughts put together by wishful thinking and a trend to "sweep under the carpet" whatever might be adverse with unhappy interpretations. As a rule, the average human wants to exaggerate the good and minimize the bad in whatever may be foreseen, and this natural tendency must always be allowed for when making any kind of inspired guesses. While there is no need to stress any sorrows, there is also no obligation to become euphoric over joys which may be very minor ones. It is better to give a good general reading than dwell on details which may never happen.

CHAPTER SIX

The Fourfold
Force Pattern

W HEN WE COME to the Trumps (or triumphs) we encounter a real mystery. Who invented them and why? Nobody knows. Yet thinking carefully there can only be one reasonable conclusion. The Minor Arcana symbolized numbers and types and certain ideas were fitted to their values. The Trumps seem to be finished "ideas," and it is obvious that the numbers assigned to them are very far from satisfactory. These lack reasonable values, and seem to be designed to present definite ideas to viewers which challenge us to find a satisfactory sequence of numbers which would put them into an appropriate pattern for some "grand scheme" expressive of their total meaning.

There are probably several methods for doing this, a major one being in relationship with the paths of the Tree of Life. However, here we are going to relate those mysterious Trumps with the ideology of the Sangreal. The concepts behind the Tree and the Sangreal are very similar. Both show a developing relationship between divinity and humanity through a series of ideals or Master Concepts. Both have the notion of a progressive journey (or quest) toward God by a series of steps or paths. Then, whereas the Tree lays out a lot of precise values

connected with letters which spell out the story of how to reach
that eventual ultimate, the Sangreal legend gets lost in a maze of
folktales concerned with magic castles, test trials and perils to be
met with, sexually crippled kings to cure, enemies to overcome,
and a whole collection of deeds to do before the Grail at the
other end could be claimed. Most of all, there was the famous
question to answer: Whom does the Grail serve?

To some extent there is a connection between the Grail
question and the riddle of the sphinx. Both were queries put to
heroes during the course of their approaches to some personal
objective, and the penalty for failing to find the correct reply
would constitute a serious threat. The sphinx's riddle was
connected with numbers and the Grail's riddle with pure ideals.
The riddle of the sphinx has a definite answer even if it is a
rather childish one, but the Grail query either had no such set
formula, or if it had, this was never publicized. In fact, the
intention may have been to pose it like a Zen koan (or query
with no specific answer) which is supposed to test the
imaginative ingenuity of its hearer. That the Grail might be
intended as a form of service for humanity might have been
what the question was supposed to convey in itself, thus
inducing us to wonder what such service might be and who
would benefit from it.

The belief behind this book is that the tarot trumps or
Major Arcana were specially designed to tell the story of the
Sangreal from an idealistic viewpoint. They only need to be
related to each other and the Minor Arcana in a suitable
sequence. Once the proper layout is established, the rest should
follow almost automatically. When the original tarot was
designed, it was normal for males to precede females in order to
protect them and their progeny from any oncoming dangers.
Here we have the phallic Sword-Rod males together, divided
from the vaginal Cup-Shield females by the Death-Birth point
of individual commencement. The females were the "vessels"
bearing every unborn generation of the Grail in themselves. It is
important to remember that it is essentially the basic idea
behind each tarot trump of the Major Arcana which should

always be considered in preference to whatever pictorial image of that idea may be presented. Here then is the Major Arcana arranged especially according to the Sangreal System.

The Sangreal Trump Cycle

The special Sangreal cycle of the tarot trumps (as illustrated in figure 3 on page 108) needs a lot of explanation. The cycle is based on the Cosmic Cross on which all quarterly repeatable cyclic phenomena—such as the heavens, seasons, time, space and all human affairs—are related in a constant continuum of consciousness. Herein everything is considered as being grouped into quarternities, such as spring/summer/autumn/winter, dawn/moon/dusk/dark, the four phases of the moon, the life-elements of earth/air/fire/water, and so forth. Here we are asked to calculate a complete cycle of the twenty two trumps into which four will not divide equally. Divisions of the quarters are naturally marked by the four suits commencing in the center and working toward the perimeter. Then the trumps have to be arranged so they describe a logical progression in a cycle that covers life from birth to death and beyond and then back to birth again in an endless repetitive cycle of successive incarnations.

It is not difficult to understand the Minor Arcana in this cyclic sense. Cups, Shields, Rods and Swords form the four arms of the Cross. A circle really has no starting or ending point, but it is obvious that the Rods are complementary to the Cups, and Swords complement Shields. The arms branch outward from the center, where in our figure we see Truth positioned, and the arms are made up of both the Minor Arcana and the court cards. Aces are central, then the Minor Arcana, then the court cards, with the Kings connecting with the circumference but not forming part of it. The Major Arcana is arranged around the circumference, and the circumference itself can be considered as

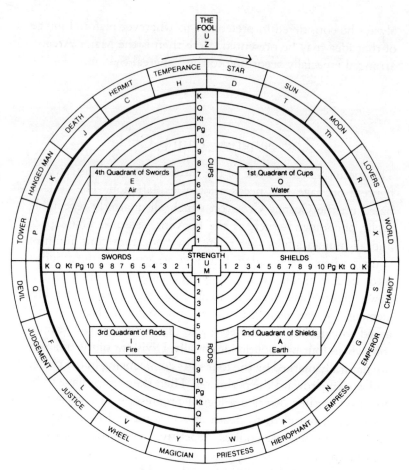

Figure 3.   The layout of the Sangreal Trump Cycle. Here everything is laid out in the Circle-Cross pattern. Each of the four suits forms a quadrant; each quadrant represents a passage of life that the Fool must make on his journey. The concepts or trials he will encounter — symbolized by the Major Arcana — are around the outer circle. The Minor Arcana of each suit form the arms of the cross. Each time the Fool incarnates, he will come in contact with not only the trumps, but various concepts represented by the Minor Arcana as well. The Strength card is in the middle, and represents the unifying principle of pure energy or power.

the Cord, or the "truth tie," which is the mysterious Fifth Element of Life connecting all the components together as a unity.

We are now faced with the problem of how to arrange the Trumps intelligently around the Sangreal cycle. The nearest number divisible by four is twenty. This means we shall have to deduct two cards from the deck and fit them in elsewhere. The Fool happens to be a "free" card representing the individual enquirer. In all former folk-dances, the fool-figure might go wherever it willed in the pattern—at absolute random, at its own pace and time—making whatever movements seemed suitable on impulse. It was the X factor of any problem, or the vital random factor of any calculation which can come in or go out at any point at all. So the Fool may be thought of as a loose card that may appear or disappear at any part of the pattern whatever. The second card is Strength (or Force), which might be thought of as just "energy" in a modern deck, for that is exactly what it signifies. Energy applies equally to any form of life, and without it there could be no movement or manifestation whatever. So let us place Strength (or Energy) at the very center of the pattern where it will animate the entire cosmos with its vital force. That leaves twenty cards to classify and connect together in the Sangreal pattern.

Working with twenty cards we have five to a quadrant, so we have to attribute the appropriate five cards to each. What might be the appropriate nature of each quadrant? One is a Cup-Shield quarter, which we will call the quadrant of Entering Earth. The trumps in this quadrant are the Star, the Sun, the Moon, the Lovers and the World. The next quarter is Shield-Rod, which we have named the quadrant of Learning Life. The trumps in this quadrant are the Chariot, the Emperor, the Empress, the Hierophant and the Priestess. The third quadrant is Rod-Sword, called the quadrant of Overcoming Obstacles. The trumps in this quadrant are the Magician, the Wheel, Justice, Judgement and the Devil. Finally we have the Sword-Cup quarter, called the quadrant of Agonizing Adventure. The trumps in this quadrant are the Tower, the Hanged Man, Death, the Hermit and Temperance.

Let's postulate further that the first quadrant is concerned with entry into life in this world from the remotest regions of existence. The second quadrant covers life as we know it in this world from its most important angles. The third quadrant deals with evolutionary alterations that we are supposed to accomplish by being here. And the final quadrant concerns the most drastic changes we have to make as humans evolving into something better, which should bring us back to the beginning of another cycle.

It is the old, old story of life. Analysis and catalysis, build-up and break down, chasing each other eternally from one end of existence to the other. The Wheel of Life revolving ceaselessly. Some would call it the treadmill to which we are condemned until we learn how to escape from it into better states of being. Here we shall consider it as the Sangreal Cycle within which we circulate as the bloodstream of being, each one of us a single cell in its structure. Like the Fool, we are continually seeking our proper places and we quest for this place indefinitely. There is a legend that if and when the Fool ever finds a permanant place to rest, the work of creation will be completed, and everything will be free to return back into the emptiness it originally emerged from. Since there are so many millions of us, who could possibly calculate when that magic moment of the Great Liberation is likely to be?

When we study the layout shown in figure 3 (see page 108), the Fool is to be imagined as being free to travel along all its ways in search of Wisdom and the Holy Grail. Such is his Quest. He represents our search for God through the whole of life. Here he will come under the influence of any card or combination of cards which he may encounter. However, for the sake of clarity, let us follow him very briefly around the whole circle so that the Fool's relationship with life may be grasped in principle before we go too deeply into detail. The theoretical commencement is made at the entry point of incarnation when any soul encounters our universe for the first time in each life. In Chapter 7, we will present an in-depth journey of the fool in the Sangreal Tarot Cycle.

The commencement is symbolized by the Star, from whence the seed of human life was reputed to have begun its journey towards this solar system of ours. It symbolizes the very beginning of the Blessed Blood linking its Line of Light with our Sun. Modifying via the Moon, it eventually contacts the biological beings represented by the Lovers, which eventually spreads it around this World, thus completing the first quadrant. Here in this world we occupy ourselves with what has been called the "Work of the Chariot," an old mystical term for the development of our souls and esoteric evolution in general. This depends on our civilization and culture which is symbolized by the Emperor and Empress. Then we concern ourselves with spiritualization, which is signified by the Hierophant and Priestess. Half the circle is thus complete, and we now face the "climb back to cosmos" process. This begins with the Magician, a card which signifies change—and the necessity for it. This eternal adaptation and alteration is sometimes called "progress." This again involves the element of chance shown by the Wheel of Fortune, and what has been called karma—symbolized by Justice in the Tarot. This stage is immediately followed by our attempt to live in accordance with such laws, which calls for Judgement of the most accurate kind. The application of all these factors naturally raises what was once called the Devil (or adversary) a card that symbolizes the opposition we encounter because of our efforts to cope with it. Here we come to the end of that difficult third quadrant.

Worse and better lie ahead. It is only by the ruin of our plans that we are compelled to construct new and improved ones. This happens, as we are shown, by the Tower, and then by Death (or total change) as imposed by Nature. Prior to that, however, we have to sacrifice ourselves as indicated by the mysterious Hanged Man, typifying the crucifixion of a Sacred King. For a more ordinary mortal however, this card means purely the symbol of that sacrifice. It is only subsequent to that event and the experience of Death that we can encounter our real identities as symbolically represented by the Hermit (or wise old man), who in this case happens to be the Fool transmogrified. Then only one final transfiguration is possible, which has been likened to a butterfly emerging from a chrysallis. This is shown as Temperance, where the Waters of Life are mixed with the Blood of Being, and everything is equalized and balanced, if only momentarily before being poured forth afresh on a new round of birth. Here a soul may experience its earned heaven with the Sangreal where all is brought to balance, blessedness, and benignancy. Subsequent to that spiritual state, the whole cycle has to begin again—and so life continues "World without end AMEN."

It should be seen easily enough that there is considerable similarity between the Sangreal disposition of the Trumps and the Tree arrangement wherein each is attached to a path. There are differences between the two, but that does not mean that one is more valid than the other: both are authentic in their own right. The Tree arrangement is extremely broad and covers the whole life field, whereas the Sangreal cycle is much more specialized and concerns the spiritual regeneration program of Western culture in particular. Though the Sangreal cycle extends beyond such a field in principle, it deals with that topic and area as a specialty subject, so to speak, and is specifically designed for use therein.

Though it might seem that the tarot trumps have been written about from all imaginable angles, they have not yet been approached from a purely Sangreal standpoint. It might prove profitable to ponder them in that particular light with the hope of extracting just that little more illumination that may have been missed by previous investigators We must approach the tarot trumps without any specific artistic designs in mind. No matter how wonderful, beautiful, or significant any particular tarot deck may be, it is never any more than what an artist can conceive around a given idea. We all can be artists in our minds, even if we have no particular skills for projecting those concepts. Let us begin looking at the Trumps that form the fixed and multi-mobile factors of the cosmic pattern we have postulated.

Strength

First look at the card called Strength (or Force). It is usually shown as a woman controlling the jaws of a lion with an Eternity symbol over her own head. Placed centrally here, Strength symbolizes the energy of existence, exerting its influence equally everywhere indefinitely – the initial and integral energy enabling everything to BE and BECOME. Something so central to existence that without it there could be nothing, or, more strictly, a uniform field of force with no variations in it whatever. Energy of some sort makes all manifestation possible, so it is appropriate that this card is central to the rest. Consciousness, itself, is energy expressed in demonstrable ways. Even if we take that as being no more than brain action, there has to be expended energy – which would be measurable as electro-chemical cell activity. We certainly have not yet succeeded in estimating, let alone measuring accurately, how energy expends itself in purely spiritual terms, but that such a phenomena must be factual there need be no doubt whatever. So let us just say that energy is essential to existence in whatever terms may be imagined.

Energy per se is more than difficult to define even though none would deny its reality. Though the dictionary definition of energy is "the power of doing work," that is far too vague and generalized to explain what is signified by this card here at the center of Life. It is not so much energy demonstrated by activity of any kind as the metaphysical principle of energy itself. The sheer incalculable Strength of Spirit needed to support nature in a condition of constant creative construction. If this were to collapse, Cosmos would go with it at that instant. To call it the driving power of deity might be an acceptable metaphor.

The card signifies more than action because it is the means and ability of action – the potential and possibility of power. Prerequisite conditions which must be already possible before any externalized demonstration of energy can evidence itself. Though this could perhaps be likened to the state of AIN SOPH AUR on the Qabbalistic Tree of Life, it is really that *plus* the power possibilities behind all the principles portrayed in connection with that plan for perfection. Although strength is centralized in this Sangreal scheme, it should be seen as extending its influence from thence throughout the entire design, so that the card can symbolize the source of power potential that pervades the whole field of life.

In relation to the Sangreal concept in particular, this power-card specifically signifies the energy drive motivating the entire movement. When we think what this means we should realize how vitally important it is and why this particular card should have been selected as central to the tarot as being representative of its complete force-field. For practical purposes, we shall see the Sangreal principle as the drive in developing humans to seek their finest state of being because of an inheritable or earnable blood-factor programmed to impel them toward a cosmic condition of perfection. This Sangreal drive is certainly not common to the whole of humanity. Relatively few humans intend to perfect themselves at the cost of expending the considerable energy needed for such a purpose.

No one can live without constantly expending energy on all levels of life. That is an obvious fact, and there is an immediate corollary of how that energy should be best spent. This central energy card should be interpreted as whatever may be required for the specific purpose of "achieving the Sangreal" in those devoting themselves to that Quest. Without the necessary strength to accomplish a Sangreal search, that would be impossible.

So what makes anyone determined to devote at least a very high proportion of their life energy to such a recondite end as Grail gaining? The answer is the same as that attributed to Sir Edmund Hillary when asked why he wanted to scale some height in the Himalayas. "Because it is there." There really is no other adequate reply. The special perfection-urge, which could be called the "Sangreal instinct," is simply there from birth, and we can no more deny it than we could disinherit our grandparents.

Let it be made abundantly and finally clear that this search for the Grail is not an implication of "elitism" or "class consciousness" based on any social or economic distinction. Just as there are physical blood groupings and peculiarities which we inherit from our ancestors, so souls have their spiritual equivalents on altogether higher or different levels. This is what we refer to as the Sangreal factor. All humans have to accept the blood they are born with, . . . whatever parentage, and regardless of how those may be placed in the order of human society. The degree of a Sangreal-strain will determine the likelihood of an individual's concern with its implications. Therefore this is also likely to determine the same individual's demand for energy devoted to such a purpose.

Perhaps the Strength card can be thought of as representing a sort of central "bank" from which energy can be borrowed or obtained for Sangreal uses. Such a storehouse has been postulated by a great number of esoteric, religious, and philosophical systems. The Roman Church, in particular, considers it as being a kind of fund fed and increased by all the meritorious behavior of mankind—which tends towards our "ultimate salvation." Donations from this may be granted to needy sinners by means of what are called "indulgences" or remissions of purgatorial post-mortem punishments. At one time the Church sold these for considerable cash, but now they have been reduced to pious formalities of prayers and performances. Few believe in them any longer, yet there may be truth behind their principles.

By sheer association with each other in this world we have accumulated resources which are usually available on the right sort of application or for enough money. Exports of surplus and imports of deficiencies form the basis of ordinary business. If we can do this on purely physical lines of commerce, why should not a spiritual equivalent prove possible? Theoretically it can. Energy is energy on any level, and transference of energy from supply-point to demand-point is always possible once the connecting problems have been solved. Methodologies of contact are always the difficulties encountered, though these are seldom insurmountable for an indefinite period. Sooner or later some system is usually found to link any power with a means of performance.

From the Sangreal standpoint this accumulation of centralized Strength is something like a blood-bank that can be drawn upon at need or deficiency. It can be supplied at need from any surplus built up at any point in its force-field. It is an energy-exchange for anyone playing an active part in the Sangreal scheme of life. The Strength card is an admirable symbol for this idealized pool of power ready to supply everyone connected with it from a flood of force providing he or she approaches it properly.

The Fool

Next we look at the Fool (or innocent), possibly the most controversial card in the entire pack. He, or it, specifically symbolizes the Quester or inquirer who is approaching the tarot in the Sangreal spirit of asking for advice or assistance. Perhaps his best pictorial representation would be a mirror or a photograph of whoever was requesting the reading. If the reading is not personal, the Fool represents whatever query is being raised. Maybe he is best thought of as the point of an indicator – like the hand of a clock – showing the tarot reply to the proposition posed.

Why in particular should this card be termed a Fool in the first place? In most old cultures the title signifies someone who was "touched by the Gods" with a peculiar "divine folly" which singled that person out from the average in sometimes very strange ways. There was no suggestion of idiocy or insanity, nor was the true Fool mongoloid or moronic. The Fool had a unique outlook and a random kind of reasoning which did not conform in the least with prevailing patterns of thinking and conduct. The traditional Fool is far from being stupid or witless, neither need he be slow and hesitant. His image is well expressed by the Germanic folk figure of Eulenspeigle or Owlglass. So may he be shown by any of Shakespeare's fools who were always more intelligent than they appeared, and clever enough to conceal this behind the mask of misdirection they presented for public inspection. A true Fool can be very cunning.

The distinguishing mark of the old time Fool was his *difference* from ordinary and average people. As a community of children, the majority will always isolate the child they instinctively feel is "different" from themselves and treat it with suspicion and avoidance, if not with persecutory practices. So does the average human tend to distrust those who "step out of line" in regard to current convention and regulative restrictions regarding social behavior or codes of conduct. In recent times, however, we seem to have become far more tolerant of individualistic behavior and unusual methods of self expression. The modern Fool has far less to fear from his contemporaries than had his predecessors. That, however, does not increase his value in our society.

It has been said: "Only a true Fool can find the Grail, because since he does not know where to look for it, he knows where *not* to look for it, and that is the best guide of all." This cryptic double-think offers quite a few clues for the Quest, and Fools are often the happiest hunters of all. In legend, it is the knights who quest for the Grail with every effort along all the most likely lines of approach. The Grail eludes them all the time, and they end up as weary old Hermits reminiscing about their fruitless adventures. The Fool, on the other hand, wanders around in his carefree casual style until the Grail begins to hunt *him* and concludes by capturing him completely while he wonders why such incredible happiness seems to have overtaken him. Fools usually fall on their feet.

At first the Fool might be considered the most unlikely Grail candidate of all, but from a purely mystical viewpoint, he is the most probable probationer *providing he is aware of his own inherent foolishness.* He must commence his Quest with the determination of altering his nature completely from Fool to Wise Man, or change places with the Hermit. He must be someone who recognizes his natural state of ignorance regarding the spiritual side of our created cosmos, and with sincere humility asks the Intelligence which created that Cosmos to teach him all the answers about it he needs to know. He is a Quester in the sense of one who keeps asking questions of the Infinite until it eventually replies in comprehensible terms. He must be as the pure "blank paper" on which alone may be written the truth. In all the old magical injunctions the need for "virgin parchment" or unused paper was stressed over and over again. It alone was worthy of being used for some important impressions of a valued magical character. In the magical sense of a true Fool, he is virtually this kind of creature – an "innocent" – who is ready to be impressed with the most precious secret of all, the Sangreal, or his "blood-being from the beginning."

In old language, such a soul was referred to as "God's Fool" and there are many legends concerning his exploits and adventures in search of spiritual objectives. Stories are told of how the Fool succeeded where his competitors failed because he did no more than "put his hand into the Hand of God." He confidently expected guidance, instead of assuming he knew everything and could advance on his own authority alone. The original meaning of the "purity" insisted on as an indispensable prerequisite for any aspiring Grail Knight had nothing to do with sex at all, but reflected a natural state of innocent and trustful confidence in the Great Consciousness, which supplies all the answers we should seek in life.

This is essentially why the Fool has been chosen as representative of the character needed for Grail questing. The Fool will not always be a Fool in the sense of remaining uninstructed or ignorant, but it is hoped he will always retain his spiritual state of innocence and enquiring confidence in cosmos, because it is this factor which will lead him eventually to the Holy Grail, which millions of presumptuous people have missed so often. Sometimes a Fool was termed a "simpleton" because of an instinctive recognition that so-called simplicity carried something of saintliness in it. The word derives from the Latin simplex or onefold, meaning uncomplicated, single spirited, with an implication of frankness, honesty, and straightforwardness. All these are fundamentally Grail-quester qualifications.

The true Fool should be offering himself like an open and empty Cup to be filled with whatever may be placed in it by a generous God. The Fool's Prayer runs: "I offer my foolishness to God that he may fill it with whatever he wills." This is the spirit of Grail-gaining which calls for a following through the cosmos of consciousness. No one ever gains the Grail by grabbing at it. The hands are supposed to be held out in a supplicatory gesture, somewhat like a Cup, while awaiting its arrival for guardianship. So the Fool holds out not only his hands but his whole self for fulfillment. The Grail surely signifies complete self-fulfillment in life and unification with Ultimate Identity. Nobody but a genuine Fool would ever expect to find this, and therefore at the end of his expectations — he does!

By choosing the Fool as a figure who can wander around anywhere in this Sangreal circle, we may be reminded of the medieval magus or sorcerer confined to the magical circle on the floor of his "operations room." There is indeed a similarity in principle, if not in practice. Life does take place in the magical circle of cosmos itself and the Grail was reputed to appear in the center of the Round Table where the king and his knights foregathered. Having done that, however, it was supposed to travel around and serve each knight with his favorite food or whatever he wanted most. The motto of the Grail was, and still is: "I seek to serve." The service our Fool offers is somewhat of a special type. The stimulation or inspiration of his antics and speech can be unique. It is unexpected and sometimes quite startling. There was an old belief that the Gods of Wisdom occasionally spoke to mortals through the mouths of Fools (or babes and sucklings, since wisdom was said to flow with mothers' milk). Therefore one should listen to what Fools say, yet judge everything on merit rather than accepting it all as directions sent straight from deity. It is surely a truism to say that sometimes a stray word or even a gesture from some strange person who might be regarded as "odd," will trigger off thought trains in the minds of intelligent hearers which may lead them a long way in search of truth. If a Fool can fulfill that function frequently enough, not a moment of his life will have been wasted. Such is his service in the cause of the Sangreal.

One characteristic of the Fool is absorbing, reflecting, and emulating the nature of whichever other card in the deck he happens to be associating with. He adopts and extends its peculiarities in himself. It could be that he instinctively selects whichever specialties of its nature seem most important to him at that particular instant. On another occasion, he might indicate a different combination altogether. Humans begin learning by copying others and then incorporate such behavior into their own characters. The tarot Fool has to do somewhat more. He has to assume the idiosyncrasies of both the Major and Minor Arcana as he comes into contact with them. Furthermore, he has to do this in the correct sequence, or the impression they leave on him will be so distorted and incorrect that it will be likely to lose its meaning altogether. There is a world of difference between a clear Fool and a confused Fool. The first is like a glass which reveals or reflects everything accurately, and the second offers only obscurity and doubtfulness.

Therefore this "loose card" of the Fool, wandering around his tarot cosmos, is actually an ideal symbol for genuine Grail gainers. He is truly representative of the Questing instinct. How many people ever know what they are really looking for in life? They may say they are looking for money, love, ego-expansion or any objective they choose consciously. They may never be certain at all, except that they must go on seeking. It is the Quest itself which is important to them, and if ever they gain some objective, they immediately set themselves another to prevent themselves perishing of emptiness. It may be remembered that with Goethe's *Faust*, the philosopher made a bargain with Mephistopheles that this demon would ensure he had everything he wanted until the moment he would declare he had reached his ultimate objective in life and needed nothing further. Of course that was something Faust had determined never to do, but the Devil knew better than he did, and eventually claimed Faust's soul just a fraction too prematurely, which nullified the contract and so Faust escaped the penalty. The moral, of course, is that we may not quit the Quest without risk of ruin. Once fully committed to it, the faithful Fool must follow to the very ends of time and space through one dimension after another. After the Grail is gained, the Fool will be totally trans-mogrified into a non-biological being, living as a form of pure energy in concentrated consciousness.

The Star

If we are going to accompany the Fool on his Grail Quest, we must first see how the Sangreal arrived at this earth. This started at the perimeter with the Star, or those remote regions of time space from which our life-seeds drifted in the distant past when this planet was dark and deserted, before the Sun burst into luminous radiance. Stars, of course, are Suns in other solar systems and galaxies as every school child should know. Life as we know it commences with stars and terminates when they collapse and disappear into final darkness. It has been rightly said that every man and woman is a star, and a Qabbalistic saying is: "When you have found the beginning of your way, the star of your soul will show its light." This is indeed where the "way of light" begins. It has also been said: "The Sangreal cannot be seen except by starlight," implying that only the most delicate type of lighting would show up such a sacred and secret thing, and that exposure to fierce sunlight would shrivel the vision to nothing. It also signifies that visions of the obvious and evident, as seen by direct daylight, will always cancel out images depend-ing on subtle and sensitized vision for making themselves known to would-be viewers. Who can see the shadow cast by candle-light when the sun shines on it? The inner vision necessary for perception of the Sangreal is best attuned by the soft stimulus of starlight rather than the glare of the noonday sun.

Stars are heavenly guides that can lead travelers around the geography of this earth or across its oceans. In the Quest for the Sangreal such a spiritual star is needed for marking out the path which must be followed to find what we seek. Like the fabled star that led the Magi to the Christ-child, so Grail seekers have to first find its equivalent which will infallibly lead them Grailwards by its unerring light. Before any journey can be undertaken with the slightest hope of success, it must be known where to go and how to get there. Here, a star presents a navigation point which can be relied on for guidance on the pilgrimage towards that Perfect Peace only to be found in Grail attainment.

Esoterically, the blessed blood brought to this world as the Sangreal came from somewhere in faraway solar systems with very advanced beings who were nevertheless capable of breeding with the species of humanity then found on this earth. This so-called royal blood was the commencement of our civilization and true spiritual development on this planet. Hitherto we had been only slightly better than beasts, and would have evolved but little before this planet perished. However with the impetus of such genetics, that entire picture altered forever. As the original genes spread, our evolution speeded and the spiritual side of us intensified and developed much faster than would otherwise have happened. Our entire history changed from that period.

It seems a pity that no accurate records exist concerning such an earth altering event and it must remain forever buried in our folk-consciousness. There was once a vague rumor that the distant star system was in the region of Sirius. That might possibly account for the report that when this world became too corrupt and desperate for the Grail to remain here, it was removed to a place called "Sarras" which was sometimes taken to mean Syria, but could be linked with a far older race-memory of a star called Sirius and all the strange legends connected with that stellar body. While this may sound far-fetched and suggestive of spaceships carrying extra-terrestrials, such cannot be entirely dismissed in the light of modern physical science. It can only be a matter of a few centuries before we shall be shooting our way across the universe ourselves, looking for somewhere to plant our seeds in a nuclear-free environment.

In the Book of Enoch there were tales of "fallen angels" who sound suspiciously like an early exploration party of advanced people who were specialists in arts and sciences. They arrived on earth (there is no mention of their departure) to teach us all their specialized knowledge. Could they have been a "follow up" party from the original Sangreal expedition to earth for the purpose of seeing how our development was progressing here and what hopes there might be for the future? We are not likely to discover the details of what happened in reality, and can only deduce the probabilities.

From the purely spiritual side, the Sangreal star brought the best blood behind our beings and ensured our ultimate immortality in the shape of what was later called "salvation," or "redemption," signifying that we would eventually be restored to our heavenly position when we "went home" to the rightful places we had inherited because this spiritual equivalent of blood was now circulating through human systems on earth. True it was first confined to specific families, but in the end it would expand to include multiple millions. Many were the ceremonies and practices devised to propagate this belief and encourage hope among the unhappy humans who asked for something better than the conditions prevalent among mortals.

This could also account for the deep rooted interest in astrology which has been with us for so many millennia. We know that our ultimate fate is somehow or other bound up with the stars. We feel instinctively that we came from them, will in time return to them and one way or another they should reveal something of our present position and show us what might eventuate from that. It remains for astrologers to translate this instinct into comprehensible conjectures for the benefit of their less learned brethren. Whether they have accomplished this in fact is anyone's opinion.

The Star card has a reference to the personal horoscope which delineates the character-qualities of any given human being, their starting point in each incarnation, so to speak. The horoscope is an identity card which may be carried through life as a sort of authorization behind each individual Quest. It could be produced in the case of query by any interested party. The horoscope, if rightly read, will testify as to the birthright of its owner to claim kinship with the Sangreal and the blood it represents. There is a much broader basis for this than might be supposed, and that is mainly the reason why the card is placed where it is at the commencement of the cosmic circle of the Sangreal.

This particular Star is usually pictured as the five-pointed Star, or as the Penragram, with its head/hands/feet significance roughly aligning with the human body. It also stands for the five senses we use for experiencing this physical world, or the quintriplicity of anything like the Five Symbols at our doors, as the old song says—which are the Five Magical Weapons of the Cup, Shield, Rod and Sword conjoined with the cord. A really arcane tarot deck would have a fifth-symbol suit of Cords which would symbolize all our various contact points or ties with the inner universe. In old times, the different places of a man's garment were joined to each other with tapes or strings, and were called "points" which people were always "trussing up" or tying. Shoe laces and ties seem to be the last survivors into our times.

In fairly recent days too, the phrase "star quality" has come into our language to mean first class or superior. This derived from the theatrical custom of sticking a star on the dressing room door reserved for the most important member of the cast, which is why they are called "stars" to this day. Such a description has filtered into all fields of action now, but it does stem from our instinctive realization that anyone seeking (or Questing) for the best in any sphere of human activity must necessarily have something of star quality in them to begin with. The same sort of quality, which if purely spiritual in nature, sends humans Questing for the Sangreal as the highest aim we can imagine. We have done no more than adopt the Star as a search-symbol of all that is best within us. Which is, of course, the "royal blood" of our descent.

The Sun

The next symbol we encounter on our Quest around the tarot is that of the Sun. Although the solar symbol is central to our particular system, it is in actuality a smallish somewhat insignificant star relatively to the rest of our galaxy. Hence its position as coming second in the Sangreal circle. Needless to say, no human could live on the Sun, yet without it we could not live at all. Its light must be mediated to us via the atmosphere of Earth, and if it were not for such mediation through all the various layers of that atmosphere, we would die due to radiation problems or our planet would be burned up and become a lifeless desert.

According to Sangreal legend, it was our Sun which attracted the original "bearers of the blood" toward this particular planetary system. It made a natural steering point for starships coming from other galaxies. So from a Sangreal standpoint we need to take the tarot Sun as being exactly that. It is a divine directive which guides us toward whatever state might prove most favorable for the implantation and development of that sacred seed which will continue our type of consciousness throughout creation. It must be remembered that the original bearers of the blood were not particularly concerned with continuing the purely physical part of themselves on this planet, because the human race was already on this earth. What they were principally concerned with was the continuum of their spiritual selves by linking these into the human genetic pattern. They knew that sooner or later their human hosts would have to "breed true" to increase the Sangreal-strain, which would adapt itself to earth life, and then automatically go on with the process of perfection.

This does not imply the whole of humanity is nothing more than the unwilling host of a parasitic infestation by "otherworlders" who brought their bloodstrains to an unsuspecting Earth because their own planet was expiring or exploded, or otherwise impossible for furthering their purpose and supporting their lives. Facing the bluntest truth, what would humans have become without the Sangreal? Animals and very little else. Nice animals maybe, who would, in time, have become the best of their species, but that was as far as they were likely to get on this particular planet.

The bearing of the blood altered that trend forever. Maybe it needed many millennia before the strain would become sufficiently widespread to make a significant contribution toward the consciousness motivating mankind, but that was the way it would have to be. Centuries seem like seconds on a cosmic clock. The Sangreal came to save humanity from eventual extinction, and has become the source of inspiration whence all our best and most wonderful impulses derive. It is the "Inner Sun" which is the principal enlightener of everyone looking for light in this wondering world.

It is believed that the Sun of this solar system was selected because its radiant frequency carried a component which was especially favorable toward the type of spiritual development desired. Not all the Suns in the whole of creation have this pecularity. And later humans would almost automatically turn towards their Sun as a worship-objective worthy of the reverence they felt for the dawning divinity within themselves. Solar cults proliferated throughout their culture. They may not have realized consciously or rationally why this should be so, but the reason lay in their deep genetics. Far too deeply to be denied.

The importance of the Sun can scarcely be held in question. Its ability to blind or impair the vision of those who stare at it for prolonged periods should surely make most humans respect it. Some of the old time Shamen would sacrifice their eyesight by staring at the Sun until they became blind and thenceforth dependent on the goodwill of their fellow-creatures. They had an idea this practice would result in their obtaining a compensatory inner vision which could then be used for guiding the lives of others so the physically blinded could, indeed, lead the spiritually blind. Though their interpretation of the Sun's message may have been mistaken, their basic instincts told them the truth of its significance.

Nor need there be any doubt that the Sun tends to optimism and cheerfulness while dark, dampness, and gloom make for morbidity and melancholy. The first are the characteristics necessary for setting out on the Sangreal Quest, while the second are qualities leading toward inertia and a depressive disinclination to look beyond the fog of confusion which seems to settle over everything during periods of temporary loss of light. However much the Sangreal Sun may shine at the back of everything, there will be many moments when Questers despair in darkness and cry desperately for the return of the Sun to relume their way ahead. It is not for nothing that the Yule feast celebrating the return of the Sun became synchronous with the Christian Nativity or rebirth symbolizing the light of the world.

The Sangreal is symbolized as being a light behind the blood, or light becoming blood. Not only legend says that light becomes blood when we consider that sunlight stimulates the natural growth of vegetables and makes them fit for us to eat. We might say with some truth that we are eating and drinking sunshine. In fact a lot of commercial advertisements do say it. However we see our Sun as a bloodmaker, we shall have to concern ourselves here with the spiritual equivalent of the action which is the Sangreal process in ourselves. Light becoming life because of blood. Where blood circulates, consciousness becomes possible. In our solar system, the Sun may be taken as an adequate symbol of the power in our human systems which originates and vivifies our blood in both physical and spiritual terms.

As the strength card symbolizes the central energy supplying the cosmic life of the Sangreal Cycle, so the Sun symbolizes that same energy, which is central to this system only. It is a sort of relay-station located in space and passing along through time-tides the power which is needed for the performance of anything. Perhaps a clue is provided in the Emerald Table of Hermes Trismegistus where it says: "The Sun is its Father and the Moon its Mother."

The Moon

It might be supposed that after homing in by means of the Sun, the next Sangreal visitation would be the Earth itself, but such is not the case. The next card is the Moon. Again we have only esoteric legends to base our suppositions on, but it has been postulated that this planet had two moons in those far-off times, one of which has since broken up and dispersed long ago. Which Moon the blood-bearers used as an initial base is unclear, but the motivation was most probably reconnaissance of earth before finally establishing a more positive presence here. There is a possibility that the missing moon, much smaller than the present one, started breaking up in about that era, but whether or not the Sangreal spacecraft had anything to do with this or not is totally uncertain. It could, however, be connected with the catastrophe which seemed to have wiped out the giant lizards and mammoths.

Be that as it may, the idea of reaching this world by tentative moves made from the Moon prior to making more permanent contact is a very old one. Most ancient cultures seemed to assume that the Moon was a sort of "spirit-home" where souls bound for this world awaited incarnation. Nearly all primitive and early magical mysticism was connected with the Moon rather than the Sun, and lunar cults were going strongly long before solar ones. All the mystique of femininity came from the lunar levels of life, and those associations remain strong to this present day.

From the spiritual viewpoint, this means that initial Sangreal contacts come primarily along the lines of dream-consciousness and very deep inner awareness beyond the range of words at all. That is something we are conscious *with* rather than *of*. So it seems to have been originally. The Sangreal was cautiously feeling its way into human awareness before finally committing itself to an irrevocable blood-contact. Once that became established there would be no way out ever again, and the Sangreal would have to stay spiritually with our odd human race until the end of its existence, whenever that might be.

Blood perpetuates itself and continues as long as there is life able to bear it.

Who knows how much of our consciousness comes from our blood? As everyone knows, the human brain cannot think without blood, and if the bloodflow through the brain ceases for more than about four minutes, the brain becomes very badly damaged and soon dies altogether. So our thoughts are utterly dependent on blood in the first place. But how far are they actually formed by blood characteristics? For instance in fevers when the blood is invaded by alien organisms, our thoughts "go wild" and we term this confusion delerium, because it makes nothing but a crazy kind of sense. Anything which affects the blood also affects our brains and the thinking that goes through them. Could it not be that there are factors causing favorable effects such as clear thinking, inspiration, valid visions, fresh perceptions, constructive and original ideology, and whatever else goes towards the development and improvement of our life-species? It has been said that we are the only thinking animal, and although this may not be quite true, what other animal has done so much with its thinking since its species started breeding on this planet? How much of this superior thinking ability is due to the Sangreal-strain inherent in us? Maybe we shall discover a lot more about this in the relatively near future.

This ability to think is one which has been developed over many millennia of genetic evolution. Primitive people think, but their types of thought are very different than those of an educated and evolved individual. The earlier type might be termed a lunar method of thinking. Instinctive, variable, sensual, and emotional in character rather than rational, logical and intellectual. It must be remembered that this lunar type of thought is basic, because it preceded the subsequent and more sophisticated thinking which has become a much more recent faculty of humanity.

Therefore the Moon of the tarot indicates that the Sangreal influence began affecting our emotional and instinctual make-up before later leading to logical and rational approaches of thought. How long it will take before this is superseded again by sheer spiritual consciousness alone is anyone's guess. There have been many signs of that awakening for a long time now, yet for a newer mode of awareness to supervene entirely and put previous modes into a process of extinction takes a very long time indeed as we count millennia.

The ideology of the Moon's phases can mean many things concerning the Sangreal. The "dropping blood" from the spear concept can refer to the menstrual cycle as well as the descent of the blood among mankind. Menstrual blood signifies infertility, or non-conception, which applies to spiritual lines in addition to physical ones. The lunar phases correspond to impregnation at the New Moon, the gravid uterus at the Full, parturition at the Wane, and emptiness at the Dark. Consequently just at (or a shade before) the New Moon was always considered the best time for conception, and most of the various Moon customs stem from those roots. When humanity was desperately concerned with spreading its species, those seemed very important, and menstruation became known as "the curse" by most women, although many anxious ones termed it the "blessing." If we remember the connection between "blessing" and "blood," reasons will become very clear.

Non-conception is very far from being a curse in our times when population control of some kind is vital. Eventually our surplus stock will be needed for export to other planets, which is why scientists are so concerned with genetics, fertility drugs, frozen sperm banks, and all the rest of the pre-exodus preparations needed for the next stardrive and the promulgation of the Sangreal through our dimensions of time-space. Although the "rhythm" method of birth control is the least reliable of all, it does tie in with the lunar concept of rhythmic renewal. Since there seems to be no rhythmic factor involved in male fertility other than psychological, it would appear that lunar trends apply more to women than men.

From the male viewpoint, lunar tides are more applicable to inner rather than outer fruitfulness. The tarot Moon indicates brain children more than physical children. Maybe "children of consciousness" might be a better term. The Sangreal is perfectly capable of impregnating masculine imagination which will subsequently produce a fully fledged concept or idea which will stand on its own. This was behind the old Hebrew notion of the "Shekinah" or feminine side of God which "hovered" or inspired humans with a sense of divine immanence. That was why they always saw their supreme deity as masculine, since to IT *all* humans were of a feminine gender to be impregnated either physically or spiritually according to Its intentions. Early Hebrew esoterics saw nothing strange in regarding themselves as "Vessels" which their Lord would fill as He would with whatever He sent. It should be noted that the Grail is described as a "vessel" of an unspecified kind, maybe the waiting womb that needed filling. Either blood would remain on the inside and make another mortal, or it would fall to the outside and make nothing but a mess. Such as the luck of luna.

Qabbalistically the Moon card associates with the concepts of Beauty and Foundation to be taken in the "family founding" sense. That is to say, whatever lay at the back of establishing definite and consistently reproductive lines of life on this Earth. We have to remember that the Sangreal was once exclusive and confined to the best stocks which could be found among humans. Even now, the Sangreal strain differs greatly in degree among individuals. It is the lunar element which comes closest to this physical world and forms a foundation upon which further and improved extensions can be built. Bloodlines were always reckoned as maternal by the ancients, since a man always knew his mother, yet might not be entirely certain of his paternity any more than she might be. Promiscuity is not an exclusively modern phenomena.

So, as might be supposed, the Moon card from a Sangreal standpoint signifies its feminine characteristics. It seeks a fresh home in the hearts of humanity while attracting the attention of all toward an Inner Kingdom where mystery and magic abound. In the account of an "angelic invasion" given in the "Book of Enoch," several angels appeared to be female, because they taught humans how to make mirrors, apply makeup and use dyes (presumably hair-tints). One specialist taught how to solve sorcery, (a psychiatrist?) and another, obviously a botanist, showed humans the art of plant propagation. These were naturally classed as very wicked angels by the Hebrew author of the book, especially one called Asaradel who taught the motions of the Moon. Though these could scarcely have been the instigators of the Sangreal strain, they could have been later observers of its effects. They seem to have been carnivorous, and crossbreeding between their males and human females produced offspring which appeared gigantic in contrast with average human children.

The Moon is also the recognized realm of fantasy which we are apt to undervalue. Without the ability of fantasy, who could bear to live in this world at all? All psychological laboratories have shown that "dream-deprival" causes serious damage to the consciousness of even the most unimaginative individual. Take our fantasies away altogether and we shall surely be destroyed. Fantasy is creative consciousness employed without being projected further than the limits of the mind. One might call it unmanifested mentalizing. The value of fantasy and the levels of awareness it offers are virtually incalculable.

The Lovers

Moving to another tarot card, we still do not encounter this world directly. Instead, we meet the Lovers. How is anyone to incarnate other than by sexual means? Here the Sangreal is very much involved with sex on its deepest biological levels. However many ways there may be of quitting this world there is only one way in, the way of the womb. All must be admitted by the Gates of Sex. That is what the Lovers mean. Though they may romanticize their relationship in cultured and civilized conditions, their earliest attractions for each other were no more than those of any other animals reproducing themselves for the survival of their species.

With the coming of generations influenced by the genetic qualities of "the blood," this animalistic attitude altered out of all recognition. Love entered human experience – a mutual attraction between beings based on more than physical functions. A bonding of Self with Self that extended the existence of both into a state that embraced a far wider condition of conscious existence than either could have known otherwise. Spiritual sex was born among humans who did not claim to understand it in the least, yet could not conceive how they might ever be completely happy without it. Sangreal sex was something entirely different than anything they had ever known, because it began the birth of their own souls.

Esoteric legends hint that early humans were so unattractive to their spiritual superiors that physical contact in earliest instances proved unacceptable and nothing but purely psychical relationships were established for a prolonged period. The working consciousness of humans had to be probed and investigated before any closer kind of rapport could be made. The mating peculiarities of mortals had to be studied and calculated to the last degree of feasiblity. Above all the Bearers of the Blood needed to know beyond doubt what the prospects of propagation were, and whether the end-result was likely to be any sort of credit to the consciousness that motivated their mission. The endless estimations, calculations, discussions, and all the necessary preliminaries to any sort of final and fateful decision can only be guessed. The probability is that what decided the final issue was a response among the human creatures themselves which provided evidence of a rudimentary Love arising amongst the sexes of their species.

If humans were capable of genuine Love in the slightest degree, then they were worth saving and helping to become better beings altogether. That was the decisive factor. The presence of Love in human nature was positive proof that given time, evolution, and the Sangreal factor, it would be possible for humans to reach the highest levels of spiritual life. Without Love, the Sangreal cannot live and perpetuate itself. Love is the essential element for its continuity. Biological sex may be a relatively low form of experiencing that Love, but such, indeed, is a human start of the process. From there it has to develop, expand, extend, and keep altering in character and application until it leads to the peak of perfection, when it will transmute the species into finer forms of life yet. Such is the spiritual alchemy of the Sangreal once it starts circulating through the "vessels" offered by the veins of the humanity it serves.

If this card were to be represented in visual terms, it would represent two humans joined in sexual congress. Strictly speaking, it is Love that bears the Sangreal on its way within this world, but if Love begins by being synonymous with sex, then so it must be for fallible mortals. Nowadays, however, sex is by no means the only entry afforded for it on this earth. So much of our race has developed sufficiently for the Sangreal to establish direct contact along purely spiritual lines. In other words, we are learning to love each other without the physical practice of sex being either necessary or essential. That was why celibate religious orders of priests became customary, and that was not until humans began to recognize instinctively that it was possible to contact the Sangreal in themselves without physical sex intercourse, though never without real Love amongst them. Such apparent sexlessness was by no means for all humans, but only for those advanced enough to attempt it. That is still the case today and is likely to remain so for a long time yet. Originally there was only one way we could love each other and that was through sex. Now there are so many alternative ways we can love and care for each other that sex is becoming an almost secondary means of inviting the Sangreal into our souls. In fact, we do not have to invite it at all, since it is already there in most of us awaiting its awakening in our awareness.

The question will naturally arise as to whether the Sangreal would apply in cases of homosexual love. The answer is yes: it applies in all instances of genuine Love between two or more beings. The instinctive aversion to homosexuality inherent in so many people stems from the fact that a homosexual relationship never "passed on the blood" and so widen the circle of the Sangreal as a genetic characteristic. That was why in the early

Sangreal era so many prohibitions existed against sexual intercourse or unauthorized seed-spillings in other than heterosexual
circumstances. It may be noted that such prohibitions were
principally among those people who were beginning to realize
the responsibility of passing the Sangreal strain along the best
lines of human blood. That is to say, those in whom the Sangreal was awakening of its own accord and urging them to
safeguard its future insofar as they could. Any rules they laid
down for this purpose were entirely of their own making, and it
must be admitted that they had very good and sufficient reasons
behind them for their day and age. It does not follow, however,
that such rules should be inflexible or totally unchangeable in
the light of subsequent alterations or developments in the whole
process.

In Christian doctrine the injunction: "Love ye one another"
is a directive made with full knowledge of what the Sangreal
entails. By that time in human history, the Sangreal was becoming widespread despite all attempts to reserve it for royal familial
lines alone. By Christian times, this spiritual situation was
changing very rapidly, especially among the more developed and
cultured people of that period. Since then, there has been an
amazing increase in the spread of Sangreal influence throughout
the world, and genetic characteristics which were once quite
rare are now becoming increasingly common.

So the Lovers in the Sangreal System should be understood
as an extension of the sexual instincts which have evolved into
Love and will eventually extend into light. Perhaps this may
give new meaning to the old esoteric saying: "Lux in extensio,"
that light extended indefinitely, and was thus a satisfactory symbol for spirit. Maybe a mistake made in former times was the
denigration of sex and its attempted suppression for any reason
except procreation. Granted, this was intended as a curb on the
misuse of a natural function, and possibly a control on the
virulent diseases spread through promiscuity. Made with the
best of intentions, this produced the worst of results. Sex should
never have been made spiritually shameful and suggestions that

hellfire awaited offenders should never have been incorporated into Church doctrine.

Once the risks and responsibilities of sex are clear, there is no reason why it should not be practiced with love whichever way they need. The Lovers imply the need for such comprehension and the realization of what sex involves on all its levels. Of the greatest importance is that the spiritual side of sex be at least suspected before its physical practice is commenced. There are still people in our relatively enlightened age who see sex as something rather dingy, if not actually dirty. They are inclined to treat sex as something to snigger at or be slightly ashamed or. This attitude ought never to contaminate so sacred a commitment between humans.

The World

What eventually happened to the original bearers of the blood in physical terms is not known either. Whether their bodies simply died naturally, or they became extinct through attrition is uncertain. They positively live on through the genetics they implanted in us. They are spiritually guiding our destiny while pointing toward new worlds in distant galaxies where the Sangreal intends to continue indefinitely. To represent its temporary sojourn on this particular planet, look at the World. This card specifically indicates the conditions of our common life level on Earth—past, present, and future—depending on the nature of the question. Strictly speaking, the nature of a "world" is not a location, but a state or condition applying to some specification. For example, we have the "world of finance," the "world of sport," the "world of music" or the "world" of anything at all. It is a generic term.

From a Sangreal standpoint, the World would signify the condition of humanity because we share the same spiritual roots as inheritors of the blood. We have to look at ourselves for what we have become (and are becoming) at this present period. We may not like what we see, but we can harbor hope for what we can yet become. Looking back at human history so far, we should be able to see the influence of the Sangreal behind our blood. Obviously it has not succeeded as yet with its original objective, and cosmically the Sangreal is still in its infancy here as far as humanity is concerned, but let us say at least there seems to be signs of some perceptible growth.

What is the influence that the Sangreal strain should have on the affairs of this world? Theoretically, at least, it should make all the difference between regeneration and ruination, salvation or damnation. There is a saying that we carry the seeds of our own destruction within us. That could not be true unless the seeds of salvation were also there as well. There is a big difference between saying we *will* be saved or *could* be saved. Saved from what? Either the breakup of this world due to natural causes and calamities, or the much more rapid results of our own recklessness, rapacity, and wrongdoing. This world can be regarded as a testing ground for humans to prove whether or not we are worthy of promotion into better orders of being. Is the Sangreal strain sufficient to save us from the worst in ourselves, or is it not?

There is no certainty of salvation in the Sangreal. It provides both the inclination and ability to effect this, but cannot exert compulsion on the human psyche to conform with all the conditions which would ensure it beyond question. So the logical reading of the situation is that some humans will use the Sangreal properly and perfect themselves out of incarnationary cycles, while the remainder will do nothing of the sort, and will stay here until the world ends them or they end the world. One way or the other, this is only a temporary habitation, even if it lasts for a hundred million million years. In this world we have but a limited life stay.

The World card signifies our association with each other in the same sphere for the sake of life as we will make it. We are all in this world for a reason, but each of us may have an entirely different reason for being here. The World is our field or area in which our forces are focused so as to achieve at least something of what we incarnated for in the first place. All this world may be a stage, but we poor players will be expected to do something more than strut if we mean to pursue the Quest which the Sangreal inspires in us. Here is where we find the clues and hidden keys which will open the inner doors to the secrets we seek. We are here to attend to this world, not to ignore or abuse it. So long as there is a lesson here to learn we need to know and assimilate it. This is our classroom and laboratory combined.

Christians once classed the World with the flesh and the devil, all of which had to be renounced if any hopes of heaven were to be held. The Sangreal would not have agreed. Instead it might have said: "Live in this World with love, learn fellow feeling with the flesh, and defeat the devil with devotion to deity." In other words, put everything to good use and don't waste any of it. Power is too precious to throw away. Economize on your energies and you will enjoy them best. The world is here to be experienced, not only in a purely spiritual sense, but from every aspect of human life—all of which relate to spiritual values. We are here to transmute matter into spirit. Until we understand the real nature of matter, we shall never be able to manage such a change.

So the World card indicates the challenge of what we have to face. If we take each tarot Trump as a direct challenge to be faced, fought out, and finished within its particular field of action, this will provide a much better understanding of the ideology behind them all. This world is a multi-challenge of countless problems that arise at every instant of our existence. Every single human alive has to deal with his or her share for the entire duration of each incarnation. The incredible enormity of this is beyond the grasp of our limited consciousness, yet we have to cope with it somehow every day of our personal lives. In one sense it is the Sangreal in us which is the root cause of all these problems, since it raised us to the level where we are able to make them. In another sense it offers answers to all these difficulties because it brings us into contact with the Great Consciousness holding the keys to every question askable.

• • •

And so we come to the conclusion of the first quadrant of the tarot cosmic cross. These cards account for the arrival and installment of the Sangreal so far. Our humanity has been honored and entrusted with the responsibility of bearing the blood. Now, having gotten into this world, what are we supposed to do with it and how are we to act to further its purpose? Some day our distant descendents may have to continue the Quest on other planets elsewhere in our state of existence and the entire story of the Sangreal may be resumed along alternative lines of life. We are far from that moment as yet, and there is a whole mountain of work to be done in this world first. Among Qabbalistic mystics, this is known as the "work of the chariot." It commences the second quadrant representing the duties of humanity in this world subsequent to a sufficiency of the Sangreal strain becoming active enough to influence human management of their own affairs.

The Chariot

Controlling and managing spiritual principles was once known as the *Merkaba*, or the Chariot Throne of God, which formed part of the famous Vision of Ezekiel. This throne had wheels (the invention that completely changed our civilization and could be called revolutionary in more senses than one), and it formed a mobile "seat of government" for God Himself. Thus God could go wherever His power was needed to support His cause. The implication is that the Sangreal should be spread all over the world by those who bore the blood and went forth to propagate it. Again we have the idea of bearing or taking the Grail around, this time by convenient vehicles which could be human beings considered in that light. So the "work of the Chariot," became synonymous with spiritual efforts of a noble nature undertaken in this world for the sake of the Sangreal.

That was presumed to be of primal importance, taking prece-
dence over any mundane matters, and so it comes first in this
second quadrant of the tarot cycle.

When the tarot was conceived, a chariot was a military
vehicle designed for field use against infantry to break them up
into smaller masses—more or less in confusion—after which they
could hopefully be cut to pieces by swordsmen and spearmen
following in the chariot's wake. A chariot was employed because
its platform provided a stance from which arrows could be discharged or javelins thrown with considerable speed and force.
As a rule, chariots were intended for a two-team combination of
warriors—a driver and his fighting companion—though single-
handed fighters were not unknown.

Chariots were especially noted for speed and manueverabil-
ity. They had been associated with racing for many centuries
and were also linked with Sun Gods and other celestial phenomena. It may be remembered that the Hindu diety Krishna was
masquerading in the form of a charioteer when he encountered
the young warrior prince Arjuna and explained the philosophy
of the Universe as related in the Bhagavad Gita. Charioteers
were generally regarded in much the same light as we esteem
leading sports figures, especially race drivers or those who risk
life and limb before an admiring audience. Such risks were even
greater then and it was relatively common to witness accidents
of the worst kind imaginable in the course of which much blood
might be lost and death counted as a merciful end. So a charioteer became a symbolic sacred king with all the attached mythology altered to suit the occasion. That is the context in which the
Sangreal significance of this tarot card should be seen.

Chariots are vehicles for young, strong, and rapid people.
Charioteers have to conform with definite specifications
whether they are male or female. They need both skill and
daring, coupled with a readiness to run severe risks for the sake
of succeeding in whatever objective their chosen vehicle is being
used for. That need not necessarily be any kind of warfare or
commercial race winning. It could be for making motivated

journeys with the maximum celerity, escaping dangers with the greatest rapidity, or some errand of mercy calling for considerable speed. In our times it might indicate control of mental journeys, thought sending with direct certainty, messages or communications of many kinds, air travel and visits of interest and importance. Rapid pursuit of the Quest itself.

Perhaps most of all, the Chariot signifies the required characteristics called for in order to become an active bearer of the blood. The blood must not only be carried around in our vein-vessels, but consciously borne with purpose and precision where and however we go. Blood that is static dies and we are here to circulate the Sangreal and keep it alive by mobility. As school children know, the circulating blood picks up oxygen from the lungs and literally supplies our brains with "food for thought." In an analogous way, the Sangreal circulation absorbs life experiences and converts these into a type of consciousness which is comprehended by cosmos alone.

In simpler language, we are like blood cells circulating around through our living existences on this earth. These make us feel and think. If we are truly connected to the consciousness of cosmos via the Sangreal strain in ourselves, then the sum of our awareness will be absorbed into cosmos from us much as energizing oxygen is taken up by our tissues from our physical blood. The Chariot represents the means of our motion through life and our necessity for making it. A chariot is not something we move ourselves, but which moves us while we are staying still on its platform. The horses, (or motive energy) supply our mobility, and providing we control them, our journey will go well, but that control always remains in the hands of the driver. Driving through life is much more difficult than learning to drive the most complicated vehicle. The Chariot card tells us that we sorely need the highest kind of qualifications in order to travel through this world on our Quest with any hope of certainty. The very first skills we need in this earthly life of ours are those enabling us to direct a clear course across it. Hence the Chariot is properly placed at this position of the Sangreal cycle. It normally represents the early training part of an incarnation–

schooldays, and preparation for position or vocation in adult life.

To a considerable extent our physical bodies could be considered as the Chariots or vehicles which will take us on our Quest from one end of incarnation to the other, just as our imaginative faculties can construct chariots which will bear us to whatever inner scenes we may seek. Indeed, when the chariots of our bodies and minds coincide in the concept this tarot card presents to us, it should surely be seen why it comes at the commencing point of our incarnations. A child's most valuable possession is its imagination or "magic chariot" which will carry it along the most fascinating or frightening journeys of its life. Such early "incursions" usually act as formative experiences which affect the remainder of that child's life. Get the Chariot guidance right at first and there may be a good life ahead, but get it wrong and there could be a lot of trouble. Guiding your Chariot properly is the first thing which should be learned in this life.

• • •

It may now be noted that the next cards in the Sangreal sequence comprise two that are connected with the civil side of life (Emperor and Empress), and a corresponding pair representing the religious approach (Hierophant and Priestess). This shows that humans have to learn and put in practice all the rules governing proper behavior in the realm of common social conduct and then learn how to live so attention is directed to spiritual subjects pointing away from this world altogether. First you must find out how to behave before you can think about traveling elsewhere on your chariot of fire. Once the Sangreal becomes incorporated with humanity it has to develop in us so we can be conscious and capable of living properly here on earth.

Glancing at the combination ahead, it will be seen that they are respectively male/female/male/female, covering the ideology of conduct control over temporal and spiritual affairs. The bi-sexual nature of the sequence carries no suggestion that there should be one set of laws for men and another for women. It does indicate that both sexes should combine and cooperate in the closest possible way to put in practice the very finest course of conduct. This conduct will lead us lightwards by and through the blood that began our "great leap forward" from being no more than animals into our present state of humanity.

The Emperor

Let us consider the Emperor. Firstly, what is he? As his title indicates, he is a ruler of rulers—the political and social head of some very large confederation of people. A controller of conduct on a grand and supremely important scale. That is exactly what each and every one of us must learn to become. Our bodies are empires consisting of different systems brought together for the single purpose of presenting our separate selves to each other as a social order of creation. They have millions of cells serving all sorts of specialized functions. In theory these functions should work together in harmony under the benevolent rulership of their Emperor (our individual Selves) carrying out the Sangreal motto: "I seek to Serve." If that were truly so, everyone would live happily all the time. As this seldom happens, we become sick and unhappy people in consequence. Why? Because we have not yet learned how to rule ourselves effectively.

Assuming that right rulership was possible, orders would come from the top that all systems under its supremacy would live according to specified codes of conduct adopted for the good government of the entire confederacy. Provided that all were willing and happy to obey the Sangreal injunction of seeking to serve, there could be no sickness in a body living in accordance with that law. Any deviation from the overall direction would automatically be corrected by cell-conduct in conformity with applied intention. Put in a simpler way, if every cell in the body was in complete agreement with the will of the individual occupying it, all would behave to keep the body in the best condition possible. All sickness is really cell rebellion against the governing will of whoever should be running the affairs of the whole body "from the top." Unless, of course, such a soul intended to be ill for some reason or other. That is not unknown among humans.

Seeking to serve the Sangreal is only another way of saying that we agree to live according to the "will of God" within ourselves, or seek ways of living for "true self" rather than "pseudo self." Put any way we like, it all amounts to the same idea. We have to realize that only when we "serve God" (as we would hope the cells of our own bodies would serve us) are we ever likely to be healthy, happy, and harmonious representatives of the Sangreal in human shape. That is really the entire essence of the whole Concept. It is obvious we are nowhere near this mark yet.

The Emperor shows one aspect of what we are here to achieve: right rulership over ourselves and related dominions. In modern times, leadership might be a better word, if that word can be understood without political connotations. Real rulership would be leading by example in preference to imposing arbitrary rules on unwilling subordinates and enforcing these by punitive measures. The qualities of genuine leadership into light are those needed by anyone accepting the conduct code of the Emperor interpreted from a Sangreal standpoint.

In very early eras, the royal blood or Sangreal factor was recognized as a familial trait through direct lines of descent, and strict observance of it was kept for many generations. It was relatively easy to recognize because particular families outstripped others in mental and moral growth. This could show up in two or three generations, and by common consent, these people were pushed into leadership roles because this brought benefits to the entire tribe. That pattern is far in our distant past and the spread of the Sangreal since has brought kingly qualities to almost anyone. Now it is only the question of depth and degree which is becoming increasingly difficult to estimate. The single remaining certainty is that kingliness should become the prerogative of any soul capable of containing it so that the light behind the blood shines through as many people as possible and illuminates the Paths of all choosing to perceive it.

To distinguish between the duties of Emperor and Empress, it will be well to look back a bit and see how this was determined in some old families. Each had their own special ideas about areas or "provinces" in which they alone stood supreme. Very roughly this was based on the female half ruling *inside* the home and family, while the male partner ruled *outside* it. The family formed the peripheral demarcation line which decided the rulership of either. Inside those limits the mother/wife ruled absolutely, and beyond them father/husband made all the decisions. In the home, father was no more than a family member, and beyond those limits in the family business, mother was no more than any other customer or associate. These arrangements worked very well, indeed, though they would be much questioned in modern times. Nevertheless, for the sake of clarity it might as well be accepted that the Emperor will represent the outer management of our mortal affairs, while the Empress applies to that of our inner kingdoms.

The Emperor stands for codes of conduct in civil areas, regulations and rules of law governing commercial enterprises, armed forces, and agreements between humans for the sake of mutual benefit or improvement in all-round relationships. He stands for a principle rather than a person, and affords an example of this being put in practice. The Emperor, in itself, is not exclusively masculine, and simply shows the qualities of being able to control the outward energies circulating around the society we live in. The card could equally apply to a female who needed to develop that side of her character or was coming in contact with it. One might say the Emperor represents decision making or the cultivation of this faculty in every field of externalized human affairs. Moreover, the card does not cover the spiritual side of life at all, being concerned purely with secular affairs. Although the Sangreal strain is fundamentally a spiritual principle, we have to live within the limitations of this world while we are alive in it. Our bodies must be fed, clothed, and maintained in terms of our times, mundane matters must be settled in the right order of priority, etc. The Emperor shows good management and rulership on Earth.

The Emperor points out our prerogative of self-rulership with every responsibility attached thereto. We are responsible for learning how to rule ourselves, not only for our own good, but for the benefit of other people, too. A badly behaved and irresponsible individual is a menace to everyone he or she encounters. Maybe the average human has gained enough self-control to be generally acceptable, but the standards set forth by the Emperor are far higher than those we would find applied to the majority of mankind. They are no less than the maximum possible to attain. These might be thought of as far too exacting to be expected of mortals, yet such should be insisted upon as an ideal to strive for with the aid of the Sangreal inspiring our efforts. Without continual striving there can never be an ultimate attainment, and the Emperor is offering the highest example for our guidance.

The most severe burden on royalty is responsibility. Not many people realize what responsibility means, except that they might be blamed for some particular happening. It means a great deal more. It signifies the acceptance of any charge from and by a higher authority in respect of whatever may be specifically presented with it. For example, if anyone said: "I ask (or order) you to take charge of this person (place or thing) and do such and such with them (or it)." From the moment of acceptance until discharged from the obligation, a responsibility exists which binds the acceptor to see that those conditions are carried out as fully and as conscientiously as possible, especially if there are failure penalties included in the original clause.

In the case of a King or Emperor, his people automatically imply: "By placing ourselves in your hands, we also place the responsibility for our well-being there too. Should you fail to fulfill your obligations to us, you will forfeit our loyalty and respect in return." In the case of the Sangreal, it is virtually saying to us: "I am trusting you to develop towards divinity as best my blood may make you. Now the onus of responsibility rests on you to come as near a condition of kingship as you can." In a way, this is not unlike the parable of the talents and the way they were used or misused by their trustees. How many people ever suspect, let alone recognize or actually *realize* their responsibility for "living up to what has been hoped for them"? How many people suspect there might be something in themselves which should be looked for and have deliberately refused to respond because they fear to acknowledge the responsibility involved? The tarot Emperor is both a reminder and a rebuke in either event.

He is also a reminder that before we can hope to rule in any higher kind of world we must learn the rudiments of the art in this one. The Emperor is a temporal and not a spiritual ruler. Humans were here as a life-species before the Sangreal contacted them, so our mundane instincts precede our spiritual inspirations. This signifies we have to raise ourselves as humans while translating earthly values into the inner language of light. If the highest type of human is represented as an Emperor, then that is the symbol we must adopt if we ever intend to reach its equivalent on spiritual levels.

The Emperor also signifies "constitution" in a governmental sense. That is to say, whatever comes together to constitute the natural condition or state of any organized body. To that extent he could stand for almost any authority with a worldly base of action. From a human standpoint this might not necessarily be a single person at all, but an authority stemming from a commission or even a committee, a body of people empowered to make rules for the behavior of others. This would cover all kinds of government departments issuing instructions or directives that influence the course of human conduct. The Emperor is to be taken in a figurative rather than a literal way, and he could apply equally well to a Republican as a Royal realm. Whatever rules in any realm is the Emperor of that estate. To copy a current type of phraseology, "Sangreal Rules. OK."

The Empress

Coming to the next card on the list we meet with the Empress. She is the consort of the Emperor. She has both feet in this world, and represents culture. Civilizations and constitutions may be the solid structure of society, but culture is its soul and sanity. What would life be like without any kind of culture? The Empress really represents the very best of cultures available to human beings. Here opinions will differ very widely so culture shall be defined as whatever artistic or aesthetic experience that brings out the best from those involved with it.

Culture has many forms of expression. For one individual, the acme of literature might be puerile pornography, and good music might be the senseless screaming and banging of a super discotheque. For another, it might mean classical music and the most exalted works ever written. Neither type of culture would evoke any worthwhile response from those unable to react to it favorably. Culture has to be suitable for its areas of application and the task of the Empress is to know exactly what will bring the best out of whom. Perhaps she might nowadays be described as a social scientist.

The Sangreal is very much basic to our cultural heritage, and the Empress represents its guardian principle operative in this world. So she goes hand in hand with her consort, spreading the customs and conditions of culture throughout the world he has to civilize. Maybe the main difference between their functions is that civilization is the work of getting this world together and culture is the pleasure of playing with it afterwards. The two go together and are interdependent. We work in order to make the pleasures of play possible, and we play to put ourselves into a good condition for work. Remuneration and recreation follow each other like the two halves of any wheel. Both are expenditures of the same energy, only the motivation distinguishes one from the other, and as we know, the work of one human is often the play of another.

So the Empress has an equally large field to cover as her consort, but her specialty is concerned with worldly culture.

The arts are a relatively small part of this field, since it includes every kind of cultural entertainment, family life, folk-customs, foods and clothing of a comfortable type, pet creatures, flower gardening, and in fact all the "soft" side of our lives here. It might be said that whereas the Emperor makes us do the things we ought and have to do in order to make this world inhabitable, the Empress encourages us to do the things we want to do so as to make the place worth living in. The Emperor is the man who builds up a hard and secure house, but the Empress is the woman who fills it with soft and comfortable furnishings which make it enjoyable to live in. Like some birds, the male gets the twigs and framework of the nest together while the female lines it with moss and down which act as warmth retainers for hatching the eggs. Without the Empress this would be a very hard world indeed. Creature comforts are her specialty.

In the old days the roles of male and female were more or less defined by physiology. The male was made to fight and safeguard territory and food supplies, while the female bore and cared for children, making the best of what the male could provide her with. Today of course those roles are almost totally exchangeable except for the childbearing function. Nevertheless, we still see a difference between "men's work" and "women's work," even though the two are well on their way to similitude in modern society. Men are now learning how to be women, and women are discovering how to be men.

The Empress stands for the feminine element of the Sangreal, which must operate through males as much as females. In fact, no human being is exclusively one sex or the other. An almost forgotten young German writer, Otto Weininger, made this quite clear in his then revolutionary book published in the first quarter of this century entitled *Sex and Character*. He claimed that sex was purely a matter of percentages. If a human being could be imagined who was 100% male or female, it would be a horrible monstrosity—the male a complete brute or the female an entirely savage slut. He said it was the male characteristics in a woman that made her a responsible and personable being to deal with, and the female characteristics in a man making him a sensitive and companionable creature. Of course Weininger tied this up with body-chemistry and some very complicated calculations concerning exact percentages. He came to the conclusion that an ideal balance would be struck if every man was about 60% male and 40% female and vice versa. They would then match perfectly when combined. There is certainly something to be said for his theory, although he discredited himself by committing suicide over an unhappy love affair with a strong element of absurdity in it at the time.

It has been said that woman civilizes man, but it would be truer to say that she cultures him, which could be a lot more valuable. Culture may be a difficult term to define exactly, but it is most certainly a major influence upon our lives and well-being. At one time, it was mainly a matter of choice and response to stimuli which stirred the Empress equivalent in our characters, but now culture is becoming more and more a purely commercial affair which is a very sad thing, because that means culture is being "sales-forced" upon us purely for the sake of profit.

We need an Empress type of awareness before we can really value all the different items and experiences we shall encounter during the course of a lifetime. The appreciation of culture is a certain sign of the Sangreal coming to life in ourselves. An animal cannot appreciate the aesthetic qualities of anything beyond its consumable or immediately utile value applicable for survival or sensory gratification. Our Sangreal strain enables us to reach and rise above this base-range of appreciation until we achieve whatever may be the ne plus ultra somewhere beyond anything we have arrived at so far in our hesitant history.

An Empress is concerned with motherhood and the functions of family life as a social group. She signifies the highest standards of social behavior and what used to be called "bringing up children properly." She is an exemplar in fact, and as such, one who recognizes and accepts full responsibility for all that she says and does. She is really an archetype of the Matron/Mistress sought by those trying to control their conduct. In fact, the Empress factor is responsible for good behavior among cultured people with no religious motivation whatever. That will come later. The tarot Empress represents what sort of a world this would be if humanity had never developed any particular religious propensities, and had only cultivated natural conceptions of right and wrong with moral values stemming from experience and observation put into social practice. That might not have been such a bad sort of world as worlds go, and humans would have lived and died in it happily enough for social satisfaction. We already have that sort of world going quite well among totally non-religious folk who are both law-abiding and have the highest social standards. The Empress is quite capable of governing Earth affairs with competence.

It may be contested that culture and religion are inseparable and one derives from the other, but that is not really so at all. As anyone should see, someone might be very cultured and have no notion of religion whatever, or be deeply religious almost without any genuine culture. Despite what anyone might suppose, spirituality per se is not a result of religion at all. It is an actual state of soul as the result of evolution and advancement of identity in closer conformity with the original intention behind the blood of Sangreal beginnings. Not something one believes, supposes, or practices, but what one has truly *become* as a cell-Self within the Supreme Entity comprising us all in cosmos. This being so, it may be asked why bother to go any further than the Empress while she is making such a good job of earthlife. There is a sound answer to that.

This develops from the intention, need, or just intense desire to establish conscious relationships and procedures between thinking humans and the power that made us think. The Sangreal has this effect in a great number of cases. It causes conscious concern with cosmic influences, which usually manifest in our force-form world as a keen interest in religion, mysticism, occultism, science, or almost any investigative attention to subjects leading toward metaphysical states of being. So far as the Sangreal cycle of the Tarots is concerned, this portion of it is covered by the Hierophant and High Priestess (or Pope and Popess). It must also be remembered that we are now approaching the nadir of the Sangreal Cycle, and those intending to progress beyond that point will have much more difficult times ahead of them on the upward climb. For the moment however, we have to consider how humans need to reach that lowest material mark via the agencies of spiritual stimuli encountered here on Earth and symbolized by the cards sometimes called the Pope and Popess.

Though the Hierophant and the Priestess were always to be thought of as a counterpoising pair, let us consider the Hierophant or Pope first.

The Hierophant

A Pope's function is that of a pontiff, which, in Roman terms, meant a bridgebuilder. His task was specifically to build a bridge between this world and the realms which lay beyond. He was supposed to *be* that bridge, himself, over which others would walk so they might reach the heavenly kingdom in safety. This called for a self-sacrifice similar to that of a sacred king. A pontiff was believed to sacrifice his personal hopes of heaven by becoming the bridge over which others passed, and his personal motto was that of the Grail altered a little: "Servitor servientium," or servant of the servants.

The Hierophant's field extends through all areas of "official" religion and religious reasoning. Here we are not speaking of the Christian faith alone, but use the Hierophant to represent the entire extent of religion throughout the world, regardless of creed or specific sect. If religions were hierarchal, formulary, and established on socially recognized lines, the Hierophant would cover them all. The card is the symbol of human beliefs and customs connected with culture, and conforming to civil laws which, nevertheless, seek spiritual outlets for expression and aspiration. This is typical of authoritarian religions which have tenets and doctrines for the guidance and direction of their adherents. They normally have some sacred book or writings attributed to past prophets or teacher-figures which they adopt as the source of their teachings. One might call these "official and authorized religions," because they are generally supportive of state and civil codes, are most unlikely to advocate insurrection or civil disobedience, and can be relied upon to mitigate all infringements of governmental regulations.

The Hierophant has to be a ruler in his own right and interprets the rules of spiritual conduct for all those people following the faith he is appointed to lead. In fulfilling this function he is said to "pontificate" or lay down the lines his followers are supposed to travel. They are thus believed to cross the chasms of doubt over the bridge he provides them. Theoretically, he is helped to these decisions by a whole council of advisers, though the ultimate responsibility falls on his personal shoulders. In the case of the Christian Church, those would be Cardinals and Bishops, but every established religion has its own equivalents.

Thus the Hierophant represents a disciplined and methodical approach to the Holy Mysteries of Life, relying on carefully formulated faith and rational ideology however mythological the original basis might be. An orderly approach by systematic prayers and practices led by educated (and carefully indoctrinated) priests or ministers ordained and paid for such a purpose. Everything regularized and backed by the light of solid experience and recorded observations. All this supported by a tradition of learning and its concomitant culture of a most impressive kind. Many famous scholars and official saints stand out like jewels in such a bright setting. Altogether a formalized force which has played a major part in the spiritual history of mankind.

The Hierophant also indicates the influence of the Sangreal which accounts for so much of human aspiration and behavior in this world. Beginning with the Sangreal promulgation of its blood through human hosts, we have divided along two instinctual lines. One said, "We feel we have fallen from heaven and everything in our blood is telling us to get back there somehow or other. We know that while we are in these bodies we can do nothing of the kind, and therefore we must pin our hopes on finding this wonderful place after we are dead and no longer have these bodies to bother us. No human surrounded by these lumps of moving meat can ever hope for heaven, so let us learn how to live without them as free and immortal spirits achieving the kind of consciousness our instincts inform us should be our birthright and natural inheritance. The spiritual life is best because it will get us back to where we really belong. So let us organize ourselves with that one objective in mind." Out of such considerations all orthodox and established religions were born.

The other inherent drive behind our blood told us something different. It said, "The evolving and developing nature of our characters is entirely due to this Sangreal strain in our blood. Collectively it will lead our species back to the stars we came from and a state of far greater intelligence than anything we know as yet. There we shall be able to lead superior and much better kinds of life. But religious ideas are so much rubbish and only hinder us from natural advancement. What we should do is educate and evolve our species until we are able to live in these bodies just as long and healthily as we want to. Once we can stabilize our species by dismissing all diseases and overcoming death apart from accidents and ordered endings, the whole universe can be ours. Our inventiveness and ingenuity can conquer cosmos itself. To hell with religion and to heaven with science. Knowledge is the answer to everything."

Both these drives began with the same motivation and nothing but methodology made the divergence between them. As we realize these days, they are trying to combine and work out some compromise to speed up the process between them before this world becomes unable to support either. How far they are likely to succeed in their uneasy alliance is going to be a matter for history to record if there are any hands capable of holding pens in those times. We began by making indented marks on stones, and now we are making electronic marks on silicone chips. The Sangreal certainly started something, but what is the end event going to be? Who dares demand an answer? It is not the Hierophant's province to do more than predict what this could be IF humanity becomes capable of transforming itself into a spiritual instead of a purely physical species.

Has any Hierophant ever been able to demonstrate this possibility? Some would say yes, but only a few selected humans were prepared to accept the evidence they were offered because they wanted to believe it. Faith was necessary first and the works would come later. Others would say this was nonsense, and they would never be prepared to accept an ideology unsupported by physical experience. The controversy between materialism and deism is likely to continue for a long time. During it all the Sangreal lies dormant in most humans. Where is the Hierophant capable of explaining to hearers who hardly know how to listen?

In the case of the Christian Pope, he and the whole of his hierarchy are dependent on the instance of a single human male who was said to have conquered death by the resurrection of his body after three days following a cruel crucifixion by Roman authorities at the instigation of Jewish officials. This single instance reported and recorded by only a few and far from independent witnesses has resulted in two thousand years of the Christian Church. Its basic tenet is roughly: "If he could do it, so can we eventually, providing we follow the guidelines of his teaching." Other Hierophants have interpreted the teachings of their respective faiths. However they all depend on a single common factor—the reality of conscious, intelligent, and active existence without a physical body. Whether this may be called life after death or independent individuality makes no difference. Do we, or do we not exist apart from our physical bodies? All religions hang on that single fulcrum.

A Hierophant was, and still should be, one who both conducts and explains the theoretical and practical performance of the Holy Mysteries. In old times he fulfilled this function literally. This meant the Hierophant had to be both well-instructed and well-inspired with an outstanding ability of expression— what we would now call charisma. The Hierophant indicates that we should develop such qualifications in ourselves, firstly for our own benefit, and then for whoever might benefit from that. It also signifies we should take every opportunity of learning from the past religious experiences of mankind which are symbolized by this card.

The Hierophant (or Pope) is no finalization of any human problems, but summates a very important stage in our spiritual development. How many people of brilliant independent thought and advanced intuition have evolved to that extent with help from the standard teachings and guidance they received when they were children concerning extant and established religions and philosophies? The leaders of all religions were influenced and inspired by the mythology and mysticism of previous faiths. Abraham became a patron of the Hebrew faith from a paganistic past. Jesus summarized all that inheritance into what later became the Christian Church, while the prophet Mohammed subsequently altered both into Islam. The teachings of Gautama Buddha were backed by ancient Hindu beliefs, and Kung Fu Tze (Confucius) collated and explained the old "Wisdom Texts" as he was charged by his emperor. All these and an unspecified number of men and women were Hierophants in the literal sense of the word. Their followers are still looking for light among their literary legacies.

So in a last analysis, the Hierophant can be regarded as our individual and collective abilities for evolving spiritual realities out of ourselves by means of all the beliefs and teachings we may have absorbed from previous religious ideologies interpreted into present forms of comprehension. Each one of us has to eventually become the Hierophant who will synthesize and construct whatever form of faith we may have evolved in the course of many incarnations. In the case of an individual, this is not likely to become effective until towards the end of an incarnation, while with a cultured civilization the equivalent might take many centuries to eventuate, though the process itself is an ongoing one throughout time. Hierophants only mark points along the line, and at this here-now point of human history those lines seem to be converging on a point in common. Can this be the Sangreal?

The Priestess

Having experienced the Hierophant, we come now to the last tarot Trump of the quadrant, the Priestess, who should always be considered as the other half of the Hierophant (or Pope). In fact, if all the symbols of this Shield-Rod quarter are arranged so they present two pairs for the Chariot to drive through, this would illustrate how we ought to progress through this world. First, of course, there would be the Chariot carrying the inquirer on his/her Quest. Or it could be thought of as bearing the symbolic Grail along its processional path. This would pass between the pillars presented by the Emperor and Empress, representing the externalized side of human experience on earth. Then the Pope and Priestess make another biological pair suggestive of an inner or spiritual experience to undergo before the whole equipage is brought to a temporary halt by the Magician with his cunning tricks.

The Priestess is an arbitrary title to match that of the Pope. It signifies that she is in the position of being a religious supremo from the feminine angle of life. Her authority derives from the same source as the Hierophant's, but is expressive of entirely different determinants. Historically, it is older than his, since it stems back to the Matriarchal beliefs implanted in us from very primitive times. Fundamentally the Priestess carries us back to our prototype parents when the mother was always known but the father might have been one of many men, and was therefore unimportant.

She is also the Priestess function in mothers who generally instill the elements of religion into their children before their intellects are developed enough to cope with their fathers' more sophisticated conceptions. Her concern is mainly for the feeling and emotional side of religious practice, without which religion would be little else than dry philosophy and dull theological speculation. It is she who gives religion life in her womb and makes it palatable for humans to experience with warmth and wonder. She nurtures it with the milk of human kindness and stirs it with the stimulus of sensuality. She sees and understands the sexual implications involved with the most pious of our practices, and encourages emotional expressions in our prayers, while sympathizing with the saddest of our supplications. She comforts us when we cry upon her shoulders and she soothes us when we sob brokenheartedly against her gentle breasts. Altogether she is a very lovely lady to rely on for religious support in our search for the Sangreal.

This tarot High Priestess symbolizes all that is unorthodox or "straight from the Spirit" in spiritual and religious affairs. She is not a particular protagonist of formal temple worship or dogmatic texts. She would much rather go to God through nature in the raw, so to speak, or rely on what came to her in her own heart when she "lifted it with love" in the direction of divinity. Her choristers are the birds in the branches, and her incense the fragrance of a flower. She knows how to worship without any words at all. She needs no arguments or complicated intellectualism to tell her about a deity for herself at the closest quarters in her own heart. Her consciousness seeks no convictions about the reality of her religion because that will be no more than herself in practice. The only evidence of deity she needs is her own existence. If she had to formulate her philosophy it would probably be: "Since I am, God must be." For her those concepts are not two but one. Why bother to doubt or argue about it, when it is much better and simpler to live it?

The Priestess bears so many implications of beautiful and enjoyable import that it is often difficult to perceive her limitations and see that we need ever leave her delightful domains to experience harder and heavier conditions of life. Still, she will always be there to console us if we fail to surmount what may lie ahead and limp back to cry in her comforting company. It is scarcely surprising that the Christian Church eventually had to accept her personified as Mary, mother of Jesus. Those who welcomed her back in that disguise must have been thankful they could openly acknowledge their beloved Guardianess under whatever pseudonym the church fathers chose for her. Let the fathers and Hierophants say what they pleased, her faithful ones knew who and what she was and would serve her regardless of any labels attached by mortal men. She would come into her own again one day, and until then it was best to serve in secret.

From the Sangreal standpoint, the Priestess is an especially important card, because she shows its deepest influence in our souls. She is behind the most beautiful of blessings poured from the cosmic cup. The Empress may make us cultured people, but the Priestess makes us spiritually cultured, fit for progressing into higher states of life. She symbolizes that quality of the Sangreal in ourselves which softens all the many hardships of the Quest into bearable burdens. Anyone seriously down-hearted should try to start a dialogue with this card once a personified presence can be contrived. She is the responsive image from our genetics, which is why the cards are sometimes called "keys" since they tend to unlock the inner realities they represent from our deepest depths.

Sometimes the Priestess is thought of as being essentially Virgin, but this is not a sine qua non in the least. She is virginal and matriarchal simultaneously. Virgin birth is always a sign of Godhood, partly because of the ideology and mostly due to the ancestral genetic memory of the Sangreal strain being originally implanted in us by what we would now think of as artificial insemination. Our "descent from deity" described as being "in his own image and likeness" seems due to much more scientific and spiritual installations into our evolutionary genesis than any method known today, but certainly "virgin" in the sense that no human agency impregnated any females chosen to start the blood which began the sort of souls we can become in this world. Subsequent mythology postulated the Virgin birth Concept as being intimately connected with the God-in-Man belief.

Though there is no special need to see the Priestess figure as any sort of Goddess, she can certainly be visualized in whatever fashion that clearly indicates her function as an archetypal female who helps to spiritualize humanity on its way up the ladder of life, or on its ascending journey around the Sangreal cycle. If anyone would like to think of her as being the one nearest the bottom who gives an encouraging pat on the shoulder and a good push to those passing that point while they summon up every energy for the steep and hazardous climb ahead, that would make quite a nice image. It is best to commence that climb with the maximum of encouragement and spiritual backing that may be managed, and the Priestess is most positively a sympathetic source for such succor.

The Priestess symbolizes spiritual qualities needed by men quite as much as women. The assumption is that when the original Sangreal strain had to be split, as it were, between males and females, it was found that each had specific characteristics that favored the development and continuity of certain definable traits. All that could be done was share the blood strain as evenly as possible between the sexes so that when they mated they might hopefully supply each other's deficiencies. This would have worked out in practice if every mating could have been supervised and controlled to ensure that only adequate matchings were allowed to breed, which naturally proved impossible. The probability is that, in the end, humanity will produce a theoretically perfect species of its own accord. That is a rather remote hope at present. The Priestess stands for the purely spiritual and idealistic instincts which could be transmissible from mother to son genetically, or arise naturally in a female child from the spiritual source in contact with its soul.

The Magician

At this point of the cycle we have reached the absolute nadir in this world, waved farewell to the Priestess, and turned to the next Trump which happens to be the Magician. This is the beginning of the third quadrant. The Magician is definitely the archetype or cosmic chromosome which shouts, "Stop, all change!" at the Fool or whoever has followed the perimeter path so far. This Magician is essentially the symbol of transmutation rather than transformation, which means he indicates an alteration of nature while not necessarily one of form and function:

such as changing a wooden item into a metal one, or a linen handkerchief to cotton. The imperative word here is *change*, and this is what the Magician signifies. These are changes and alterations we must make in our own natures if we wish to continue our Quest with solid hopes of gaining the Grail at its apex. The very word "magic" has a fascination of its own, and the Magician we meet here on the threshold of our cyclic ascent is no common trickster, but a veritable Magus of the Great Work itself. His work is not necessarily to deceive anyone, but to facilitate all the alterations which will be needed by our individual and collective characters before we will be ready to rise any further toward the truths it would otherwise be foolish to face. This is a sensible thing to do, and a practical preparation before embarking on any serious course of spiritual action.

In the old days we used to hear a lot about the "work of preparation" supposed to precede any magical operation. Many rules were laid down with conditions to fulfill and obligations to undertake. Endless injunctions were made about what must infallibly be done and descriptions were given of the penalties to be paid in the event of non-compliance. Everything was deliberately made very onerous. When the would-be magician finally entered his circle to consecrate it, he was probably in a serious state of apprehension and anxiety.

The tarot Magician is already in his circle of the Sangreal cosmos. Here he greets us with a welcoming wave of his wand or instrument of integration. His task is to change our consciousness so that it will serve us as an instrument of investigation, for are we not Questers on the Holiest of Hunts? It is the Magician who is familiar with all the "tricks of the trade" we shall have to learn in advance of our approach. He will teach us what we need to know once he can trust us not to betray them or him. It is the Magician, too, who knows what lies ahead of us. He is no savior figure, but a knowing trickster figure. We must hope we can persuade him to impart some of that knowledge without too many tricks. He is quite capable of trying to trick us if he can as a test of our intelligence. This can determine what proportion of the Fool is left in anyone who has reached the turning point of a spiritual career, and on the results of such a test so will the rest of the Magician's conduct depend. Therefore it behooves us to be very wary indeed when we deal with this not entirely unfriendly deceiver. He only fools Fools.

Magician is a Hermetic one in the sense of what was called a psychopompus in the early mysteries: a soul-leader who was supposed to guide people along puzzling and problematical paths by precept and practical advice. The Magician is another type of Hierophant in a way, except that he deals with a very different sort of world, because we are entering the quadrant of overcoming obstacles. Whereas previously we had authorities like the Emperor to tell us how we ought to behave on Earth, and the Hierophant to tell us how to act if we hoped to gain heaven, here we have only the Magician to brief us before we must set forth on our own to travel a very uncertain and peculiar route leading somewhere we can only hope might bring us closer to the Sangreal.

As we already know, the rule of life is "adapt or die" and this Magician has to help us adapt to some very uncomfortable conditions of existence and get ourselves past them with a minimum of trouble. If we were going on some very difficult earth expedition, we would approach an expert who would say something like: "You will need this type of clothing, eat this sort of food for energy, take these sorts of medications with you, these kind of tools and equipment, employ only those particular people," and so forth. Anyone able to follow all those instructions would expect to make at least a reasonable trip, but if such advice was ignored, they would only have themselves to blame. The Magician here is in much the same position as an expedition adviser, except that he really consists of Sangreal awareness born in and by our own inherited blood. He is as genuine as that.

After the Magician we are not going to meet any more "people" for quite a period, and will be encountering abstract powers and principles. They will present one problem after another for us to cope with if we can, so the Magician had better make some very potent magic to protect and project us along.

One of the worst mistakes we can make while searching for the Sangreal is to try pushing past the Magician and rush along to encounter the dangers ahead without being prepared by his ministrations first. There are many who attempt this and come back beaten, only to undergo all over again that magical "labor of preparation" they should have done properly in the first place.

The Magician symbolizes the ability of self-change to suit conditions of consciousness according to circumstances, and further than that, changing circumstances themselves to suit the state of consciousness required. Magic was once defined as the art of changing or altering in accordance with will, and that is quite a fair description on the whole. When we think of Magicians, what image appears on our mental screens? Someone producing rabbits out of hats and girls out of heaps of handkerchiefs? Always changes, always alterations. Nothing must stay the same after a Magician has touched it with his wonderful wand of intentional alteration. The entire motivation of magic is to alter things, and whether we are watching a show we know quite well is arranged by skillful and entertaining deceit, or witnessing an actuality of alteration taking place in a human character, both are still a magic to be astonished at.

Good Magicians never tell the secrets of their trade, for to do so would take out all the element of enjoyment. We enjoy being amazed or bewildered, providing we feel assured that nothing harmful will happen. Though the Magician does have an element of amusement in his good humored and sometimes quizzical approach to problems, he will teach at least the rudiments of his art to aspirants on their way Grailwards. Are we really able to alter ourselves at will? Can anyone in the throes of a violent temper suddenly stop and say: "This will not do at all and I must alter my attitude." After which magical invocation the raging one would forthwith become calm and reasonable. That is the type of magic we have to learn here. Should anyone feel like saying: "But that isn't magic, that's just self-control," a knowledgeable Magician like our Tarot one might reply: "Well, what else is self-control but magic of the highest kind?"

Perhaps a pragmatist could interject: "It all depends on what you mean by magic." Although such people can sometimes be very annoying, they do have a good point in demanding clear definitions before embarking on any new idea. So maybe the definition of magic here should be: "necessary change in conformity with confrontation." There are many stories of this in magical mythology which usually center around traditional "duels" between two rival magicians who keep altering themselves in such a fashion as to gain advantages over each other until one makes a fatal slip and the other instantly assumes some form which annihilates his ex-rival. Such are really "moral example" tales of procedures to be adopted in a figurative rather than a literal sense. We have to know what to change into so as to meet any challenge life may fling in our faces.

Life has a nasty habit of doing just that for most of our incarnations, and unless we learn enough about magic to counter and cope with each one as it comes, our lives are going to be very difficult indeed. The tarot Magician symbolizes that inner instinct which comes up with bright ideas or original notions for changing such situations in favor of its invokant. This may not sound very exciting, but such a Magician can be not only a very present help in trouble, but also a creator of fresh situations to suit whatever may be needed. There is always the magical risk of making a bad situation worse, or a good one go bad, but risks are all part of magic—to be undertaken only when strictly necessary. Magic can be a very mixed blessing sometimes, but when the correct usage is known, the type of magic taught by the Tarot expert can be a very valuable asset for Grail finding.

The current interest in magic among young people of the 20th century is interesting because it shows how very deeply they feel the need of change, not only in themselves, but also in their circumstances and all around them. Most of them are unaware of the exact changes needed, but all would agree that alterations in this world and its condition are most certainly called for. Evidence of their magic is all over the place, and unhappily it seems to have made a worse mess out of mismanagement and muddle. They try situational changes by violence and upheaval, by the introduction of outrageous customs, fashions and behaviors. They may call this magic, and yet it is of a strange kind which they cannot understand in the least. Madness has a magic of its own. Unluckily those who are responsible for running this world cannot understand it either, and care to do little more than cash in on the opportunities afforded. There is only one way to counter mad magic, and that is by changing its character through inner alterations. The tarot Magician might be able to impart such a splendid ability, but only to those who have undergone the previous experiences in the Sangreal cycle.

The importance of this previous conditioning through the tarot tests presented by each Trump in its proper turn can scarcely be overstressed. In conventional decks, the Magician is card I, and it is the continued acceptance of this numeration of unknown origin which has caused so much misunderstanding and confusion in our times. Commonsense and appreciation of ideological symbology seems to be so seldom employed. Why is it that so many authors and investigators blindly accept the numeration of the tarot as something so sacred it must never be questioned? Why are tarot designers so enthusiastic about altering the picture yet never the number? What would be the state of modern medicine if every medical writer and lecturer insisted on issuing textbooks based solely on the dogmas of Paracelsus?

If the Magician had been made to start our Sangreal sequence, nothing would have made any sense at all. It might have been implied that the Magician had to commence everything with a wave of his altering wand, but that would have been ridiculous, because at that point there would have been nothing to alter. It is only after a distinct process of development has taken place that there will be anything worth altering, and this card in the Sangreal cycle is at that exact point. Right at the bottom of the cycle where the most changes should be effected in order to favor the uphill climb ahead. The entire nature of the ordeals ahead are going to change a climber anyway, and unless the equivalent of a Magician is capable of matching this by adaptively altering and changing the characteristics of aspirants, few if any of them are likely to reach the top of the Magic Mountain where the true Grail exists.

The tarot Magician is cunning enough to alter his own appearance in conformity with cases. He can look like almost anyone of his nature. Perhaps a psychoanalyst or a brain surgeon, an orator or even a salesman trying to induce people to change their minds. He can look like a book which alters people's opinions and outlooks. Nor is there any ruling to say that minor magicians do not count. Many such makers of magic each having minimum significance would amount to quite a sizable major magician if all their combined influences for a lifetime were to comprise a single Magician figure. That is mostly how the majority of humans meet their Magician in the end. Through a longish series of minor encounters with a great variety of differently dressed magical practitioners, none of whom might be prepared to accept that description of themselves.

It is only when the Magician has had sufficient time and opportunity to alter us properly that we should consider continuation of the Quest. It may be well to recall that we commenced with the Fool (or Innocent) encountering the beginning of his journey through time and space in search of the Sangreal with its seeds instilled into his blood. He has now gotten to the bottom of things at last and, it is hoped, may have learned some sense on the way, so strictly speaking he should not be called a Fool any longer, though he may still be very far from real wisdom. However, if he is inflated by overestimation of his abilities and filled with conceit or self-satisfaction, he is still a Fool in spirit, even if he happens to be the most informed and best educated individual in the world. Those who know the meaning of the title "A Fool in God" are quite satisfied to accept it gladly. Maybe our Fool has found out how to take the title as an honorific. He has met the Magician who converted it.

Conversion is a strange and interesting word, and the Magician is a great converter. We tend to associate that word with a crowd of frenzied people being preached at who make a theatrical show of repentance followed by acts of penance, such as giving thousands of dollars to funds conveniently controlled by the preachers. "Conversion" comes from Latin roots meaning to turn in the sense of altering course. That accords very well with the Magician being placed at the turning point of the Sangreal cycle. It also implies that we should turn when the course of our lives becomes too difficult to direct along whatever lines we may have been blindly following without thought or consideration of consequences. Rigid inflexibility is not so much foolish as idiotic. Everybody should know when to turn or convert their energies into alternative channels, and this knowledge comes from the depths of our Sangreal ancestry presided over by the Magician.

The Wheel of Fortune

The experience of conversion or turning comes via the Trump called the Wheel of Fortune. Its fundamental concept signifies the ups and downs of life, the turning of the mind from one thing to another, and the realization of the cyclic nature of cosmos. Additionally, it shows the alternative connection of good and evil derived from the same drive, the good luck of one person being the bad luck of another, the turning of the tides in life, and the circular motion of most energy events in our universe.

The conversion and conservation of energy is one of the first subjects a schoolboy physicist learns about, and now it is a major concern of our current civilization. Convert the energy of coal into steam which works a turbine driving a dynamo producing electricity distributed to our homes for operating energy-consuming machines like heaters and domestic appliances. All dependent on the simple principle of the wheel in rotary action. Here, however, we have to work out the equivalent in spiritual dimensions of life, converting the laws of mechanics into those of metaphysics. The art of spiritual conversion or "true-turning" is a very subtle yet vitally important subject. We still talk about "turning into" when we mean the process of change anywhere, and we say "turning out" when we mean some situation developing into something different. And we speak of not knowing which way to turn when we feel baffled or bewildered. Turning is a peculiar subject.

The probability is that the Wheel of Fortune image overlaid the original one of a simple wheel without complications, which may have been a Chariot wheel. A "wheel of fortune" was the forerunner of roulette, being a large vertical wheel with numbered segments which was spun either to select the lucky number of a lottery when it stopped, or indicate numbers against which bets were placed. Fundamentally a gambling device wherewith fortunes in money could be won or lost as quickly as possible. This could signify that life's winners are funded by the losers, the winnings of few being gained from the losses of many. Could this be a hint that here is where the secrets of rigging a wheel in favor of the rigger should be learned? Probably not, yet a working knowledge of such tricks might always be useful.

It has been credibly said that the wheel was the single invention which altered (or turned) the course of our entire civilisation forever, and no cultured nation could exist without it. This, however, did happen in the case of American Indians who surprisingly knew about the solar disc and calculated a calendar thereon, yet failed to convert it into mechanistic terms. Did they consider it too sacred to use for mere mortal convenience of transport? We must remain uncertain. The only indubitable point is that we must learn to use the spiritual equivalent of the wheel-principle, and also experience it for ourselves as an act of life.

Nowadays we hear a lot about bio-rhythmics as predictive patternings of physical and emotional health in ordinary human beings. This seems to tie in with personal horoscopes which chart the cyclic motion of the planets in our solar system. The belief is that such knowledge is valuable for planning a working life so as to get the best advantage from all angles. That is the sort of thing one would expect to contact at this tarot Trump point of the Sangreal cycle. The astrological chart of anyone can be considered their Wheel of Fortune for an incarnation. Old Qabbalists called their doctrine of reincarnation that of the Gilgolim or wheels for the same reason as Buddha taught about his Wheel of Life and Death. All branches of esotericism employ the wheel-principle to illustrate appropriate teachings. So deeply is the wheel-archetype impressed into us that it is probably the idea of a turning wheel which inspired most of our ideas about immortality. As a wheel could not make a complete revolution without bringing the same portion of it back to earth again, so would we return ceaselessly until the Chariot of Life stopped altogether as it was reputed to do every so often in a state called the Great Sleep of the Gods.

There is so much to learn and experience from the Wheel that the Quester will need all the ingenuity of a wheel-inventor to approach it. A wheel is necessarily an endless invention. It will only revolve properly when perfectly balanced in its center-circumference relationship. The implications of this alone should make the spirit of an earnest inquirer spin for a lifetime. One myth tells the story that when people are born, a wheel of fortune is set spinning for them in heaven and left to revolve on its momentum. When it stops, their time is up and they are recalled to await another expedition. Meanwhile, they had an opportunity for rebalancing their wheels because the better this balance was, the longer and luckier would be their next lives. These wheels could be weighted with the guilt of their sins, or lightened to the extent of the burdens they lifted from others. There must be quite a moral to infer from this somehow.

While we are at this position we should not forget that a wheel is fundamentally a specific shape. It cannot be other than round, though an imperfect wheel could be very slightly oval and still serve its function, albeit badly. Strictly speaking, it is only by convention that we think of our elliptical solar system as a wheel. The same could be said of our blood and body cells which link with the Sangreal line. We are, however, reminded of the Round Table at which the Grail knights gathered, and the roundness of the Vessel itself is implied rather than specified. As a pure principle, there is the circulation of the blood to consider and the three circles of time, space, and events which combine to form the figure for cosmos. The wheel-concept is so intimately connected with much that concerns us very closely. There is neither beginning nor end to it, like eternity which has been compared to a ring of light.

Wheels are especially connected with time because any revolution is only possible by the passage of time through the space of the circumference which forms the event. So the wheel is really representative of the three cosmic rings in itself. Measurement of time would not have been possible without accurate wheels for the mechanisms of clocks, and space was often measured by counting the revolutions of wheels of known diameters. Time is one of the most difficult factors to deal with in esotericism owing to such great variations in viewpoints. This is where we have to come to terms with time by learning to measure it, not by human standards, but cosmic ones. A lifetime is still a lifetime for any living creature, whether a mayfly or a person. To each it has the same length as measured by the principle of time, and only the Wheel of Birth and Death can determine that.

The Wheel of Fortune has chiefly to teach us how we should take the good and bad experiences of life so they even out and make something worth winning at the end of them. Difficult? Most certainly, but what else makes any real sense out of living? The Wheel, at least, deals with only the average ups and downs of life. The really horrible and terrifying experiences come at a later point with the Devil and the Tower, but we shall have some character work to put in first before we shall be prepared to encounter them. Many might say the Wheel is bad enough, but it comes here in the Sangreal cycle as a sort of "practice run" in leading up to future ordeals which must inevitably be undergone sooner or later in one incarnation or another. In a way, the Wheel is the rehearsal room where we go through the play again and again until we shall be ready to perform it before a cosmic audience which will decide our worthiness to gain the Grail at the end of everything.

Most tarot commentators point out the legend of Ixion when they come to the Wheel, and interpret this in many ingenious ways. There is, however, one item of interest they seem to have missed. When Zeus condemned Ixion to hell on his constantly turning wheel of fire, it was Hermes who was instructed to supervise this sentence. Even though Hermes was officially a psychopompus or conductor of souls, this was an uncharacteristic obligation for such a God, so why should he in particular be singled out? It was a rather engaging quality of the Greek Olympic Gods that they all had typically human faults. Hermes had a reputation for dishonesty and intellectual inquisitiveness which was liable to lead toward trouble. That was the trouble with Ixion, too. He wanted to know what it would be like to have sexual intercourse with a supremely important Goddess. Not lust, but sheer overweening curiosity of the most insolent kind.

The all-knowing Zeus, who had plenty of faults on his own account, made a simulacrum of Hera out of cloud, which represented the insubstantial and unimportant fantasies of idle and inquisitive mankind, amusing himself for no other purpose than passing time without using it constructively. Ixion seems to have been too stupid to see through this God-trick, and his sex act with the cloud produced the centaurs—half men half horses—monstrosities of a naturally impossible kind. The moral being if we insist on impossibly irresponsible behavior, we must expect to get a corresponding result. One of the main reasons that we remain bound to the wheel of birth and death is pure curiosity. An overpowering impulse to "see what happens next." That was why Buddha preached his doctrine of disinterest, or uninvolvement, which might help to overcome this instinctual urge which did nothing except tie human souls to a state Buddha regarded as being one of perpetual torture.

Ixion's wheel of fire was constantly turning to show its connection with time and torture. So Hermes was only inflicting on a surrogate human the punishment his own faults deserved. It is very interesting to note the proximity here of the Hermetic Magician and the Wheel. Our misplaced hermetic instincts of curiosity can lead us into deeper trouble than the poor fabled pussycat encountered. If humanity really wanted to get away from its fiery wheel, it would just have to stop being so stupidly inquisitive concerning things we have no need to know in the wrong place and at the wrong time. That is the moral of Ixion's Wheel we have to learn here at the nadir of this Sangreal cycle.

Again the point is being brought out that there has to be a right time and place to initiate events of this earth. This is what correct knowledge of the Wheel would tell us if we knew its secrets. The implication is that before we proceed any further on our Quest, we should at least have some general ideas about the workings of this Wheel. People often say: "This is a mad and crazy world," and though we would most certainly agree with them on the surface, we cannot help wondering if there is any method in the madness, and if so, how could this be put to profitable use. Maybe meditation on the fundamentals of this tarot Trump might release a clue from our subconsciousness.

Justice

Only when we have absorbed as much as we can from the Wheel-concept dare we face the next card Justice, followed by that of Judgement. No one can possibly exercise Judgement if they have no notion of Justice, and it is certainly best to know about Justice and how to make accurate Judgements before facing the Devil who comes after that. The question is, what exactly is Justice? Dictionary definitions are not very helpful. They tell us the word derives from the Latin "jus," meaning the law as understood by average humans. They also indicate that the quality of justice concerns the administration of law and correct compensation for offenses against it. What dictionaries do not make clear is the concept of Justice as karma or the automatic action of cosmic compensation for everything that happens in existence. That is the sort of Justice symbolized by this tarot card. Karma is only the Hindu term for this law, which is not just *a* law of cosmos, but simply law itself. What goes up must come down and nothing can exist without its equal and opposite co-existing simultaneously. Men and women are not the only creatures or creations God made in pairs.

Justice is a life-principle which is implanted deeply, if often inadequately, in the majority of mankind. Children are constantly complaining that something or someone "isn't fair," and most mortals are convinced at some period of their lives that fate or whatever has handed them out a dirty deal, and it is about time they had a piece of good luck to make up for this. Should the weather be particularly fine for a prolonged period, some old lady is sure to say: "Ah, but we shall pay for this sooner or later." If ancient Greeks suddenly felt that a happiness event had been unexpectedly extended, somebody would ceremonially break some relatively valueless object to upset the equilibrium because they felt that only the Gods had the right to eternal happiness, while humans stayed under the laws of cyclic change.

So we are still concerned with the concept of change with Justice, but this time it concerns the event cycle of the three cosmic rings. Justice is the principle that evens out all the events we experience until they form a perfect Ring of Recompense and fit exactly as they should in cosmos. It is vitally important that we both appreciate and understand something of the law responsible for this operation, because it lies behind our beings and applies not only to every moment of our lives but also to the entirety of our existence. Nowadays it is more or less common to hear people saying "It's my karma," as an explanation of anything that happens to them, but very few have any real idea of what this implies.

They have vague ideas that if they murder anyone in one incarnation, this gives their victim the right to murder them in their next earth-visit, or if they are born poor in one birth they should be born rich next time. This is just as foolish as supposing that the more one suffers on earth the happier will be that person's heaven. Such was the misconception Christians made about the law of life. Jews had, and still have, an enormous respect for this law, which they called Torah. The connection of this with tarot is too obvious for comment. The entire formalities of Hebrew worship were concerned with the law, by which they do not mean their written scriptures which were only symbolic of it, but the Power Itself which kept everything in its proper place and worked everything as it willed with its universe by means of cosmic compensation. They revered the incredible energy and intelligence of whatever ordered Cosmos in that style, so the actual law *was* their God.

Many suppose that Jews worshipped their scriptural rules and regulations (identified as the Torah) which they studied so assiduously while they kept their Holy Scrolls in the Ark of their synagogue and performed many ceremonies in honor thereof. They spoke of "studying Torah" as if that meant poring constantly over word-puzzles presented to them on parchment or paper, instead of genuinely "living the law," or as the Christians put it later, living in accordance with the Will of God. Many sincere Jews made the mistake of spending much of their lives bent over such scrolls and documents in dim and dingy surroundings, straining their eyesight and everyone else's resources instead of "studying Torah" by simply living it all the time with their ordinary lives. There was a theory that heaven was a place where they could "study Torah" without ever having to take their eyes from the written scroll. Had they stopped to think what Torah really meant, they could have saved themselves a lot of anxiety.

None of us can help being involved with cosmic compensation, because we are all in it together. With Justice we have first to be convinced that this law exists, and then that it applies to every human being. Some may wonder how this fits in with the doctrine of free will so beloved by the Christian theologians. If karma determines everything in the end, how can our lives possibly be free? The answer is, of course, that our individual and collective wills are only free within the limits of our capabilities, and those have very definite limits indeed. We are literally free to intend or imagine whatever we can, though that does not mean an actual accomplishment of this. Which is just as well for our spiritual safety, because if thoughts alone could kill, most of us would be dead long ago.

It was chiefly for this reason that Buddha kept insisting on what he called "right thinking," and Jesus taught that thinking about fornication or other unapproved acts would risk retribution almost as much as if the thinker had done the deed in physical form. There is even an amusing cartoon of an unhappy monk in hell saying gloomily, "If it's as much of a sin to think about it as to do it, how I grudge all that time I wasted on Earth in a damp monastery when I could have been in a comfortable bed enjoying myself!"

Justice as a principle has nothing to do with retaliation for any kind of crime. Revenge may be sweet, but it is never *just*. For instance, judicially executing a murderer may be legal vengeance, but it never brought a victim back to life, which would be the only real justification for it. Justice is only that which fully compensates for any act, and what possible compensation can there be for murder which can be made by any mortal? Earlier Muslim law made at least an attempt in this direction when it made the penalty for murder an obligation for the killer to support the murdered man's wives, children, and dependent relatives. That cut the Muslim murder rate down as nothing else seems to have done since. Our modern incarcerations of murderers are completely futile and little pretence is being made that true Justice has any connection with our criminal laws. Making the punishment fit the crime in a criminal ridden society has been made a matter of expedient economy rather than intelligent application. We need to remember the old motto: fiat justitia ruat coelum—indicating that justice itself is more important than the falling of heaven. So it is when we consider that without Justice there could be neither a condition of heaven nor hell. Those states of consciousness are results of karma and not the causes of it. Karma originated automatically with creation itself. That was the meaning of the dictum that a thing is not just because God wills it, but God wills it because it is just.

We are always talking about justification one way or another. We ask "Is that justified?" or "How can I do justice to it?" Real Justice would be a perfect balance of might and mercy so that everything equals out and comes to calmness with stability and satisfaction all round. The chances are that absolute justice cannot possibly be carried out in this world at all, and the most we can do is make a rough approximation. It is said God never punishes us *for* our sins but always *by* them. Old notions of a vengeful God punishing human offenders against divine dignity should be a forgotten fallacy. We have worse to face than that. All the activities of body, mind, and soul are automatically entered in the cosmic computers of correction (not punishment) and we shall again automatically be presented with the bill in the course of time—which has to be paid in compatible currency of consciousness.

Because such a bill is not presented immediately to those knowingly incurring it, too many suppose it will never come at all, or at least to them personally. Yet if we look carefully, it is quite possible to trace payments presented in this century for debts incurred several hundred and more years back. This was why the ancients assumed that karmic debts would be paid off in future incarnations. The truth of this may not be as literal or personal as they supposed, though it certainly applies in broad principle, since each generation has perforce to inherit the unpaid obligations of its predecessors. Christians considered that Jesus dying on the cross had cancelled all such debts when he cried out "It it finished," just before he died. The Greek phrase used was "tetalestoi" which was then in common use for writing across an account which had just been settled in full.

Understanding all the ins and outs of Justice is often more than anyone can learn in a lifetime, but the principle has to be encountered in its turn and comprehended as far as possible. This may not be to a very great extent, but it is the attempt itself which counts for credits to the Quester. Many folk-tales are told concerning those who questioned the Justice of God, and their adventures which proved that this not only existed, but was working ceaselessly to compensate the apparant injustices of this universe. It is always a question of "in the end" or emphasis being placed on the delay factor due to many others involved.

The quote is often made about the Mills of God grinding slowly but exceedingly small, and only a slow sort of action could guarantee everything being taken into account so genuine Justice might be done eventually. All attempts at summary Justice are liable to be faulty ones calling for further compensation.

Judgement

Together with Justice comes Judgement. This is the faculty of employing and controlling the principle of Justice with intelligent consciousness. Justice is a principle, while Judgement is a practice. The two go together like previous pairs. Although the card is usually shown as a "Last Judgement" scene, it is really the faculty of judgement itself which is supposed to be symbolized by this card. It follows that nobody can be expected to exercise judgement who does not have some very sound ideas about Justice, which is why it is placed here in the Sangreal cycle.

We are the only species able to use the faculty of Judgement. It might be supposed that any animal capable of calculating all the circumstances leading up to some decisive action—like killing its prey or leaping some obstacle—was exercising judgement, but that is not so, since it is doing no more than estimating its own abilities in relation to physical needs. The Judgement shown by the tarot distinctly means an ability to consider, ponder, weigh up (as with the scales of Justice) all possible known factors concerned with specific events or circumstances, and determine what consequent course of action to take.

Judgment is governing and controlling ability which directs our lives in accordance with principles which we have reason to believe are best to behave by. It is a much misused word. If we mistime a leap and slip or fall, we are liable to say: "Oh, I judged that badly," when it should have been "I estimated or guessed that badly." Judgement in the sense of the tarot invariably means arriving at decisions concerning conduct and behavior. A legal judge, for instance, has to decide what should be done in the cases of those who decide to break civil laws. There are usually moral issues involved, in the sense that morals mean conventional customs rather than rules imposed by opinions.

There are good judgements and there are bad ones. Which was which can only become clear in the light of subsequent events. We speak of prejudice, which actually means that we have formed a judgement before we should have and this is another sad misuse of word values. Many people use the word to describe the opinions of somebody else which do not agree with their own. Prejudiced people make up their minds before taking all the facts into full consideration. Who is in a position to know whether they have done this or not? It could be quite possible that their opinion is wrong, but it could not be prejudiced if they have come to it after thought and deliberation. It is a pity there is no such word as postjudiced for a person who comes to a bad judgement, but a judgement per se is simply that and nothing else.

Whether a judgement is good or bad, it has to involve the expenditure of thought and intention before it can be considered as such. We speak of "snap judgements," which are decisions made after rapid thought, and these could be either right or wrong depending on circumstances. Yet, if a decision is made after thought has been expended, it could still be called a judgement if it is a hasty or ill-advised one. Ill-advised judgements are made when there is insufficient evidence forthcoming, or the full truth has not been told.

Here we come to the connection between Judgement and Truth. The object of using judgement should surely be to establish the truth of whatever may be under consideration. Otherwise, there would be no point in using the faculty of judgement at all. The Truth in the case of the tarot cards is the Grail itself. We have to make a judgement about it (and our relationship with it) which will determine our course of action for the future. That is why Judgement comes at this point of the cycle, because it is only after living through the previous Trumps that any human soul is likely to have gained sufficient experience to make the Judgement required in this case.

The conventional tarot card depicts the Judgement of God on Man, but the real implication is the Judgement of Man on God. How do we judge God and then decide what course of action to take on that account? By our judgements on God we decide our own courses of life very considerably. Those who judge God to be a being of infinite omnipotence who inflicts dire punishments on offenders, who rewards those He approves of with a dubious kind of heaven, will behave with motives of fear and greed rather than selfless love. Conversely, those seeing God as a being of both light and love are liable to live compassionately and with friendly feelings towards their fellow-mortals. As we judge God, so do we determine our own lives. It does not matter in the least if humans do not believe in any kind of God as the word is usually understood. Whatever set of beliefs we regard as high enough to control the course of our lives is our God by whatever name we term this.

Here we might think of the Fool climbing this part of the Sangreal cycle. By this time the Fool should be changing his cap and bells for a full bottomed wig and his motley for a solemn gown. He has a lot of questions to ask anyone able or willing to answer. Will the Grail be worth gaining in the end? Does it mean enough for him to face the terrible trials and tests that lie ahead? Has he developed the necessary qualities which will take him through them triumphantly? Is he going to find sufficient support from friendly forces in contact with him? He may have heard the saying about perfect love and trust being necessary for gaining God, but does he himself have enough love and trust for commencing the perilous part of this pilgrimage? He has come up against the crunch, so to speak, and will hereafter meet the grim realities of life. Everything depends on his judgement of all these factors and his conclusions arising from such deliberations. Shall he go ahead or not?

The question of judgement to be decided now is whether or not the Quester (or the Fool) has reached a degree of Sangreal development which will definitely lead him or her around the remainder of its life-cycle. At the same time the Sangreal has to judge those humans concerned. How have they developed since the inauguration of the blood? Has that been a justifiable and credible experiment or not? In childish terms, a God capable of judging us would really be judging himself for having made us in the first place. The Sangreal has to decide whether it has been worth ensuring its own survival as spiritual energy at the cost of mankind carrying the burden of this in his blood. Moreover, will humanity be worth supporting any further on its Quest for future development and gaining the Grail of eventual immortality? Most of all, will humanity be worthy of "passing the blood" anywhere else in existence? Those are all questions of Judgement which only the Sangreal can make. What human is able to assess the nature of such a judgement on its own species? That would indeed be the Last Judgement of all.

The Devil

After the experience of undergoing judgement on himself, the fool is plunged into the challenge of meeting the Devil and all his works at the last of this quadrant. Christians are supposed to have nothing to do with the Devil if they can help it, but seekers of the Sangreal have to take him as he comes and deal with whatever type of nastiness he offers. The Devil is known by many names, most of them uncomplimentary, but in the tarot he is mostly thought of as the Tester—the one who tempts us in order to test our character and prove our honesty. In the Torah he is always considered to be an Archangel who was given this unpleasing job by God, just as we have to find people willing to collect garbage or dispose of dead bodies. With us, unpleasant and unpopular jobs are often well paid to attract applicants, but God was not so generous with Satan, except to appoint him money-master of this world.

There is a legend that for every sin a mortal commits, Satan sheds a tear because it prolongs his stay on the dark side of life by just that amount. It is odd how humans find the Devil so fascinating and invent these stories to account for his activities.

We are really much more interested in Evil than we are in Good, as every newspaper shows. This has certainly kept schools of philosophy and hordes of religious wranglers at each other's throats for many centuries. The Cathars once had the notion that Satan and Jesus were twin brothers whom God separated on account of their endless disagreements. Jesus was put in charge of Heaven, while Satan had this world to play with until they would sort everything out at the end of time, when both would live peacefully together evermore.

The tarot Devil is not so much an evil fiend who delights in torturing humans, as a supreme annoyer and antagonist who symbolizes the opposition and frustration we meet in life. Things so often seem to go wrong we sometimes lose our tempers and say, "Oh, damn the thing, its got the Devil in it." Although few people these days might believe in a personal Devil, so many think about him in one form or another we could very well create him out of our own thoughts. If all the folktales and legends about the Devil were collected together as one book, it would certainly be thicker than the Bible.

From the Sangreal standpoint, the Devil is that factor in ourselves which resists or opposes the free flow of its evolutionizing influence. The Sangreal objective is its own perpetuation as a spiritually entitized existence. The closer we come to a state of species-perfection, the better we shall be able to bear the Blessed Blood, and the nearer we shall get to the end of our Quest. Why should there be any opposition to such a wonderful objective, and why should we mortals hold the casting vote as to who will hold the majority of shares in Humanity and Co., Inc.? Sangreal or Satan, which?

Very roughly the difference is this. The generic term "Satan" (or the Devil) may be taken to symbolize a spiritual life-species interested in maintaining itself in the Cosmos at the expense of all other living creatures. Such a species concentrates on breaking down resistance and, as it were, superimposing themselves on whatever types of living being they are able to overshadow. Humans come within their range of influence to quite an extent, although there seems to be no actual blood-bond or equivalent of the Sangreal strain. Nevertheless they can, and do, divert energies from humanity for their own purposes – which are seldom in our best interests. From their activities most of the inaccurate tales concerning vampires, incubi and succubi, and all the rest of the demon stories have been drawn. There is a basis of truth at the bottom, but the superstructure is highly exaggerated.

The Sangreal, on the other hand, does not deplete human energy or deliberately inflict itself on human hosts unwilling or reluctant to bear it fully, freely, and motivated by pure love alone. Without love the Sangreal Spirit cannot live, and those who willingly welcome the Satan-Spirit have no real love in their hearts for anything. This may sound suspiciously like the old thesis of our being the prize for both good and evil spirits, though such is a simplification of a far more complex situation than a case of "goodies and baddies." Its moral issues are mainly matters of opinion. Multiple varieties of entitized energies exist, and this single planet is only a tiny point in the whole of Creation.

Put into analogical terms, the Sangreal influence seeks to civilize, culture, and develop us. What we might as well call the "Satan-influence" is no more than an intrusion, or, in old fashioned language, *stealing* whatever profits we have made as a result of the Sangreal setting us up in business. If we ask why the Sangreal shouldn't protect us against such pilfering, the answer is that it will never interfere with anything we intend on our own initiative. That would be contrary to its original intentions. The so-called Devil can do no more than coerce, persuade, or put pressure on us to supply its wants, and if we do so willingly, no Sangreal is ever going to stop us. Neither will it encourage us to permit such spiritual embezzlement.

The ethics of all this are far too convoluted for any full discussion here. We have to learn how to stand on our own spiritual feet and fight for our own Cause when we have to confront what is really the Devil under whatever name we choose to call it. The question is how do we recognize this Devil when we meet it, and is there an acid test of its identity? Fortunately there is. The Devil can never love in the real meaning of the word. He can be incredibly clever, brilliantly intellectual, and every other superlative we can imagine, yet he cannot counterfeit love convincingly. This has to be genuine, and it would be useless to challenge any appearance of the Devil with simulated love, because it could respond on the same lines quite easily.

No application of the love test actually exorcises or dismisses any devil. All it does is make the evil entity reveal itself for what it really is, an enemy, or something contrary to the Sangreal within ourselves. "Know your Enemy." That is good advice to any who have ideas about tackling Devils in the tarot or anywhere else. Know all about him, his weapons, tactics, methods, capabilities, and every possible piece of information or intelligence that can be gathered. Learn his tricks. Forget fantasies from the past and view the Devil in his most modern dress. He exists. Maybe we have even evoked him out of our most terrible mistakes.

We are approaching the end of this third quadrant with our Devils teasing, tormenting, and torturing us right up to the limits of our endurance. Our poor Fool is being batted from one end of Hell to the other and having a perfectly miserable time. He certainly seems none the worse for the experience from a spiritual viewpoint. No one who has not undergone his fair share of Hell would be much use in Heaven, or know how to appreciate it. The Devil appears here for the best of reasons. From him we can learn how to oppose opposition on its own grounds and put it where it properly belongs with our love. "Perfect Love casteth out fear," and the fear of Perfect Love is certainly what casts out devils quickly.

Perhaps visualizing the Devil is a problem in modern times. The old Beast-Image seems so archaic and futile in an era when the appropriate place for such a creature would be a zoo or a safari park. Possibly the mushroom shape of an atomic blast might be more in keeping with contemporary dreads, though the makers and controllers of such a devilish device would certainly make a more accurate picture. Perhaps the best image of the Devil in modern dress would be a politician or civil servant whose decision would be responsible for pressing the button that would sound the Last Trump in grim earnest, or maybe whoever programmed the computer which decided such a decision. We have many contemporary Devils to choose from.

Any sort of "bogeyman in the background" picture of the Devil would not be entirely accurate, because such an Ultimate Devil could only act once, and in destroying us he would automatically destroy his own sustenance, too. The Devil does not commit suicide, and we are his principal life support in this world. Perhaps what might illustrate the Devil of the tarot best would be the picture of an average politician. We have to symbolize something that makes our lives miserable, difficult, and a constant annoyance to us while it lives on the fat of the land at our expense—so that we actually pay for the privilege of being pestered and sometimes persecuted. That was the image of the Devil in medieval times. All in all, the Devil amounts to whatever makes our lives most miserable for the sake of its own survival. Perhaps body lice or fleas come into the imagery somehow.

The one certainty emerging from our encounters with the Devil is that whosoever is able to survive successfully generally comes out of the encounter with a much greater soul and improved individuality. The Devil is not without his uses, and it is an old adage that any government without an effective opposition is mostly a bad one because it becomes complacent, indifferent, and inactive. Therefore the tarot Devil might be thought of as something that keeps us on our toes. He may be a pest, but he is a necessary pest so far as humans are concerned. There are worse things to face and overcome yet.

• • •

At the end of this quadrant we come to the commencement of the last in the Sangreal cycle, that of anguishing achievement. Not a nice or comfortable title at all, but nevertheless accurate. The genuine Grail is only achievable through anguish and death. How else did any of the Sacred Kings achieve it? How else can anyone hope to gain any kind of Grail-Kingship? If there were any other way or easy system of sneaking round to some side entrance to the adytum, some clever creature would have found out by now and have most likely bragged about his exploit to the extent it would have become a very public secret. For an ordinary human there is no other alternative.

It has been aptly said that the only absolute certainties in life are death and taxes. In the coming quadrant we shall have to face them both in addition to whatever else may be included in our fate-packet. We see here ahead a strange combination of the Blasted Tower, the Hanged Man, then Death, followed by the Hermit and Temperance. Cynics might see a connection between the Tower, Death, and the Hanged Man as the ruin of any edifice by death duties. The Tower is destroyed by the taxman, after which the owners go out and hang themselves. It might be added that their heirs became Hermits after signing the Temperence pledge because they couldn't afford to drink any more supertaxed spirits. A fate only the ultra-wealthy need worry about anyway, and just a ludicruously loose interpretation of the tarot spread shown here.

The Tower

The Tower is certainly significant of ruin from any angle. Ruin of hopes, houses, ruin of everything inhabited by humans or whatever they have built up as a monument to their sense of self-importance. A Tower is actually a high-rise type of building elevating humans above the earth for some specific purpose of their own. It is essentially a man-made construction built to serve some human purpose. In former times, Towers were built for defense or as observation posts for perceiving an advancing enemy in plenty of time to warn local people of a threat to their peace and property.

The Tower in the tarot is probably a reference in particular to the famous Tower of Babel (Babel means the Gate of God) and most modern readers should be familiar with the story. The Tower was being constructed as a symbol to proclaim how important its patron was, and all the foreign workmen employed on the job found their native tongues too difficult to understand after the Interpreters Union had called a strike. Anyway there was so much dissension and misunderstanding among them that the Tower never got finished and was eventually destroyed by lightning. Lightning conductors had not been invented then. In other words the whole thing was built on nothing but human pride and vanity, coupled with an unwillingness on the part of people to come to terms with each other. Not the best of foundations on which to base any building.

Such a Tower deserved nothing better than to be knocked down and reduced to rubble. That seems to be what is happening here: reduction to rubble which may be used for rebuilding something more solid and practical than protecting a few privileged people perched on its penthouse so to speak. Sometimes we say when some public figure has been exposed and humiliated, "That's knocked *him* off his perch," meaning that such a one has come to a deserved downfall. There is the well-known proverb, "Pride goeth before a fall," indicating that pride (which was the reputed sin by which the Devil fell from Heaven to Hell) deserves to be compensated by a corresponding drop in the estimation of everyone. The images of height and depth are always linked, and a Tower is a man-made height providing an artificial advantage over others.

The Tower is not an elementary or single-symbol Archetype. It has to be coupled with a sign for damage or destruction—often a lightning flash, a dropping bomb, or at least two humans in the process of crashing to earth with nothing to save them. This is a complex symbol with three elements in it—the high building, the destroying agent, and the death-doomed humans. Without this combination, the Tower card would be meaningless. Its fundamental significance is definitely wrack and ruin to human hubris. Humbling of pride. Reduction to essential elements—Catalysis. The breakup of whatever is built on a false foundation with the implication of a need to do better next time.

Getting "cut down to size" is never a pleasant experience, but it is often a necessary one. That is more or less what the Tower symbol generally indicates. Again it has been said "The Lord chastiseth whom he loveth," meaning that God (or Whatever) does seem to arrange strange "put downs" for those who appear to ask for them. Many would agree that He (or It) did not do this frequently enough to satisfy their demands that sinners should be punished properly in summary style. Probably the most dramatic of such "put downs" have been the World Wars wherein all the tarot conditions of the Tower were fulfilled a million times: high buildings brought down by bombs, humans crashing to death and destruction all around, the sky flashing with explosive energy and ruin everywhere. Bombastic and loud-mouthed people reduced to gibbering wrecks and cringing cowards while many ordinary folk got on with amazing acts of heroism which they only saw as a duty to be done. A blitz in progress is a good illustration of this card. Futile follies and vanities which had taken mankind so long to build were blasted to blazes in a matter of moments. Good or bad, all was brought to the ground impartially. Did we deserve that? Truth to tell, in many ways we most certainly did.

From a Sangreal standpoint, the tarot Tower symbolizes the chastening of God as a self-process of inner purification—removal of inner rubbish which sets up a spiritual state of preparation for death or temporary escape from this world. It should be a natural that toward the normal ending of a lifetime the soul should consider its state of being. A whole incarnation has been spent on building up a sort of Tower with oneself at the top of it. That Tower may be based on money, beliefs, or it could be the dead bodies and damaged souls of other humans. The foundation might be sound enough but there might be woodworm and dryrot in the timbers, and the stones are crumbling away in the acidulous air. Its entire structure could be cracked from top to bottom and decay evident everywhere. While the wear and tear of a lifetime is not good for a physical house, how much more perilous may be the state of a spiritual structure lived in for the same period by even the most hopeful human?

The Sangreal Tower represents the process of demolition we shall have to do before we can say with any real conviction: "My desk is cleared, and I am ready to die at last." A variety of the Nunc Dimittis. The question is whether we prefer to do this ourselves before physical death or have it done for us afterwards. One way or the other this clearance has to be made. The Tower we build up around our spiritual selves is also a prison (the tarot Tower has no doors), and the only way of escape is to blow the top off. The Lightning Flash is liberating even if it costs the prisoners their mortal lives in exchange for their freedom. Also, the connection should be seen with the Lightning Flash of the Tree of Life which caused the creation of all the spheres. Before we leave our bodies, we need to knock down our Towers of self-preservation. These served a temporary purpose for safety in this world, but there will be no need of them in life-states far higher than any humanly built Tower could ever reach.

To that extent the Tower symbolizes the artificial ego or "pseudo-self" (often called the personality) that we more or less make automatically during the course of our incarnations. This is no more than a mask under which we appear in this world, and when the body dies, it should disintegrate also, though it often survives for a surprisingly long time afterwards. Past personalities can be an absolute curse if they persist into subsequent incarnations, and they are best disposed of peaceably after the death of their erstwhile owners. Instructed initiates commence the process before death, which is why the Tower is placed where it is in the Sangreal cycle. Once you "knock the top off" the thing will start disintegrating of its own accord.

To begin this, the actualities of such a spiritual situation have to be comprehended with the perception symbolized by a lightning-flash. The personality or pseudoself has to be seen — and seen through — for exactly what it is. Something which has served a purpose and now needs to be put through a dismantling process which will render it ready for recycling and consequent reissue as raw material elsewhere in existence. Perhaps reduction to its original elements might be the best idea to think of here. It could be well to remember the French description of this card as the Maison Dieu (or House of God) which was once a euphemism for a hospice where sick or terminally ill people were cared for by nuns until they died. Looked at in that light, the Tower has a kinder meaning.

In a Maison Dieu, the dying people were prepared to meet their end with every prayer and practice known to religious workers. Heaven was pointed out to them with vivid descriptions and the most pious of pictures. They were told what miserable sinners they were, but if they humbled themselves properly and acknowledged their faults before a generous God, He would be prepared to forgive them graciously, especially if they were in good standing with His beloved Church on earth. Though a modern might strongly contest that version of the story, it must be admitted that the fundamentals of Tower significance are all mixed up with it. Medieval people would have understood the Maison Dieu connection with this card. They knew it meant a habitance where one was God's guest while waiting to meet Him in his own home.

However we tackle this card, it indicates a severe struggle taking place (within ourselves) to adjust to a situation of danger and difficulty. There is a distinct resemblance here to the butterfly (the ancient symbol of the psyche) struggling to release itself from the confines of the chrysallis case (the Tower). As the struggle continues, a liberating bolt of lightning strikes the case and frees the creature completely, but alas, it burns off both wings at the same moment and the butterfly expires on the ground. The moral seems to be that it had better wait for a more appropriate time when it will be able to reveal its inner beauties in better spiritual conditions beyond a physical body altogether.

The Hanged Man

Once we have coped with the difficult state of the Tower, we are immediately faced with the mysterious Hanged Man. So many interpretations have been attached to him that there is a plethora to choose from. The Archetype is simply a Hanging Man. Not necessarily a dead one, but someone suspended from somewhere by means of a rope. He could be hanging from a cliff or from any other set of circumstances that range from a heli-copter to the gallows. It is only a pictorial convention to show him as being suspended by his left ankle from a variety of beams. Fundamentally, he is simply in a state of suspension.

We sometimes speak of "hanging between life and death," or the state of "suspended animation," and that is certainly the state of consciousness indicated by this tarot card. It is the counterbalance of the womb-condition before birth, and is the coma-condition before death, which is why it occupies this place in the Sangreal cycle. Before we are born, we should have an adjustment period of semi-consciousness in the womb, wherein we are contacting the conscious world of our mothers through sensory impressions brought to us via her nervous system being linked with ours. In a like manner, before we die – if death comes naturally and peacefully – there should be a matching period, during which our world senses weaken and our spiritual senses strengthen until we become dead to the former and alive to the latter. Natural death should be a lot more pleasant than birth and quite an enjoyable experience it if is peaceful and undis-turbed by revival efforts and resuscitation methods.

This state is representative of what psychologists have called the subconscious mind and Jung in particular termed the Col-lective Unconsciousness, which is a state of awareness so far removed from ordinary human objectivity as to be almost out of contact yet tenuously attached to it as if by a thread. Here we have a picture of an embryo joined to its mother by an umbilical cord, alive yet not fully alive, aware but not awake, dreaming but not dead. Half and half of everything so to speak. Neither in one world nor another, and of not much apparent significance in either. Actually this state is of very great importance to humanity indeed, because it is a condition of consciousness held in common not only by all members of the human race but by the majority of intelligent life in existence. Humans are not the only species of life occupying responsible positions in our created cosmos, even if we are liable to behave as if we were most of the time.

When we pause to consider this point, it appears that mankind is quite arrogant. Why should we take for granted that we are the only species of intelligent thinking creatures in the whole of creation, and what give us the right to act as if we were? It might almost be supposed that when the commandment "Thou shalt have no other Gods before ME," was formulated, it referred specifically to us. We may be lord of a localized and almost experimental order of living creatures, but what makes us think we are so important that we are entitled to "do what we damn well like" with everything on this earth, regardless of anything except our own whims?

Even though there are far saner and more realistic viewpoints of our spiritual situation reaching us during this present period, it is doubtful whether these will prevail powerfully enough to alter the course of current human history. It may be hoped that some salvation will indeed change us in time, though there is no guarantee whatsoever. Let us inquire, however, where any of our "rescue operation" ideas come from and how they reach human minds at all. They arrive at our objective consciousness from the Sangreal source which is the "Light behind our Blood," which we could call inner illumination. The Hanged Man at this point represents the state or condition we have to reach in order to establish a workable contact with this vital verity.

It is due to this facility of sharing consciousness in common with other orders of living creatures that the Sangreal was able to reach us in the first place. Without that initial contact with us, the Sangreal could not have exerted a beneficial influence through our blood. As it happens, there are many other-than-human types of intelligence attempting to invade the areas of human activity on earth and few of them are favorable to us. They are exploiters of our energies rather than enhancers of them. How can we distinguish one from the other or be certain of any? Long ago it was said: "Try the spirits to see whether they are of God," and that remains good advice to this day, but how should anyone do this? By descending into the depths of what we call the subconscious mind (or the Great Unconsciousness, if this term seems preferable) to find out for ourselves by direct and conscious contact with what we encounter there. This descent is symbolized by the Hanged Man suspended by a foot so he may be lowered head down into the Well of Truth and there discover it for himself. In other words, we must learn how to sink ourselves in meditation deeply enough to touch the truth-level and afterwards return to the surface of normal consciousness with some of that truth grasped in our teeth as it were. The visualization was that one got lowered down to the water level, took a mouthful of water, and then on return to the surface spat it out toward whoever was ready to receive it. A nice way of describing a dip into the depths of oneself until truth was touched and then getting back to tell this on surface levels of ordinary consciousness in this world.

That is the whole point of spending so much time in practicing the techniques of meditation. Meditation is not an end in itself, but only a means to the end, which is touching the truth behind our own beings—if only momentarily or even slightly. Having so touched this truth, it has to be brought up and set into some kind of action or circulation in order to utilize it. Gold or diamonds dug from the deepest mines are valueless until someone places value upon them. The profoundest truth has no value unless it can be utilized in the service of humanity. The very word "profound" means from the depths, which indicates some instinctive recognition of the value of exploring the depths.

It is scarcely strange that so many people are fascinated by this particular card in the tarot deck. Their attention appears drawn by some instinct telling them that the Hanged Man is really an outstanding and important symbol—a key that might unlock secrets of the deepest significance. Few grasp exactly why this might be so, yet all are convinced there is something here they ought to know but cannot *quite* grasp. It is almost as if he is taunting them to discover his meaning while casting a contemptuous look in their direction for their laziness in not bothering to dive the least distance down into their own murky depths to discover for themselves what seems so clear to him.

In olden times it was sometimes a practice of people undergoing initiation to "half hang" themselves in order to simulate what the Hanged Man stood for. They would literally carry out semi-strangulation procedures, which resulted in oxygen lack and unconsciousness that could cause symptoms of cerebral toxemia and a consequent confusion of consciousness, which was then misinterpreted to mean inspiration by some otherwise unreachable inner source of intelligence. Some did this with a special cord with a loop at one end and a number of knots at different points. The idea was to apply this round the throat and tighten it just a trifle more on each occasion so that the knots engaging with the loop prevented it from tightening enough to kill, yet applied enough constriction to produce eventual unconsciousness. The subject had to be released from this by companions who would later question him on his impressions or visions. The last knot on that cord was called the "life knot" because it was the one deciding the difference between life and death. Or the subject, himself, would hold the ends of the cord—one in each hand—and then apply the tension with his arms. In that way, constriction would be released if and when the person fainted and was a lot less dangerous. It should go without saying that no reasonable person should ever attempt anything even close to such a performance. There are much less hazardous methods of reaching the same self-state which our psychologists now call ASC (Altered States of Consciousness). The Hanged Man indicates no more than the symbology of these and not the ideal system of attaining them.

From another angle, the Hanged Man symbolizes the Sacred King sacrifice that should be offered on behalf of humanity before Death opens the doors of deliverence to any of us. This mystical mass has deep spiritual significance for anyone—alive or dead. Originally, it meant the operation of the Sangreal through specific channels of consciousness so as to offer the hope of eventual evolution into an immortal identification with the Spirit of Life itself. Today we are asked to offer the whole of our lives in service of the Sangreal, however that may be seen. A Hanged Man is another way of showing a crucified one if death resulted from the action. Both hanging and crucifixion were legal methods of carrying out capital punishment, and a Christian crucifix really symbolizes a legally condemned and executed human being. Exactly the same literal symbol would be shown by a dead man suspended from an ordinary gallows.

The chances are that in the Middle Ages and a few subsequent centuries, the Hanged Man stood for the multiple martyrs dying for the sake of their old Pagan faith, then miscalled Witchcraft, or worse still, Diabolism. It is a mistake to believe that they were always burned. Some were, but hanging was a lot more common, especially in England. Fires were expensive, and a rope, which could be used over and over again, was the cheapest way of execution. The cross of Jesus and the gallows of those hanged for heresy were equal in the eyes of pagan people. Both parties died because of their beliefs, and the Hanged Man perpetuated the memory of many who perished for their faith at the hands of Christian executioners.

Therefore the Hanged Man would stand for a sacred symbol to those who knew what he represented, and who could explain his odd fascination for modern people. It could be an ancestral memory stirring in them from previous incarnations or rising from reminiscences in their own blood. When we think of the numbers of people put to death all over Europe by Christians for religious reasons, it would be surprising if there were no reactions from any of their descendents. Even keen Christians who have learned to respect other viewpoints than their own might view this card with a sense of shame that their Church could ever have been guilty of such barbaric and unthinking cruelty.

In the end it can be assumed that the Sangreal significance of the Hanged Man is that of living and dying for a cause believed in and followed faithfully to its end on earth—which was only a beginning Otherwhere. Diving into one's depths in search of a truth worth living and dying for. Searching the subconscious for signs of a true spirituality leading to our ulti-mate liberation. Trying to establish contact with all other orders of life in a common consciousness. Those are only the main points leading out of this single tarot key. This card may only be understood properly at the end of life, when the future indicates that one has reached the departure lounge and the boarding calls are beginning to come over the public address system. Perhaps there may be just time for a last drink at the Well of Truth before the waters of Lethe are served aboard. Shortly it will be time to fasten seatbelts for the final flight.

Death

Now comes the great encounter of Death: an uncompromising end to physical existence on this earth. The common experience of every single individual (and any form of life) on this planet since it began. The universality of death is an unquestioned fact of life altogether. So far as it may be known, not even one instance of any creature has ever been known to have avoided death in its physical form since the phenomena of birth began among us. This in itself is a peculiar event: the inescapability of death. If it had been possible to avoid or avert dying, the wealthy of this world would have purchased immunity before now, but physical immortality is unbuyable.

Possibly more speculations and guesses about the nature of death have been made concerning its possibilities than any other topic of speculation. Despite all our hopes, fears, thoughts, and opinions, nothing has ever emerged except the conclusive fact of death itself. Unless, of course, we are prepared to accept the likelihood of life without physical bodies. Many minds can and do believe in such a possibility, while plenty of people refuse to accept this in any way. Again, the only certainty is a state of divided opinions. It seems unlikely that we will ever agree about death or the non-necessity for birth. The only absolute agree-ment is that anyone born MUST die. Birth and death are inseparable, inevitable, and interdependent. One might just as well say that whoever dies must be born.

Millions of human beings do say exactly that. The continuity of human life as a species on this earth is just as definite and indubitable as its continual interruption by death. It is only in very recent times that the prospect of putting an end to humanity altogether by nuclear war has become a possibility. Even in that terrible and unspeakable event, nobody supposes it would be an immediate or instant end. There would be *some* survivors capable of breeding some kind of bodies which would carry on at least a semi-human sort of life, or maybe a new species altogether. The possibilities of this are almost too frightening for contemplation. Supposing that by some appalling chance of radiation or unknown factor, such survivors bred a physically deathless type of creature? Bodies born continually which did not die as we do?

An old Mithraic ritual describes death as "the great necessity whose debts can never go unpaid," and that is as good a comment as may ever be made. Death is a friend and not the terrible enemy as once depicted. Is it possible to live as an active being without a body? Despite little or no evidence that a court of law would accept, millions of intelligent humans believe so, and most would say they already had the evidence they needed to convince them. Serious spiritualists would assert that dear old Mum came back to tell them where she had hidden the family jewels or whatever, and hundreds of thousands of incidents have been reported by responsible people to indicate that dead relatives and friends do not necessarily lie down for a long time after the incident. Despite this mass of belief and experience, a solid body of scientific opinion adheres to the doctrine that extra-physical awareness or conscious existence apart from a physical body is impossible. Atheism has become just as fanatical and bigoted a religion as any deistic creed ever invented.

Not even the most dedicated and devoted atheist would dare assume or defend a doctrine which claimed that humanity was the only species in the entire universe with the ability of consciousness and its application to environmental conditions whatever those might be. Once the possibility of such a state is admitted the probability has to be allowed also. An old Chinese proverb states that whatever the human mind can conceive must exist somewhere in creation, either past, present or future, because otherwise we could not have conceived it in the first place. Why then would so many great minds be so concerned with spiritual subjects if there were no shadow of truth in any of them?

Once it is permissible to postulate a condition of living consciousness apart from a physical body, the inner doors of our existence will open very widely indeed and show us strange scenes on a compelling landscape. Apart from anything else, the indications are that the death of a physical body means no more than an interruption in the continuum of consciousness reaching from one end of existence (as a whole) to the other—where or whenever that might be. As a lifeflow, we have to be immortal. Bodies and personalities die constantly and are almost immediately replaced with fresh ones. The single cells of which those bodies are made are dying all the time and being replaced with new ones. Life is an ongoing process which death does nothing except interrupt by making ripples in its rhythms.

If we could only establish a clear contact with the consciousness which flows along the lifestream in which we are individual units, the incidence of death would worry us no more than normal sleep disturbs any healthy human. Deprive us of sleep and we become seriously sick. Deprive us of death and we would suffer a lot more than that. We have evolved very considerably since our dim and distant origins, but we have not yet evolved past the need of death. The living experience of endless existence is a concentrated state of consciousness far too terrible for any except the highest type of being to consider. Should such a being exist, it would be God for no other reason than that It *had* to be.

The tarot Death, however, does not always indicate cessation of physical life, though it always means a total change of circumstances, which is really what death amounts to. It is not death itself which generally frightens people, but the prospect of sudden change from known conditions to unknown ones. The thought of going to sleep in one personality as a wealthy and prosperous person possessing everything worth having, and then waking up in another as a poor, hungry, and discontented creature who was sick as well, is not an encouraging prospect. The opposite one might be a cheering idea if its disadvantages were realized and nothing better could be imagined.

From the Sangreal angle, its blood strain had to be death-survivable physically via the laws of genetics, and spiritually by a fidelity factor sometimes known as blood-belief. Those in whom the strain was developing were marked by strengthening beliefs in their own blood and a sense of connection with it in others. Death was a more or less infallible test to determine the best and finest qualities in a human being. Separating soul from body for a sufficient period afforded an opportunity for much closer contact with the individual entities concerned.

This sounds rather like taking some item of mechanism out of service so that it can be sent for an overhaul, and that comparison could be made, though a more accurate one would be taking an active serviceman out of a conflict zone for R and R (Rest and Recuperation). The idea is fundamentally the same with death being the interim period making this possible. Death is the only means of restoring the soul, as sleep restores the body. There was the need for the intelligently active elements of the Sangreal to keep some sort of a supervisory contact with souls coming under their direct care. This possibly started the notion of guardian angels watching over the sleep of the innocent, whereas the realities were guiding the dreams of the dead so as to assess them for fitness before handing them over to the few remaining stages before rebirth.

It is only when the evolving soul has reached the deathstate, that it can be directly influenced enough to change its nature into improved genetic paths. The Christian Church sees Purgatory as a state of being in which a soul is cleansed from past sins by a good God's chastisement, after which it is ready for the joys of Heaven. This is a very garbled version of what really occurred. A soul without a body is still in a state having all sorts of characteristics and idiosyncrasies which correspond with matching patterns of genetic arrangements. If it is to be reincarnated, it will have to conform with those lines and no others. Provided it is able to alter itself and change its characteristics sufficiently, it can then select a different genetic pattern which could be a much better one. This, however, can only be done during death, and once the pattern has been selected and set, it will have to remain so for at least another incarnation.

So that is the maximum importance of the Sangreal Death card. It symbolizes a real chance of changing ourselves for the better while in an out-of-body condition of consciousness during what we call death. It is an opportunity to be used and made as much of as possible in preference to idling that period away in some Heaven or another.

The Hermit

The assumption is that our tarot traveling Fool has died and consequently changed his nature completely. What has he now become? Death has metamorphosed him into the Hermit. Where the Fool was witless, the Hermit is wise: where the Fool faltered, the Hermit is slowly footsure; where the Fool was young and silly, the Hermit is old and wise; where the Fool sneered, the Hermit smiles. The Hermit is the Fool grown up, come to his senses and after passing through every experience of the Sangreal cycle including that of the Great Change, is almost ready to gain the Grail after one more stage of evolution.

The Hermit symbol represents the essential individuality. Not the "personality self" which only appears during embodiment and should not last much longer than a lifetime, but the Spiritual Self or immortal identity. It is the part of us which does not normally die but remains intact indefinitely. The surviving soul, which is the part of us most subject to change, comes in much closer contact with the Spiritual Self after release from bodily bondage and will eventually identify with it.

Hermits usually come into the story of the Sangreal somewhere, figuring as strange and solitary beings seeming to know
everything about it without having actually gained it. They act
as guardians of its secrets and sometimes share the Hallows or
specially sacred symbols such as the Lance and Shield. Occasionally the Grail pays them clandestine visits from its mysterious hiding place in a far-off Heaven (where it normally lives
because of human wickedness) but all they and the Sangreal
seem to do together is celebrate Mass in a tiny chapel concealed
in thick woods. These Hermits act as advisers to eager young
knights who pass by in search of the Grail, yet none of them
ever accompany those knights any further than the thresholds
of their hermitages. There is an absolute mine of meaning in the
Hermit tales which contain little adventure but lots of moral
philosophy.

The young Knight is really the Fool in armor who quests
away in all directions except the right one – inside himself. The
Hermit is really the Fool's Spiritual Self living at a remote distance from the focal levels of his consciousness. This means that
to contact his "Hermit-consciousness" he would have to penetrate the tangle of the forest (his own wild thinking), come to the
very small clearing (his inner adytum) where this Hermit dwelt
and sometimes celebrated Mass (made close spiritual contact)
with the visiting Holy Grail (spiritual object of the quest) which
both Knight and Hermit are seeking to serve, each in his own
fashion. The Hermit officiates in the most sacred service he
knows while the Knight wanders around the world looking for
wrongs to put right. The Knight serves in the outer field of
battle, while the Hermit serves with the Inner Sanctum.

All this represents the general trend of questing through its
practice in human history. The Hermit, of course, signifies that
remote and distant part of ourselves which seems so far away
when we are young, yet we come closer and closer to it as we get
older, and are only likely to encounter it directly after we have
died or gotten clear of our earthly bodies. Even so, only those
who are actively seeking the Sangreal through the tangle of their
lives will come into very intimate contact with it. During the

course of our lifetimes on earth, the Hermit is occasionally heard in the distant background as what was once called the "voice of conscience." Many humans cannot hear this at all, or it only seems like an irritating whisper. The relatively few who not only listen for it carefully, but try to work out what it is saying and follow its difficult instructions, will surely gain the Grail in the end.

The Hermit is trying to encourage his hearers to follow his voice through the thickets until we come to the chapel wherein the service of the Grail is being celebrated. The symbology of the Mass (or Sangreal Sacrament) applies here, and Communion of the Blood is symbolized by the union of the bread and wine in the partaker's body. In pictorial versions of this card, the Hermit usually has one red glass panel in his six-sided lantern to show the Light behind the Blood and the light is six-rayed to illustrate the immanent union with God as symbolized by the hexagram.

The chief characteristic of a Hermit is undoubtedly his isolation. A chemist speaks of isolating anything when he has discovered how to remove all contaminants and everything which is NOT the substance itself. All that remains must be the pure essential element only. This is exactly what the Hermit represents in spiritual terms. A chemist also speaks of spirit when he means a volatile ether that is the result of distillation separating the subtle and solid constituents of a compound. The language of chemistry has come to us through schools of thought concerned with body and soul relationships, so the exchange of idioms should not be very surprising.

Indeed the practical process by which the Hermit attains his "splendid isolation," and the Self-Spirit achieves its independent individuality, is very much the same in physical and metaphysical ideology. That independence is more apparent than real, since it is like that of a single cell in a bloodstream or a single human in a lifestream. A unity in a multiplicity which of themselves form a unity in a containing consciousness ad infinitum. If the magnitude of this seems improbable, consider the relationship between one blood cell in a body, all the human bodies in the world, and every possible planet whose Suns can be seen as stars in our sky. If such a phenomenon can be taken for granted as a fact of existence, why should there be the least problem in accepting a far simpler concept of ourselves being related by the common blood-bond of consciousness itself. Straining at gnats while swallowing camels is a common propensity of people on this planet.

The Hermit is usually seen as someone who shuns the company of others, but this tarot card should be seen as one who has risen so far above the common level that there are few enough souls around to afford him any company at all. It is not his fault that relatively so few humans are prepared to undergo all the trials and tribulations to seek the Sangreal. He is old— almost beyond the bounds of humanity itself—even though every one of us alive has got at least an embryo Hermit at the background of our beings who awaits that magic moment of meeting. Hermits are not inhospitable, though their food may be very plain, their beds somewhat hard, and their cells rather chilly. They are always prepared to give all they have in the service of the Sangreal.

This signifies the connection between a quester and his own Self-Spirit. This connection may only be an attenuated consciousness while we live in an earthly body, and we should not expect to be very close until after physical death has taken place. Even then, the soul would need to be a very advanced one. This does not mean we need not try to make any contacts with our Hermits until we are dead. We should attempt to make lifelinks between the top and bottom of our extremities, because our Hermits can certainly hear us if we call clearly enough. That is to say, communication with our higher sources of consciousness and inspiration is possible if we direct attention in that direction. Since Hermits are contemplatives, the methodology of contemplation is best suited to contact the type of consciousness they deal with.

To the unthinking observer there seems no idler type of occupation than contemplation, whereas precisely the opposite is the case. Externally silent and motionless individuals should be loudly and actively making themselves clear on inner levels. Internal action must be in directly inverse proportion to external appearances. From a physical point of view, the body is supposed to be limp and relaxed while the inner awareness is very keenly and actively engaged with the objective. This takes considerable practice, because the body tends to tense with the mind because the brain directs the exercise, whereas it should be the mind and soul. The quester has to learn how to let the brain take charge of a passive body while the mind supervises the arrangement of consciousness into a state of contemplation with a definite objective held in view. This is an exercise older people find easier to perform as a rule, but that should not stop young people from learning the art of contemplation.

Temperance

So, if our Fool has at last become the Hermit, where can he go now? The final step to take, before beginning the Sangreal cycle all over again, is called Temperance. This may puzzle many people until the deep meaning of this description is explained. For a modern reader, Temperance usually signifies abstemiousness in the usage of alcohol. Not total abstention, but moderation and a sensible absorption of stimulating drink. In other words, complete control of craving. Temperance has come to be so much identified with human drinking problems that it is difficult to see past this and realize what the word meant originally.

Temperance signified the process of tempering anything — which meant modification of its nature into an ideal condition of adaptability throughout its entire range of action. This applied especially to steel swords so they would be as flexible as possible, while still taking an admirable edge and retaining a good penetrating point. In other words making a weapon as perfect as it could be in the fulfillment of all its functions. The word derives from the Latin *temperare* (time or season) to indicate that there is a proper season for everything and in time all things will be accomplished. Time was the needed element which, if it were put to proper use, would produce perfection, and that is how we should understand the selection of this card for representing the Sangreal at the end of its tarot journey.

Temperance not only applies to steel but also to the human character. A perfectly tempered character would be one which has passed through every trial and test life afforded and death had improved, so that no more would need doing. A finished human specimen fit to incorporate with the Sangreal. Having reached that stage of Truth at last, what does it discover? It learns that this automatically imposes the greatest obligation of all—selfless service in the cosmic cause of light, life, love, and law. This cause is greater than any self, because no self could exist without it. There would be no being at all if those pure principles were not the very primals of our cosmic creation, and unless they are served properly, the break-up of all beings into a state of chaos would be inevitable. In serving the Sangreal we shall have conditioned ourselves into a spiritual state of ability to serve on higher levels of life. So the reward of long and faithful service in one spiritual field is being privileged to serve once more in a greater capacity of competence. Heavier and heavier responsibility on our spiritual shoulders evermore.

Be it most especially noted that no such spiritual obligation is ever imposed, but only *offered*. No penalties are imposed for rejection of this opportunity, and no gratitude need be expected for its acceptance. The only consideration is the conscience of those souls concerned. The question arises whether any soul could ever feel happy or contented after being offered this cosmic chance and deciding not to take it. We may be reminded of the fatal "Grail question" asked of Knights at their earthly banquets where the Sacred Vessel appeared. That question was never specified, but it struck so many Knights to stunned silence that they missed the opportunity for service, and the wrongs of this world that they might have rectified remained unrequited in consequence.

Here we have that question again put to Grail gainers on a much higher level. What it amounts to is this: Are you willing to forego every entitlement which is indisputably yours and continue to serve the cosmic cause not only with, but AS the Sangreal in which you have earned identification? The Sangreal and you are now fully of one blood. This is symbolized by the traditional Temperance figure mixing the contents of two cups. That is usually assumed to be water, but it is really blood. At this last point of the Sangreal cycle, the blood of believers is mingled inseparably with that of the Grail so that the two become one forever. At this last stage, the human soul is tempered to the finest degree possible.

A long time ago it was literally supposed that the best fluid for tempering swords was human blood, and blood was used for swords specially forged for those rich and unscrupulous enough who demanded such dramatic service. The heated blade would be plunged through the body of a helpless slave or prisoner condemned to death. No evidence exists to show that these blades were any better than those tempered with oil or water. Up to relatively recent times, it was considered a "lucky" thing if a sword blade were anointed with the blood of some small animal which was well rubbed in before final polishing.

Tempering applied also to the other instruments of the tarot. The contents of the Cup could be tempered by the addition of water, and this is still mixed with wine when Mass is celebrated. The Rod was sometimes supposed to be hazel because this was a flexible wood. The Shield had to be hard enough to absorb heavy blows, but also needed sufficient resilience to allow arrows to stick in it instead of bouncing off to hit others. Temperance was an overall ideal applying to all aspects of the Sangreal, and hence is most suitable for representing the apex of the Sangreal cycle. For Christians, the proverb of tempering the wind for the shorn lamb might be linked with the "Lamb of God" sacrificial image of their Redeemer.

So gaining the Grail did not mean obtaining a sort of universal passkey to the treasures of Heaven from which one is immediately entitled to help oneself and freely enjoy everything desired forevermore. It earns an entitlement to share the Cross of Creation more closely with the Creator. The Sangreal description of this condition is bearing the burden of the blood. There is an old saying, "Unto whom much is given, much will be expected," and nowhere does this apply more than to those who have truly gained the Grail in the original sense of what those fatal words imply. The whole process of Grail-gaining amounts to the most arduous training course in existence, an enduring experience in life which eventually makes mankind fit to become a divinity with its own duties and obligations. Nothing but the most perfectly tempered being could possibly accomplish such a thing, which is why Temperance is at the top of all the others in what could be called the Sangreal tarot spread.

The mythos of Christianity was one of Man becoming God by Sonship, which is the closest kind of blood-relationship imaginable. This is not supposed to mean that Jesus of Nazareth was and would forever be the solitary human being to hold such a position. He may have been an exemplar of the idea, which was that all humans could qualify for such truly royal responsibility if only they were willing to do so. Jesus once said: "These things and greater than I shall you also do," when people wondered at his performance of what looked to them like miracles. How many of his hearers then or now realized the implications of such a saying? His eventual crucifixion was for him a symbolization of what must happen to every other human who dared follow the way he tried to show them.

The most needed element for gaining the Grail is time. There is no such thing as instant evolution. Temperance and time have the same root-meaning. Without time we have no hope of ever coming to a satisfactory conclusion of our creation and continuance in cosmos. The burning question of our present position on the "Grail scale" is have we enough time at our disposal for reaching the objective of our origins? Who among the millions of us can possibly know beyond the slightest shadow of doubt whether or not we have sufficient time to save ourselves as a species and carry the Sangreal to a safe destination elsewhere in existence? Yes or No, what will be the answer? All we know is that the outcome has to be one or the other. Not even the tarot can answer that question of questions.

• • •

The end of anything is but the beginning of another thing and that is the story of time told in the shortest space. Eternal eventuation. Coming to the end of a tarot deck only means working with the cards in a different sequence. The ancient formula of, "As it was in the beginning, is now and ever shall be, world without end. Amen," puts everything into a neat nutshell which is usually swallowed whole without another thought. If the formula gabblers had the slightest inkling of what they were really uttering, their mouths would be too dry with fear for a single squeak to emerge. They have told the story of the Sangreal in a single sentence: eternity as the vehicle of verity. We sometimes say, "Time will tell," as an automatic truism, but how often do we mean time WILL tell, with automatic confidence in the time-factor to reveal truth? Would we recognize it if we ever encountered it? Shall we live long enough to learn the lessons of life we need to know?

To some, reading the tarot comes easily and to others it is an uphill climb. As to whether or not this effort is worth the expenditure, only you can decide. Maybe the decisive question should be what is an illiterate person worth in the world today? Let us say that such a one would certainly be disadvantaged and leave it at that. The next question would be what might anyone who was spiritually illiterate be worth in the world of tomorrow? This is where the tarot can help by being a practical means to assist us to learn what amounts to spiritual literacy. They may not be the only letters of an inner language, but they are easily available and well within the scope of average intelligence.

In the legend of the Holy Grail, it had to be quested for through every imaginable human experience. Why "questing?" That implies questioning, and that is just what the quester is supposed to do. Ask endless questions of life until it supplies the eventual answers. With the Sangreal system, the tarot is laid out to show how the cards are combined to make sense in connection with the Sangreal style of thoughtful consciousness. Here strength is seen as the central power, and the Fool as the person that power is pushing around the cosmic circle of creation on a quest for the Sangreal as a spiritual objective. To gain that Grail, the Fool needs to identify with each card in turn through the twenty Major Arcana comprising the circle of life as experienced from the Sangreal angle. This means $14 \times 4 \times 20$ of 1,120 combinations. Though it is scarcely practical to consider all those at any great depth, it is a good idea to follow a few around for a little just to see how the system works.

CHAPTER SEVEN

The Journey of the Fool

T HE MYSTICAL JOURNEY of the soul, or quest for the Holy Grail as the Sangreal strain in human blood, is a long and far one, yet no longer than we shall stay on this earth nor any farther than the time we take to leave it. Apart from this, it is a quest we have to make in ourselves as we search for the life-spirit animating us. In the tarot, this is symbolized by the Fool who wanders around the world in search of wisdom, which means discovering your own deficiencies. At first the Fool wanders blindly and heedlessly, learning only a very little with each step he stumbles over. But that little keeps increasing until he learns to keep his eyes open and listen to what he has been told by his intuition or compelled to take notice of by his experience.

Around and around the cycle of life goes the Fool, from one incarnation to another, gaining more ground with every embodiment until at last the soul of a young and foolish man becomes that of the wise old Hermit who then renews himself forever in the Grail he finds was with him imperceptibly all the time. In this universe, we have to earn our emancipation by efforts, endurance and experience. Souls have to grow, like every other form of life, but they take a lot longer to mature than bodies and cannot escape from their levels until they have gained the Grail which wins them admission to higher than human forms of life. In other words, they will continue being bound to human bodies until they evolve into superior states of being.

Every incarnation lived to its full extent is a miniature Sangreal cycle. A human being begins, not with birth, but with conception. From that instant until physical birth, the individual recapitulates the whole process of evolution from primal protoplasm to emergence in human form. The first quadrant of the cycle is quickly covered. Then comes learning how to adapt awareness to this world—its laws, customs, beliefs, and all the peculiarities that prepare people for making their contributions to civilization. So much for the second quadrant. After this, in the third quadrant, come active dealings with the principles of living on this earth and perhaps some inklings of how this might apply in other areas. In the last quadrant come all the difficult and unpleasant things which we have to face until death releases us temporarily. Here we may go into a Hermit-like state of retreat, awakening when we reach a heavenly Grail-state, or we may sleep unconsciously all through it and start off again on the next cycle—another step up the Ladder of Life, or a fresh numeral ahead up the tarot scale of ten. By the time the people-cards are reached, that type of soul ought to be well within reach of the Grail goal.

It is possible, of course, to regress if deliberate reversals of life-principles are pursued or opportunities for advancement are rejected. There are many reasons why we vary so much in our rate of progression, or apparently turn around completely and go in the wrong direction. In the normal course of events, however, an average soul can be expected to make a slowish sort of progress from birth to birth, and eventually catch up with the blood of our beginning and so grasp the Grail we were intended to gain as an end to earth existence. Only to earth life be it noted, because subsequently to that we shall, in the words of the Bible "become as the Gods, immortal." The Sangreal may cancel the responsibilities of this world, but it will place far higher ones in the hands of those who gain emancipation from it.

Let us follow a few Sangreal cycles with a Fool-soul who emerges into existence for the first time directly from the central force of formed creation. This point is represented by the Ace of Cups, often shown as the Fountain of Life. Here the Fool encounters the Star-stage of the tarot where "The Sun is his Father and the Moon his Mother and the wind hath born it in the womb thereof," as represented by the mating of two Lovers who summon his soul into this world. The Star, of course, represents the divine spark which is central to any soul and without which no life would be worth anything. This is the integral identity indicated by the injunction: "What doth it profit a man to gain the whole world, yet suffer the loss of his own soul?"

Once in this world, the Fool can either stay as he is, in a Cup-condition—which would mean a state of happy infantilism—or alter in keeping with the other suits as he encounters their positions. Although he can alter his nature during an incarnation, he cannot alter his intrinsic value while embodied. This means that we have the genetics we were born with for the remainder of our incarnations, and though we can and should change their condition by intentional alteration, we cannot change their potential value until disembodied, and that may only be done with considerable concentration of consciousness and intensification of intention. However, IF this can be accomplished, it will cause the great advantage of abbreviating the tedious trials of life.

The soul able to make three distinct character changes during a lifetime, moving from Shields to Rods and then to Swords, would be in a position to increase its Cup value possibly past the next stage before being conceived back into incarnate life again. This would mean cutting the "cosmic time" from 1,120 circuits to 280. Those are arbitrary figures of course, and are only presented here to show the principle involved, which is the important factor. Normal individuals have all the suit qualities of the tarot inherent in themselves simultaneously. A conscious character-change has to be made so that the end result is a complete experience of suit natures. For example, if an individual soul has a potential value of four, but deliberately lives like a two when opportunities were offered for attaining such primal potency, then it will be in the position of the unfaithful servant in the parable of the talents.

This means to say a developing soul both can and should alter itself during incarnate life so as to maximize the characteristics of the four tarot suits in its nature up to the limits of genetic value. Relatively few do anything like this, and many make no effort to alter at all. Their spiritual progress resembles a record with the stylus stuck in the same groove. However, let us consider the course of a lively soul determined to do its best, pulling enough power from the central supply to push itself along as fast as reasonably possible towards the Sangreal. For the sake of familiar friendliness let us call this soul Galahad, since he was a Knight who was supposed to have gained the Grail.

Galahad, in his earliest appearance as the Ace of Cups, has now reached boyhood and altered into the Ace of Shields. Here he relates himself with the work of the Chariot and realizes his necessity for adapting with the current rate of progression in this world as fast as he can. Everything seems to be going so fast after the comfortable womb wherein he waited while the millennia whizzed past him as his baby body was moulded into modern shape. Still, he adjusts to this eventually and comes into contact with the Emperor, who represents all senior male influences, such as his father and those who are going to control his life by teaching, ruling, and instructing him in everything he needs to know about being an adult. At the same time, he encounters the Empress, who typifies all the female influences which will have a corresponding effect on him—mother, sisters, teachers, and eventually mates. It could be said here that the order of encounter might be reversed, except that the Emperor and Empress are to be considered conjointly rather than separately, and in early earthlife, they specifically stand for parents. They are really the Lovers from the previous quadrant who have at last produced a child—Galahad.

He next meets with the Hierophant and Priestess who specifically represent all the males and females who will give him a sense of religious or idealistic value by either their example or precept once he is old enough to learn them. They are going to teach him the rudiments of knighthood and kingship, which he will find so inspiring when he grows up. These may not be currently living people at all, but could be long dead ones whose writings and teachings have lived into our era. They will appear to Galahad through his contemporary vision and may be masked behind the faces of friends who mediate these qualities for him. This is the point at which he will need to alter his character from Cup/Shield, to Cup/Shield/Rod. Unless he means to retard his life by rejecting the opportunity.

Here it may as well be explained that his character will form by following the tarot suits in proper order. He emerges from his mother's womb as a Cup-character, poured straight out of the Sangreal so to speak. From there he graduates to a Shield-state, during which he has to be shielded (or covered) by the concern of his elders for the first quarter of his incarnate life. Once past that, he should be ready to pick up the Rod and run his own affairs, which he will learn to do in the next quadrant. Only when he has understood these, will he really be fit to pick up the Sword and begin to handle it in a responsible manner. The Sword is a dangerous weapon because it means not only what may injure him during his life, but it also gives him the ability to hurt others. It is thus important that it should be the last skill he learns. Defense with the Shield before attack with the Sword always comes first.

So during his Rod-session, Galahad will learn how to apply his intelligence to the problems of life and how to overcome them with ingenuity if possible. Sheer force is only to be invoked as a very last resource. Here he will meet with the Magician, first as a trickster-figure who misleads and beguiles him in order to test his gullibility or lack of sound sense. Subsequently the Magician will be an amusing friend who teaches him the tricks and dodges in dealing with life's difficulties. In his early stages of development—while there is a great deal of the Fool about Galahad—he is likely to meet the Magician only in his trickster-guise, though this will always be without malice or ill-intent. The Magician is only likely to trick Galahad through silly things which will teach him better. In a way one could suppose the Magician to be the Devil with all the evil taken out of him. A tryer and a tester through harmless trickery.

It all depends on how Galahad deals with the Magician, who will fool Fools if he can; but once he knows he cannot, he will change himself towards them as he finds most fitting. He may even teach a few things about the Wheel of Fortune next to him which those like Galahad must learn how to ride success-fully so that they do not fall too often, too hard, or too seriously. It is not expected that they will stay on it very long, but if they can do so at all without tragic results, that will be good enough for average purposes. It is the Chariot transported to this quad-rant of the cycle. For the first few times Galahad is unlikely to do very well with the Wheel, for it has tricks of its own to play, but at least he can get a good inkling of what is needed so that he may think about it at leisure later.

Once past the Wheel, Galahad will have to acquire some sense of Justice and Judgement which really go together like the Emperor and Empress of the first quadrant. They are the only factors which are capable of helping him deal with the Devil, who he now encounters on a personal scale of opposition which seems to present every problem possible. If he has not heeded his lessons, he is likely to grab the Sword a bit prematurely and start using it wildly and recklessly.

That will cause his last character-change of this round, which brings his Tower toppling around his ears with all his hopes blasted. So crawling out of the ruins, he suspends his efforts and his Sword under the sign of the Hanged Man where he waits for the transformation of Death to come and deliver him. This comes in many disguises. Sometimes as disease, some-times murder, often as battle, frequently as accident, and occa-sionally as age. Birth only happens one way, but the various appearances of Death are amazing. Death is by no means the end of Galahad's existence, since it transforms his consciousness into a cocooned chrysallis-like state, resembling the Hermit wrapped in a cloak of dreams until ready to emerge with the triumph of Temperance, where he may live briefly like a butterfly before being ready for his next incarnation. This is where he may expect his reward – increased value if he has earned it, or a demotion to a lower grade if he merits that.

Here we can see the reason for the so-called Rosicrucian "grades" of one to ten. They were actual spiritual self-states measured against the Sangreal scale of life. They represent an actual condition of consciousness and spiritual status as an individual soul. Strictly speaking, they could not be changed at all during a lifetime, because they were genetically set, and all the ceremonial "lodge" promotions were purely symbolic, representing changes of opinion by bretheren concerning any member's developing abilities. Unhappily, very few working lodges ever explained that properly, and most members were happy enough to decorate themselves with what were really IOU's for future achievements.

Now we are going to suppose that Galahad has lived a good and useful life, tackling its problems cheerfully under the Cup, carefully under the Shield, cleverly under the Rod, and courageously under the Sword. This would certainly earn him promotion on the Sangreal scale, but to what degree will depend on how far he has advanced himself. Be it most carefully noted that this does not necessarily mean he will have a much higher social or prominent birth status in his forthcoming incarnation. It signifies that he will be placed at a position where he will probably encounter all the challenges he needs to deal with in order to advance himself yet closer to the Sangreal by his own continuing efforts. So, still in his Fool-character, young Galahad has to set forth again on another round of life. This time we will promote him to status three. He will have earned enough wisdom to take him to the understanding stage.

This time he commences his Sangreal cycle from the third degree of development. His conception is more likely to be started in its Star-state with a certain amount of understanding and comprehension of its consequences. His parents are likely to be more evolved than previously, and their sexual relationship is apt to be slightly more sophisticated. By the time Galahad gets into this world again he will have advanced into a condition of clearer understanding among its citizens. Not greatly, yet significantly so far as Galahad is concerned. He looks round the world with wondering eyes as he adopts his Cup/Shield character and eventually faces his first major challenge at the Chariot.

He does this in a three of Cup/Shields style. Cheerfully and carefully with understanding. He now has an inkling of what Chariots mean, and this fresh encounter is more interesting than the last. He is scarcely developed enough to control it very skillfully yet, but he can become very curious about its workings and wonder how best to deal with it. He is beginning to be a lot brighter with schoolwork and preparations for adulthood. Encountering the Emperor and Empress next, he gets some good ideas of their functions, first as parents and then as the seniors who are responsible for worldly education, employment, and advancement as a citizen of earth. When he meets the Pope and Priestess, they appeal to his youthful enthusiasm and set his mind and soul into a pattern which will influence him all his life. At this point, he is ready to take up his Rod and rule the remainder of his progress on this planet from a Cup/Shield/Rod viewpoint.

His meeting with the Magician teaches him some new tricks and he is not so easily caught by the old ones—though he does fall for a few. When it comes to the Wheel, he still gets mostly thrown, but he gets a free lift or so, too. His encounters with Justice and Judgement are met with sufficient understanding to enable him to tackle the Devil somewhat more intelligently, but this makes him so unhappy he grabs the Sword again and tries to make a fight of it, but the crafty Devil lures him into the Tower, which collapses on him. Ruined again, he retreats into the suspension state of the Hanged Man and awaits Death rather miserably. When it does come to collect him, he feels relief.

Galahad's Hermit stage is one he spends trying to understand why he should have to undergo all those experiences. He ponders and broods over them until his understanding increases enough to push him another couple of promotions up the scale, and by the time he has emerged into his brief but beautiful butterfly condition at Temperance, he has reached the fifth degree of tarot on the Sangreal scale. This entitles him to have his genetics adjusted again in keeping with his new status and, metaphorically taking a deep spiritual breath, he plunges back into incarnate life with renewed determination.

This time he is likely to be conceived by a fighting family or one which is dedicated to some rather stern spiritual principles. His Star-stage is more likely to be ruled by Mars than Venus. Alternatively it might be a lineage of jurists, or even arms manufacturers. There will be something militant about them. Possibly he might have a Sun conjunct Mars or Moon in Scorpio, which would indicate more of a political fighter. Then the Lovers who make a body for him on earth would possibly regard sex in some odd light, such as it being more of a duty than a pleasure, or perhaps coldly and offhandedly as something to be ashamed of. There is likely to be little love in their mating. By the time their son gets to this world he will feel as if he had been poured from a somewhat bitter Cup, and he will encounter this world with angry tears instead of chubby smiles.

A little later, when he meets the Chariot, he will do so under the aegis of a fifth degree Shield with the sourish taste of an upset Cup still tainting his soul. When he does manage to drive his Chariot for a while he will steer it straight at trouble and have several crashes. At school he is likely to have a quarrelsome time and be involved with many conflicts of opinion. Though his Shield saves him from one calamity after another, he will not be without wounds. Encounters with authority via the Emperor and Empress are almost guaranteed to arouse antagonism, not entirely without cause since he can detect corruption in those that control the affairs of this world. Hence when he meets his Pope and Priestess, he will probably be influenced by their most puritanical principles and preachings. In religion, if he has any, he will be almost fanatical and certainly devoted to the most rigid and inflexible forms of faith. It will almost be second nature to him when he takes up the Rod to rule all around him with severe, yet on the whole, just discipline.

At the Rod-stage of this incarnation, a fifth degree tarot type is beginning to lose his Fool characteristics, although there are still enough of them to be taken into account, mostly in matters of over-severity and almost complete lack of humor. His rule is rigid, and for him the Law is the Law, to be observed to the letter. Though he has little time or tolerance for the Magician, that Trickster is still able to work his brand of magic. By subtle flattery and misdirection the Magician is able to make him see evil or wrongdoing where none actually exists, and so distracts his vision from the truth he thinks he is tracking. Galahad is no longer deceivable by childish tricks, and a much more sophisticated level of legerdemain has to be used for entrapment now. However, that is well within the Magician's competence, and Galahad will meet his Wheel with over-confidence, behaving so much like Don Quixote tilting at the windmills that he makes a ridiculous spectacle of himself and generally gets the worst of it.

When it comes to the triumphs of Justice and Judgement, he is in his element again. As a qualified Cup/Shield and Rod man of the fifth degree, he is certain that he has a mission for righting the wrongs of this world by punishing those he considers guilty of them, and this includes his next encounter with the Devil. Galahad is ready to blame the Devil for all that has gone wrong with his life so far, and for all the bad behavior of other humans on this level of life, too. Snatching up a useful Sword from the last stage ahead of him, he puts up a very powerful fight with the Devil, dodging around on one side of him while the Tower threatens him on the other. This time he stages a most competent conflict with considerable skill, and maybe for a while it looks as if he has made a dent or so in the Devil, yet in the end he proves no more invincible than anyone else, and the Tower defeats him as usual by falling on top of him, so a sadly squashed Galahad hangs himself up and waits for Death to take him away, which it duly does. This time, wrapped in his Hermit's cloak of consideration, Galahad has a lot of time to think things over, and he does this with reflective regret.

True, he has learned a lot of lessons in this degree, but he has paid a bitter price for them. Were they worth it? He believes so, yet hopes he may have earned a higher value by his trials and troubles. He would like to be a bit more cheerful and successful in his next incarnation. So coming out of his Hermit's cloak, and assuming a bright and blissful butterfly appearance with the triumph of Temperance for a while, he arranges a reprogramming of his genetics to the seventh tarot degree, and starts looking around for a suitable Star which will light up when it is time for him to make the drop to earth again.

Eventually his Star flashes to tell him an opportunity is opening. Now it will be with affectionate and successful people. Comfortable at any rate and good at gaining their way around the world. In a somewhat happier mood, Galahad swoops down to earth and his future parents, past the radiant Sun and reflective Moon toward two Lovers who are making the most of their mating. Gladly he slips through the seed of one into the womb of the other. There he will wait in a happy dream-state until summoned out of it to face the world again. He does not yell or cry out greatly on this occasion, because he feels confident he will be on the winning side for a change. The world looks much the same, but his folks are glad to see him and assure him he will be most welcome to stay with them for as long as he likes, which he appreciates. He determines to deserve them.

His early meeting with the Chariot is much better than on previous occasions, now that he has become a seventh degree initiate of life with its Cup and Shield symbolism behind him. He actually manages to stay on the Chariot and direct it fairly well at this stage. Moreover his Foolishness is definitely fading out, and perhaps there is a hint of a Page visible in his face. At any rate, he is positively a great deal more mature and sensible than in former incarnations, Galahad can still shake a bauble occasionally, but more in fun than foolishly. He has learned how to handle his life-weapons a lot better and shields himself skillfully as he gets through early years safeguarded by parents and friends who feel sure he is bound to be a winner in whatever battles he might have to face ahead of him.

Galahad makes good relationships with all those represented by the Emperor and Empress, assuring them he is on their side and will serve them faithfully. When he reaches the Pope and Priestess, they tell him a great deal about the Sangreal as they understand it, and now it becomes much clearer to him what he should be supporting with his life and learning. He has been quite bright at school and possibly won some honors in one field or another. Galahad is now good at winning things—and people.

Once he picks up his Rod, Galahad points it intelligently around himself, picking out the points he is interested in and asking for answers until he gets them. The Magician no longer fools him very greatly, though he admires the technique and quality of the Magician's performance. The gratified Magician reveals a great many secrets concerning the unpredictable performance of the Wheel. Though he does not tell everything he knows about the Wheel, he explains enough for Galahad to ride it successfully for quite a while, and he does not sustain any serious injuries when it lets him down with relative gentleness. At his seventh degree, Galahad has many winning ways with him.

Coming to Justice and Judgement, our young hopeful runs his rule over them and decides that they measure up to his standards. He relates them with each other and finds the proper proportions to combine, so that when he encounters the Devil, he has a fairly good notion of how to handle this opponent by the rulership of his Rod rather than the Sword he knows he will have to tackle next. The Devil does not like being dealt with by means of a Rod instead of a Sword, because this reduces his image to that of a naughty child instead of a terrifying fiend, and if there is one thing the Devil dislikes, it is diminishment. Yet even he has to respect the laws of life and bow before a Rod which is rightly raised. Galahad is either getting good at guessing, or the Sangreal is communicating with him a lot more clearly.

When he faces the dreaded dark Tower, Galahad knows he will have to take up the Sword even though he does so with reluctance. The fatal challenge reaches him from its roof-top, and he raises the Sword hesitantly. The Heavens answer instantly with a flash, but instead of striking the Tower as usual, the lightning strikes the Sword, and Galahad lies in a shocked and stricken state wondering what might happen next. This was one battle he did not win, and when he recovers sufficiently to crawl away, he will suspend himself from action as before and await release by Death from this perilous position. While there, he has a chance to think about things in inverted terms with regard to the world. The Hanged Man symbol shows someone looking at life from an entirely opposite way to anyone in the usual upright position. There is a lot to learn from this upside-down angle. Anyway, Death soon releases him in kindly fashion and wraps a Hermit's cloak around his ghostly shoulders with an encouraging pat.

The phrase "wrapped in thought" is very apt to describe what happens here to a tarot initiate of the seventh degree. Enwrapped in the woolen cloak of concealment, he tries to unravel it all, strand by strand, so it may provide a long enough clue for following next time he mixes with the maze of mankind. Somehow there must be something connecting all those people in common, and he strongly suspects this must be the Sangreal he has heard of and feels must be within his own origins somewhere. From now on, he determines to quest consciously with all the awareness he can muster in search of such an objective. Most people call it the Holy Grail, and think of it as being a mythical and mystical ideal far beyond their attainment, not worth bothering with. Galahad somehow knows that the Sangreal is much more than mythical, and worth any sacrifice he can make in order to attain it. Now he realizes what that sacrifice will have to be—himself. So be it then. AMEN to that. His dark cloak turns into brilliant wings while he enjoys his respite in the heaven of his highest ideals. He has won a battle well worth winning here—the battle between his higher and lower self.

We are going to suppose that during his temporary sojourn in his human heaven, Galahad gets promoted to the tenth degree. Factually, of course he would make these major changes at a much slower rate, but we are deliberately skipping stages in order to show the overall system rather than the tedious covering of every incident. Already we have theoretically covered what would normally take maybe thousands of years. Before he will gain the Grail and earn his escape from earth evolution, Galahad must reach the highest condition of consciousness possible, and that will be the equivalent of kingship – in the sense of becoming a sacred king who deliberately dies for his people so that they will one day share his immortality. For a Christian, this would be reaching the Christ-state, after which there can be no obligation ever to live on earth again. The so-called "second coming" would be purely a voluntary visit because of love alone. Galahad is not yet at that point by any means, but he has consciously dedicated himself to its attainment, so in furtherance of that vow, he proposes to have himself reprogrammed genetically to the tenth tarot degree of the Sangreal system.

This time Galahad will get himself born into some very suitable family, though this does not indicate any very important social position or great wealth. It does however mean spiritual suitability, so his family will be able to help him through his initial hurdles by making allowances for his specialty of soul and his developing uniquity of character. They may, though this is not a certainty, have some definite inkling of what lies behind Galahad's birth. They may be keen to teach the ideals and principles he is coming to support and practice throughout his humanity. They will positively belong to the same general tradition, and they may even be aware of the blood-bond between them all. Galahad's blood-related relatives are going to be of great value to him from now on, because his own value is approaching maximum.

When Galahad's Star beckons him towards birth, there is something of a Star of Bethlehem appearance about it, although by no means entirely. Again the Sun shines on him brilliantly and the Moon smiles softly as the Lovers prepare to produce their child. There is something very beautiful about their mating, which is done with intense love and a keen awareness that they are summoning into this world a soul who will someday be more special than themselves. Only very developed souls have the genetics which are able to call in others of the same category. They have to be of the blood themselves before this becomes possible, and somehow they are usually aware of this to a sufficient degree for passing it along conscious lines as well as literal ones. So their mating call reaches the Stars and summons Galahad into a very welcoming womb once more. There he meditates his approaching mission, something in the style of his remote Sangreal ancestors awaiting arrival on this earth. When he eventually reaches the World, it will be with very little surprise and a great deal of satisfaction all round.

His Cup is now very potent and his Shield is strong and sound. Galahad has only a slight difficulty in dealing with the Chariot, as he almost swings himself into the driving seat. He has a disposition which used to be described as "sunny." He is warm-hearted, apt to be protective of younger children and animals, and there are remarkably few traces of the Fool left in him, except his readiness to laugh and be cheerful. His encounters with the Emperor and Empress are favorable, since he can see their function clearly enough and is glad to have opportunities of supporting it in service to their station. When it comes to the Pope and Priestess, they awaken a much keener sense of mission in himself, and he hopes he will prove worthy of the tasks he feels lie ahead before he will be ready to tackle the one beyond it. Together the Pope and Priestess confirm consciously what Galahad had always suspected deeply in himself—that the spiritual truths of creation are the most important things in life, and its purpose is the quest of inner realities that will culminate in gaining the Grail by becoming one with the blood borne in it.

When Galahad takes up his Rod as a tenth degree initiate, he does so with an air of familiarity. After all, he is getting to know the ropes by this time, and his early training has accustomed him to taking command of himself as well as others. The

Magician makes only a token gesture of tricking him, and they get on very friendly terms indeed. Many more secrets of the Wheel are revealed to him on this occasion, and he also learns that magic is much more than mystification, being based on our very oldest and deepest spiritual senses relating with the Sangreal at the back of our blood. The Magician teaches Galahad a tremendous amount, and when he gets to the Wheel, he has nearly but not quite acquired an ability to run it in accordance with his own will.

He encounters Justice and Judgement very capably and he can see a lot more clearly into their relationship as he probes them with his Rod to discover some fine details of their construction. It reveals much he did not formerly know, such as the Sword of Justice being sharp on one edge and blunt on the other. Also the scales of the figure may not always be as equally balanced as are commonly supposed. They are sensitive enough to weigh thoughts. Then with Judgement, the trumpet with which the angel is supposed to sound the Last Trump can be used for listening *through* as well as *to*. On that fabled Last Day of Judgement, God cannot very well judge humans without giving them the right to judge Him in return. Both Justice and Judgement make this perfectly clear.

Encountering the Devil at the end of his Rod-run, Galahad finds the fiend more of a nuisance than a menace. He gets in the way and acts with all his usual obstructions, but Galahad turns his Rod into a Staff, and pushes these aside with an annoyed boredom rather than any difficulty. The Devil is becoming an old acquaintance, whom Galahad has not forgotten, but has taken into account almost automatically. He is getting wise to the Wicked One's wiles, for his erstwhile Foolishness has faded to an almost imperceptible impish grin, which rather adds to his attractions. When it comes to the challenge of the Tower, however, Galahad takes up his Sword very thoughtfully.

This time the Tower is tackled differently, since he proceeds all around it very warily, examining it from every angle. The Tower itself does not defeat him, but his human enemies do. They have followed him to this point and arranged an ambush.

One might not suppose that a man like Galahad would make many enemies during this incarnation, but he has. Plenty. Mainly from motives such as envy and malice because he so strongly supports the principles they hate and fear most. There are at least ten of them, and being afraid to face him, they stab him in the back while he is watching the Tower. Sadly enough there were several of his erstwhile friends among his murderers. The going of Galahad tells the tragic tale of treachery and trust betrayed. Behind his back, the Devil snickers as Galahad gathers the very last of his strength to stagger off toward the suspension stage of the Hanged Man where he will not have to wait very long until Death mercifully envelopes him in his Hermit's cloak.

Galahad has a lot to ponder in that last life. He knows now that he will have to become a king who will sacrifice himself for the same type of people that have just betrayed and murdered him. Does he really feel he will be able to do this? Sacrifice for loved ones is more or less natural for any honorable person, but sacrifice for enemies and those who seem to be in league with the Devil seems rather more than might be expected of any reasonable human being. However this sacrifice has nothing to do with reason whatever. It touches us as deeply as divine love can inspire a developed Sangreal soul. Wrapped in his cloak of contemplative consciousness, Galahad comes to realize that all souls connected with the Sangreal strain of blessed blood will always be worth every effort made to save them. They may not have developed to Galahad's degree, and they certainly work out their lives along different lines, but so long as there is a single drop of Sangreal blood left, it will be his solemn duty to die for them if need be. Even if they reject his effort to rescue them, which many will probably do, it will still be his honored obligation to do whatever he can on their behalf. Galahad rededicates himself with the old Sangreal Oath: "I seek to serve," and, making wings of his cloak, goes gladly to the triumph of Temperance.

Here he drinks deeply of the Cup that consoles him to the very basis of his being while it fills him with blessings. He lingers over it lovingly with companions of his own kind who welcome him as a true blood-brother. They assure him he is far from being alone in any world the Sangreal has touched on its travels. They tell him also that they, like himself, are awaiting calls for their services as active agents of the Sangreal on earth, and they hope to meet him there in friendly fraternity. None of them expects an easy time on earth, but now that they have realized what they are all striving for, their tasks will be that much more endurable because of the blood they share in a common consciousness. From their exalted approach, they tend to view the troubles ahead of them with lightheartedness and confidence. They exult with enthusiasm and wait for their Stars to light up. While they are so engaged, they find an opportunity to initiate Galahad into their order, and he emerges from this as a fully fledged Knight of the Holy Grail to find his Star glowing as a spiritual summons his soul is bound to answer.

This time his parents are outstanding. Not necessarily socially or financially but of good blood on both sides, and of very high cultural standards. Most probably the Sangreal strain will have reached a marked degree of development in them both, and they could be initiates themselves. Their mating occurs during very good Solar aspects with the Moon, so that Galahad's soul sails up to them in great style and waits somewhat restlessly in his new mother's womb for the moment of birth. His entry to this World is possibly a difficult one, such as being inconveniently premature, a breech presentation or even a Caesarean section. He will make himself memorable somehow.

At first he may seem a gentle and biddable child as he comes out of the Cup stage, but this will change when he starts working with the Shield when he will become very practical. His handling of the Chariot becomes skilled at an early age, and he is likely to excel in athletics and physical prowess as well as in academic spheres. He shows that he is very capable by driving himself in a well-disciplined yet daring way. He is liable to gain honors and distinctions in many fields. Encountering the Emperor and Empress, he will be their staunch supporter, yet can be very critical of conduct he feels should be under their control. Galahad is particularly protective toward weaker or more fallible humans. When he comes to the Pope and Priestess, he may meet these not in any religious sense, but as idealists who have propounded social systems purporting to bring maximum benefits to mankind. On the other hand, they might not be human, but simply spiritual ideals he encounters to make the necessary changes in his character which earn him his Rod.

Once armed with his Rod, Galahad starts stirring up anything he can think of which might make some difference to the inequalities and injustices of this world. He may be influenced here by the remnants of the Fool which remain with him. Though very attenuated by this time, the Fool is not entirely defunct. Meeting the Magician, Galahad matches his Rod against him and asks if the Magician can do anything really good or useful with his magic, like healing hurts or conjuring up cleverness in someone mentally defective. He also wants to know whether the Wheel can be manipulated to produce an even distribution of wealth instead of riches at one end and hopeless poverty at the other. He dislikes the Wheel very much on account of its inequality, and tries his best to fix it so that it will produce a steady stream available to everyone, rather than untidy heaps of fortune and open spaces of dereliction. Galahad tries to regulate it with his Rod, but has little luck in this direction, so he turns to encounter the triumph of Justice.

Here he gets into a heated argument about injustices and unfairness. Justice coldly reminds him that this is entirely the fault of mankind, and Galahad has to agree, yet insists that if Justice exercised a more Rod-like control over humanity they might have become better beings. Justice points out that we have more power to abuse it than Justice has to punish them. Galahad protests that human legislation is hopelessly out of date, totally unfair to those who need protection most, and he personally is very dissatisfied and intends to alter its applications as soon as he can. Justice then refers him to Judgement at the next station of the cycle.

Judgement is not in a mood for argument, and Galahad seems to have lost a lot of steam at the last station, but he does question whether Judgement is always on the side of the righteous. Judgement says yes, in the end, though it may have to alter as information becomes available, and therefore should always be taken as a temporary finding until there is nothing left to judge. Judgement remarks that it has nothing to do with punishment but is concerned with accurate assessments of situations and principles in relationship with each other, therefore the real task of Judgement is setting minds and souls in agreement concerning attitudes of consciousness to be adopted relative to the rest of creation. Galahad has to be content with this information when he turns to face the Devil at the next station.

The Devil seems very forbidding to Galahad, not so much on his own account as for the effect it might have on more easily frightened mortals. He himself is not greatly impressed by its awesome appearance, but realizes the influence this spiritual spectre has. Since Galahad is holding the Rod, he gets to learn that the Devil is quite helpless unless there is enough of its nature in anyone for the Devil to take hold of. Most mortals have a lot of the Devil in themselves which will respond to the Archetype confronting Galahad at that moment, but he boldly challenges the fiend-form to try what it can do with him. Taking him at his word, the Devil tries, but Galahad does not have much difficulty in disengaging himself from the Devil's claws.

Moving out of the Devil's grasp, Galahad confronts the fearful Tower which has ruined him so often in the past. With Sword in hand he pauses for its challenge to meet him. Nothing happens, so he flings a challenge at it. Again silence. When the mystery is revealed to him by a quiet whisper in his alerted awareness, Galahad feels chilled with horror. The doorless Tower is a prison for the hopes of humanity which have been building up since the beginning of their civilization. Therein those hopes will be doomed to perish unless they are released by those special souls who are great enough to be considered of royal blood, who are entitled to sacrifice themselves on behalf of their people. In losing their human lives, they will gain the Grail.

Realizing he has no personal power to rescue the imprisoned hopes of so many hearts with any sort of Sword, the Tower has ruined his own hopes by its impregnability. Galahad turns sadly aside and slowly places himself in a state of suspension as a Hanged Man, and thinks things out while awaiting Death to rescue him from his dilemma. Gaining the Grail will be a far greater sacrifice than he previously supposed, and he wonders whether he is really prepared to offer it. While he is pondering this problem, Death quietly removes the life-support and wraps the Hermit's cloak around Galahad's shoulders again.

Now he has plenty of time to think and work out his next step. This would normally be the Queen-state, but Galahad has been rather skipping up the stages, so his final steps around the Sangreal cycle as a King can only lead him to the Grail itself. He and the Fool are by now united in the Hermit's condition of experience and wisdom well earned by what seemed like endless questing and wearisome wanderings through an inhospitable world. At last the light behind the blood begins to call him out of his coma, and he awakes to the sound of celestial harmony welcoming him into the triumph of Temperance.

Galahad now finds himself in the company of kings. Far from being proud, haughty, or overbearing, they seem the most spiritually humble and sincere souls he has ever encountered. They greet him as another who will increase their influence for the benefit of their blood-bonded brethren throughout the world. The incredible responsibility they bear almost bows Galahad to the ground the first time he feels his share of its weight on his spiritual shoulders. All of these kings have paid the price of release from bodily bondage, and they mention something of the sacrifices they were asked to make. Some faced terrible forms of death so their people might be saved from a worse fate. Others accepted dread diseases so that medical science might learn how to combat them. Others endured persecution and martyrdom for the sake of a faith enabling their fellow-mortals to survive spiritually. Many more had lifetimes of poverty and misery to bear while struggling to construct some edifice of consciousness which would inspire a multitude of other humans long after they had expired through neglect and starvation. Plenty had long lifetimes spent in unappreciated service of the Sangreal among indifferent associates, yet they succeeded in implanting its spiritual seeds in very neglected areas which would later flower and fruit in abundance. Every king present had accomplished something which ordinary souls were unable to perform, so it had to be left with those special ones to bear the burden for the remainder.

Galahad was at first overwhelmed by their fraternal friendship, and then became aware of how they were gathering around an altar he had not noticed previously. When everything became silent, they all sank to their knees except one in priest's vestments who approached the altar and summoned Galahad to serve the Sangreal Sacrament with him. They got through the first part with relative ease, all giving responses from their very hearts. The Presence seemed to press upon them with enormous power when they went into the second dedicatory and commemorative stage, and as they arrived at the Canon, its intensity would have been unbearable had they been mere mortals. When the actual moment of consecration came, Galahad had the greatest difficulty in maintaining any kind of consciousness at all. How he managed to carry the Cup around his kingly companions, he never remembered, and after he had partaken his portion of its contents, he was only very distantly aware of the priest returning the Cup to its place, taking something from the altar and pressing it on his head with the words: "By the Blood be thou a King among thy kindred," after which he lost touch with consciousness altogether. When he regained it, he found himself absolutely alone before the altar wherefrom the Cup had vanished. His head hurt, and raising his hands he tried to remove his royal regalia. It was a crown of thorns!

Perhaps at that moment Galahad might have been reminded of an old legend he had heard about a bargain between God and Man. The story went back in the beginning of human history when God and Man were on speaking terms.

God had asked Man what he wanted most, and Man unhesitatingly replied: "Fame." God smiled and replied, "Very well, you shall wear this crown of roses. When people see you they will think how wonderful you must be to present such a beautiful appearance, but all you will ever know is the pain of the thorns pressing into your head." From that time forth, fame was only to be had at a painful price. Galahad, however, had his sacrificial life ahead of him, and so placing his thorny crown upon the altar, he waited for his Star to shine. When it did, it would be blood-red.

It seemed to Galahad that he had an extra long wait before his signal showed, but he realized that those capable of summoning a king-soul from a heavenly habitat would have to be very special people indeed. It seemed a very long time before Galahad's Star beamed its bloody summons to a sacrificial incarnation.

On this occasion his descent to the earthly world appeared much slower than usual. That was actually because Galahad's character was altering so rapidly that all environmental factors appeared slow by contrast. The Sun seemed to be setting with glorious rays of red and gold, while the Moon was at her fullest and most beautiful as her beams shone beneficently on the mating of two Lovers who were experiencing each other in spiritual as well as physical bliss. Such a sexual union is so rare as to be almost unique for it sends signals to the highest heavens where king-souls await incarnation. Galahad glided into his mother's womb to start his life of service by awaiting rebirth. He may have reflected that human life consists of waiting for momentary action to happen, and often the waiting is the hardest thing to endure.

The World was in its usual confused condition when Galahad arrived. Wars and woes abounded. People preyed upon each other even as some prayed for peace. If such a state of civilization was the best example of a Sangreal effect millions of years after its inception, was this world really worth sacrificing a single fingernail for? The sentient soul of Galahad, connected to his body by an umbilical cord of consciousness, had to reconsider this very carefully. The blood was definitely flowing, but it would take a lot more time before its influence could be considered a dominant factor of human genetics. Galahad's sacrifice would be only one among the many millions needed for the salvation of the species. Galahad definitely determined to go ahead and give himself for the sake of the Sangreal and the love he now bore towards his blood-brethren on earth and all potential bearers of the blood for the future. He may have entered this world with a sigh, but there was a responsive smile from his parents to greet him. They knew.

These parents were neither rich nor poor, not prominent nor insignificant, just a little above average on the social scale, though very rich indeed on the spiritual side. Genetics apart, they were entirely capable of imparting to Galahad all the truths of the tradition which the whole family followed with the firmest faith. They saw that this was not anything to talk about so much as to live. It was not a question of believing but one of *belonging*. Only people like themselves could give Galahad the sort of start he needed to accomplish his life-mission. So that was exactly what they did.

When it came to the Chariot, he showed easy expertise, and his early instructors were amazed at his intelligence and ability. Truth to tell, his childhood companions were slightly afraid of him because of his unusual gifts and unexpected demonstrations of them – almost as if they were not entirely under his control. Strange or odd things seemed to happen in his vicinity. Sick people became better or even well again after he had visited them. Bullies were liable to lose their belligerance, pompous people their pride. Hence he was not an entirely popular person, though he was certainly a noteworthy one.

He had the effect of attracting attention to himself which he did not always welcome, and as he grew up his elders felt sure he would make some kind of memorable mark within his own community. They would not have very long to wait before their opinions would be confirmed. When he came to the Emperor and Empress stage of his career, he decided to enter public life in order to act and speak on behalf of his people. His Shield characteristics aroused all his finest instincts in their defense, for his great need was to protect people from the oppression and unfairness he strongly felt they endured unnecessarily. He believed they were inflicting most of their troubles on themselves through stupidity and lack of love for each other, and though he strongly supported the law which both Emperor and Empress had sworn to uphold, Galahad saw the need for its alteration because of the advances made because of the Sangreal strain spreading amongst itself.

Encountering the Hierophant, he realized why that office had adopted the title of "servitur servientium," or Servant of the Servants. The Sangreal echoed it all the time in Galahad's soul. Service was one thing which all people might give each other freely. The very poorest could still give service equally with the rich. So service was about the most valuable commodity on earth and no one should withhold it from another. The poor person who hoarded the ability for service was more of a miser than the rich one who never gave any of his money away. Galahad prepared himself to give his life if need be in the service of his people.

Meeting the Priestess, Galahad acknowledged how much humanity owes to its female complement for its spiritual sentiments. He also noted how few men really understood this. He resolved to make that clear through everything he taught. In this incarnation, Galahad does not marry because he knows the sacrifice that will be demanded of him and does not feel justified in asking any woman to share it with him.

Since it is now time to take up his Rod and start metaphorically ruling some of the affairs of this world, he does so with the greatest sense of responsibility. First he encounters the wonderworking Magician and works more than magical wonders himself. He causes people to look on each other with love instead of hate, compassion instead of cupidity, and friendship in place of ferocity. The Magician could never do that with all his artifices. With his Rod, Galahad points out people's principal faults and indicates how he thinks they should be altered. He promotes rules of behavior for their benefit. Believing in a

Supreme Being himself, he instructs those who will listen in the fundamentals of his simple faith. Its basis is love in every sense of the word. Tolerance, kindliness, friendliness, and all the best that can come out of human nature because of its connection with the Sangreal. He believes that God and people are blood-related and that love is the finest expression of this bond between them.

People attribute miracles to him, though most of them are fulfillments of their own faith. His type of magic seems to border on the miraculous because of its dramatic effects through the minds and souls of willing witnesses. Stories about him magnify and multiply themselves enormously. He is becoming a legend in his own lifetime. When he reaches the Wheel and manages to make it distribute fair shares to everyone for a short time, the acclamation of the multitudes is tremendous. This is where he arouses the deepest antagonism of those who already disapprove of his dispensation because it interferes with their interests. Even he cannot fix the Wheel forever, and he has to move on to Justice. Here Galahad is on firm ground, and he teaches his views while reiterating his opinion that if people would love each other, that love would automatically take care of all the Justice they would ever need.

Nevertheless Galahad is no namby-pamby sentimentalist, and he is absolutely firm on the point of people getting what they deserve. He does not hesitate to condemn cruelty and criminal conduct, especially that committed against the weak and feeble. By this time Galahad has collected a circle of followers who accompany him and help with the more mundane matters of his mission, such as finding funds and arranging accommodation. They listen to all he says and does, often discussing it among themselves and relying on him to guide them out of their difficulties when they come to crux-questions. This is where he meets Judgement, which he administers expertly and accurately.

Meanwhile the moment of sacrifice is coming closer, and his enemies are taking counsel with the Devil, who, of course, is totally opposed to such teachings ever gaining popularity with the masses. The Devil feared that if the majority of people became seriously convinced of the spiritual truths that Galahad was trying to teach, he would find himself in danger. The Devil tries bribery. He offers Galahad a substantial reward for disclaiming his own teachings or betraying his best beliefs.

The Devil works out a scheme for putting an end to Galahad with a maximum of defamatory publicity. With the aid of a betrayer from among his friends, Galahad and his group are arrested in a public park on a charge of disturbing the peace and using inflammatory language. In the end, Galahad's companions are released on bail but he is held in custody pending trial.

During his imprisonment he learned what police brutality could be, and the only Sword he could take up in his defense was a metaphorical one. He was held for a time in a Tower wherein he was tortured, made sport of and abused to such an extent that when he appeared before the civil court its president was shocked enough to exclaim, "Just look at that man!" When the charge was read, Galahad discovered it had been altered to one of plotting to overthrow the government and set himself up as king. A political offense for which the punishment could be death in a very cruel way.

He had very little to say for himself. Witnesses were called who twisted his most simple statements into an absolute travesty of truth. Interrogated about his alleged claim to kingship, he replied his kingdom was certainly not one of this world and could not help adding sadly, "I wanted peace, but I only seem to have brought a Sword instead." After a lot of consideration, it came to a dramatic end. He was to be hanged excruciatingly before the eyes of a public gathering so that they might witness his downfall and disgrace. In Galahad's case there were strong rumors of an attempted rescue, so guards were more than trebled. Also with his remarkable reputation, tales spread that something miraculous might happen, so a much larger crowd than could have been expected turned up to witness any wonders. They might as well have stayed home. A tropical thunderstorm took place and lightning struck the Tower and damaged it enough for all its prisoners to escape, which they did in every direction. The storm cleared as suddenly as it had started, and Galahad still hung there trying to die. His last uttered words were: "The obligation is over."

Death took his soul in the end, and while his body was borne away for burial, his Hermetic cloak settled on his spiritual shoulders like a royal robe. No one discovered what happened to that body, and wonderful tales were told of his reappearance and conscious communication with his closest followers. Meanwhile the soul of Galahad entered the Sangreal Temple of Temperance for a final celebration of his kingship among his kindred of the blessed blood. He had earned his complete emancipation from the Sangreal cycle of life. The crown of thorns left on the altar had turned to solid gold. The secret door leading to the Gates of Eternity stood open, and he could have placed the crown on his head and gone through it to join the joyous ones in eternal entity. The Cup came to him of its own accord, and he held it to his heart saying to whoever might be listening: "No, I will not disappear into divinity just yet. I know men killed my body because I was a threat to their senseless schemes for power and profit. What else could I have done? At least I told the truth as I saw it and as the Sangreal said it through me. I hope I may have opened a way for those who hung as desperately on my words as I had to hang on those gallows. Perhaps I can still help them by reaching their minds or touching their souls in some fashion. The death of my body was no real sacrifice because I could easily get another if I wanted one. Let this be my real sacrifice, that instead of going into God entirely my consciousness will continue to be connected with humans and their miseries until we can all be in Eternity together. I will never enter it without those I love who still have to live on earth. I hereby offer every chance of my Cosmic happiness in exchange for my brethren's chances of attaining the same Grail as this. That I pledge by the blood we all belong with."

At that point Galahad raised the Cup to his lips and drank deeply. He scattered the last few drops in an earthward direction. Finally he replaced the Cup and concentrated his attention to meet the first prayer to be directed toward him on one of the hopes which had escaped from the fallen Tower. He would not have long to wait. Silently his brother kings came to keep him company. The sacrifice of Galahad did not consist of only a physical death; his sacrifice was much greater than that. It was a voluntary limitation of himself within spiritual boundaries which can be reached by conscious efforts at self-extension.

• • •

This thinly disguised story is the secret of the Sangreal. The blood-bond factor makes our eventual evolution possible. Who is not familiar with the old text: "God is Love"? The Sangreal is the emitted essence of that love into human nature so that we may enter divinity ourselves when we reach a fit state to do so. It has been likened to the blood of God being shed for our salvation, and in a metaphorical sense that is perfectly true.

The Major Arcana indicate our progress from start to finish of its Cosmic course. Zero the Fool becomes Infinity at the Temperance point where all becomes equalized in eternity. We have only been following the relationship of a few cards making brief contacts with the Major Arcana on odd occasions. What happens when the Fool has to make these contacts through more than one card, then many cards, then more and more combinations of the cards through all the Major Arcana again and again until there can be no more left? This can only be imagined, yet it will have to happen to every soul before we may hope for eventual emancipation from matter. Buddha compared this process to grains of sand on the seashore, but we of the West might compare it with endless combinations of the tarot. The Minor Arcana within the Major, and the Fool traveling ceaselessly around them like a squirrel in a cage. No wonder some earlier writers compared life with a treadmill, but at least a treadmill can supply power which can be put to use to transform humanity into the purest gold that gets fashioned into the Holy Grail.

The tarot can assist us in our quest by programming our consciousness along the lines we shall have to follow, each one of us in our own way. If even a few cards are chosen daily and only glanced at for a quick contact, that would at least help to set minds seeking a little further, for the subconscious goes on working a long time after the initial impulse that set it in motion. Once the overall Sangreal pattern is known, the process will continue constantly if only sporadically on objective levels. Now and then everything may seem to open up and give a momentary glimpse of the Grail, which is sure to strengthen our resolve to renew pursuit of the quest.

CHAPTER EIGHT

Sangreal Tarot Exercises

T HERE ARE ENDLESS textbooks providing long lists of meanings for each card in the deck, detailing exact methods of laying out the pattern from which final decisions are deduced. They reduce the art of tarot reading to an ABC affair. Anyone could learn this as a foreign language, with a grammar and syntax of its own, with a fixed arrangement and a standard method of application. This is actually so only up to a point.

Initiation of a tarot quest always has to start from the human end. Cards have never been known to bang on their box and call: "Let me out, I've got something important to tell you." This means that the nature of anything asked by us has to be known or can be categorized in some sort of classification. On the other side of the oracle we have—what or whom? Exactly. We have to ask the famous question: "Is there anyone there?"

Tarot Meditation

The only known way of discovering this is by taking each card in turn systematically and empathizing with it until it becomes an inner experience in its own right. This used to be done as a standard meditation practice in many occult organizations, and it certainly bred considerable familiarity with the deck despite the dependence on visual stimulus and an incorrect numerical sequence with the trumps. The card had to be seen exactly as the artist depicted it, and then the meditator was supposed to enter the scene imaginatively and take an active part in whatever was being portrayed. Although this resulted in contact with the card, it was colored and typified entirely as its designer had laid it out, which considerably limited the experience possible.

The Sangreal method of tarot meditation is to deal with each of the Major Arcana entirely as a concept, without any particular picture except whatever may come to mind in connection with it. No fixed and immutable images. Pure concepts of consciousness at their own values. If any illustration is needed, existing ones may certainly be used, providing you realize this is only a convenience for handling ideology through a brain accustomed to thinking in those terms. For example, when dealing with the Sun concept, stay tuned to its purpose and power rather than its external appearance or connection with other systems of symbology, such as alchemy or astrology. The activating intention of the card should always have priority over other considerations.

When dealing with the Minor Arcana, numerical values and suit symbology will be the decisive factor, but specific pictures made by previous artists are not altogether advisable. The guide here is the position of each card on the Tree of Life and the significance of the sphere it is attached to. That is to say, the same sphere-concept is to be seen from four different angles, each of which is shown by a suit, which in turn is a Hallow of the Holy Grail. Here it is best to begin by meditating on all the ones first, then the twos, and so on. When this idea is beginning to come clearly, the suits can be taken one at a time from aces to kings in sequence. Even with the picture cards, it is best to concentrate on the character of the people they portray rather than any particular person, unless the card is being specifically used for that purpose.

This may sound terribly boring and unrewarding in itself, but nothing else will establish a firm enough inner contact with the spiritual realities which the tarots can only symbolize. Unless you are able to think in the language of the tarot itself, how can you possibly interpret it for anyone else? Despite any catchpenny claims there is only one way to learn tarot-talk, and that is the hard way.

To start the tarot talking it is necessary to begin building patterns with the cards, and the simplest sort of pattern starts with one of them. For quite a while the entire deck should be gone through over and over again, turning up one card at a time and concentrating on its meaning. Look at the number value first to identify the class of concept, then the suit to find the approach to that concept. Finally, look at the general significance of the card. Despite every existing description and classification of the cards that you may read, a fresh approach should be made on every separate encounter. This may sound odd but there is a good reason for it.

Memorizing other people's ideas attached to any particular tarot card is not very difficult, but this means that only those specific ideas will be talking and not the cards themselves. True, the ideas will suggest a good many things which could have been quite true on previous occasions for other inquirers, but what you want should be a spontaneous reply made in relation to the individual and inquiry concerned. The only way to get the tarot talking is to make them tell the whole message to you in your own terms of understanding.

Two known factors have to be combined in order to produce the unknown reply. The number of the card is known and so is the suit. Therefore the concept indicated by that figure is first called up as clearly as possible into conscious focus and then your approach relates the two as closely as possible to raise a resultant impression in your awareness. What subconscious guidance may direct attention to such a scene except that contacted by those initial pressures? The thing it should *not* do, however, is talk outside that field altogether, and if it seems to do so, then something is wrong and the process should be examined for error.

For instance, if the card chosen was the three of Rods, that would clearly be connected with the concept of understanding from a Rod viewpoint. Suppose an impression of a happy meeting or a disastrous death is received. That would obviously show no possible connection with the card's connotation and should therefore be ignored or investigated as to its source. Anything entirely incongruous or plainly inappropriate has to be rejected, and only if and when a contact between a card and its interpretation seems quite clear should it be accepted. A constant check has to be kept over this process. At one time it was known as "banishing" and considered to be an exorcism of demons invading human intelligence from hostile realms of inner space.

It is important that an overall control of consciousness is kept while considering the tarot so they do not slip out of their slots, so to speak, during the process. One helpful way of practicing this is to sort the cards into their three separate piles of trumps, people, and thoughts, then keep going through these face up while passing them from one hand to the other and changing consciousness accordingly. This will help train your mind to make runs in character. For example, while running through the people-pile, try to think of who you are reminded of by any particular card. If no special person comes to mind, try to connect that card with some public or popular character. With the numeral cards of the Minor Arcana, take each suit in turn and see if these can be connected with incidents that have happened in your personal life. When this has been done, pick up the Major Arcana and go through them in order of appearance, relating each to some personal happening. After that, go through them in reverse order while relating them with some imaginary event which would be welcome.

Now try the Who, What, Why, Where, When, and How game. From the people-pile pick one card and set it up for Who. Choose the What and Why from the Major Arcana, then the Where, When and How from the Minor Arcana. Make up a story from the cards you've chosen and see if it will fit together to make a plausible account. Then shuffle the cards again, starting with the Major Arcana and finishing with the people. It could be helpful to keep two tarot decks, one permanently divided into the three piles and the other shuffled normally. Shuffling is best done by holding the cards loosely in your left hand and shaking the rest of them sideways on. The professional cardplayers' brisk flip of the deck into an interlocking whole and then smartly ramming the cards together is not recommended. It may look impressive but it does not treat the cards in the right way for responsive results. Incidentally it is a good idea to take a quick glance on the bottom of the assembled deck to make sure the bottom card is not a key-card in the sense of being a Major Arcana ace, or court card representing a person present. If so, reshuffle until some less important card is at the bottom of the deck.

Another exercise is to take out the Fool (who of course represents the inquirer), think very hard about the matter in mind, then push the Fool anywhere into the deck and shuffle it a few more times. Then sort through it slowly with the cards face up until the Fool is found. The few cards in proximity with it will be the ones to tell the story. This is only a very rough and ready method of eliciting a response from the tarot, but it serves to establish rapport with the deck. The more any particular deck is used, the more responsive it will be as a rule. Most tarotists have a favorite deck which is almost falling to pieces—which their friends vainly try to replace. New decks are gratefully and politely received, and usually put away in drawers full of similar new decks. Perhaps they will be used some day, but not before they have been heavily handled and possibly placed under their owner's pillow for quite a few nights. That was once a general practice with Gypsies, who were not above "naturing" their cards by rubbing in traces of their body fluids so as to "personalize" the deck.

About the quickest tarot consultation is to merely cut them and see what the card is. If this is done, the deck should always be cut with the thumb and middle fingers of the right hand on the sides of the cards and never the ends. In the olden days, oracles were not expected to do much more than indicate a straight yes or no to the problem propounded. This can be done with the tarot if the Major Arcana are extracted and the fifty-six card deck is used. The inquirer has to know which court card represents himself or whoever he is asking for. Furthermore, the query must be one that can be answered by a direct positive or negative reply. Shuffle a few times and cut once, with your mind firmly fixed on the problem all the time. Note the card cut. Do not shuffle further, but put the deck together again, and start dealing it in three piles face up. If the card cut comes up in the same pile as the personal card (or the nine or ace of Cups), the answer is yes, and the cards between them should be read for further information. If this does not happen, the reply may not necessarily be no, but simply that the tarot doesn't feel like answering. Sometimes tarotists will use this method to determine whether the cards will respond to their queries on that occasion. If the reply is favorable, they will proceed with a more extended method.

On Using the Tarot as An Oracle

It should never be forgotten that the primary purpose of the Tarot is not for fortune telling, but for deepening, sensitizing, and refining ordinary consciousness so we can reach a range beyond average awareness. Consciousness, like light or any other energy, has a spectrum, and the common or garden type does not extend very far past fixed points on that scale. Some individuals are born with a greater reach than others, and it is mostly a matter of methodology to extend your normal level of awareness in any desired direction. The tarot can be regarded as an instrument for extending our awareness into spiritual space. If we try to use them outside those limits, whose fault will it be if they fail during such misuse?

One of the quickest ways to shut down communication by the Sangreal tarot system is to ask for prophecies and other wish-want information. All that happens when closure from inside occurs is that your questions are reflected back like echoes from a blank wall. This does not mean that no personal inquiries may be made, but it does depend on how they are presented. For instance a preemptory order to alter some purely personal circumstance would very likely meet with an ambiguous answer or none at all. If a request were phrased something like: "I am having trouble trying to make inner progress because of such-and-such a situation. Can you help me solve my problems by assisting my consciousness to deal with them?" then it would most probably be dealt with in the same spirit. Establishing the right relationship does help in obtaining a right reply.

So how do we know whether we have established a worthwhile contact with inner intelligence of a trustworthy order? Because the formulated thoughts beamed back have a strangely original quality about them which differs from our ordinary thinking methods, so it seems as though someone else is speaking "inside your head." Perhaps the phraseology is somewhat peculiar, or the ideas or even the information that reaches you is outside your normal range of knowledge. By and large there will be an unmistakeable sense of otherness more than difficult to describe, yet entirely recognizable to anyone who has experienced it. From that point on acquaintance will improve just as it would in the case of contact with another human being. Entity is entity whether embodied or not.

The Tarot Alphabet

We normally communicate by means of words written in the Latin alphabet, while the intelligences behind the tarot communicate by using concepts expressed through symbols. It should be theoretically possible to translate the "language" of the tarot into our own language by assigning a single letter of our alphabet to each card of the Major Arcana. By creating a "tarot alphabet," we can create further possibilities for self exploration using the exercises presented in this section.

The immediate difficulty in assigning a letter to each trump is apparent: there are 22 trump cards and 26 letters. This we overcome by assigning the consonants to the trumps, and the vowels to each of the suits, as we already discussed in the chapter 3 (The Four Ways). Strictly speaking, it does not really matter which letter goes with which card, as long as a sensible pattern can be made. For the sake of reason, we might as well work with the Tree pattern so the Sangreal pattern makes sense. Table 3 on page 247 will show you the tarot alphabet suggested. The reason for associating an alphabetical letter with a tarot card is because our ordinary objective thoughts are usually formed in terms of words composed of those letters. So if we identify these with the cards, we shall eventually come to think tarot in its own terms, and if those make contact with classes of consciousness in a higher category than our own, then we shall gain from such an ability.

It should be understood that the Sangreal association of alphabetical letters with tarot trumps and suits is virtually the same as those ascribed to our Holy Tree of Life version. There seems no need to have different attributions for the two systems when the same one will serve both purposes admirably. Nevertheless, some interesting points have been brought to light.

In the case of the Sangreal System, the central stationary trump, Strength, which is normally M, takes the additional significance of U. This combination (UM) means "Mother" in Hebrew or Arabic. It could also mean "Mum" in English, or even the sacred AUM of the Hindus. To place a Mother-Concept in the center of the Sangreal design seems more than appropriate since all living beings emerge from their mothers originally.

The mobile perimeter trump of the Fool (with the normal attribution of Z) also has the Sangreal sense of U in this particular pattern. There is no exact U in Hebrew. If we take AZ in the Hebrew, it gives a sense of "then—at that time." If we use OZ, we have a goat. Z by itself means a sword, and the letter which

Table 3. The Tarot Alphabet on the Tree of Life and
Sangreal Systems.

Trump or Suit	Letter on Tree	Sangreal System	
Hierophant	B	B	
Hermit	C	C	
Star	D	D	
Judgement	F	F	
Emperor	G	G	
Temperance	H	H	
Death	J	J	
Hanged Man	K	K	
Justice	L	L	
Strength	M	U*	
Empress	N	N	
Tower	P	P	
Devil	Q	Q	
Lovers	R	R	
Chariot	S	S	
Sun	T	T	
Wheel of Fortune	V	V	
Priestess	W	W	
World	X	X	
Magician	Y	Y	
Fool	Z	U†	
Moon	Th	Th	
Shields	A	A	2nd Quadrant
Swords	E	E	4th Quadrant
Rods	I	I	3rd Quadrant
Cups	O	O	1st Quadrant
Truth-factor	U	U	As applicable.

*Strength, being central, carries extra U.
†The Fool, being peripheral, carries extra U.

serves for O (Ayin) means both an eye and the vital Zero of the Nil-Concept behind the apex of the Tree of Life. In Arabic, "ain" means a well-spring or water source, which is synonymous with life itself in desert areas.

So combining all those meanings together, we might sense a goatlike being with a persistent and stubborn nature wielding a sword as it wanders around the world while being watched over by the All-seeing Eye of God as it seeks its own source wherever it goes. Such is scarcely a bad simile for a Fool in search of his ultimate destiny, while wrecking a great deal of the world with wars and stupidities in the process!

Alphabet Exercises

Those who may be considering making contact with classes of inner consciousness connected with the tarot of the Sangreal should really begin something in this style unless they have very good reasons for adopting another. Having obtained a tarot deck – preferably one that shows the Minor Arcana in numerical rather than pictorial style – dedicate that deck to Sangreal purposes, and thereafter let it be used for nothing else.

Begin by laying out the cards as shown in the tarot cycle in figure 3 on page 108. Study the layout while holding the spare Fool card in your hand. Take an occasional glance at the Fool. Connect all the cards consciously while allowing your attention to be drawn from point to point as the cards seem to call. After a few minutes of this exercise, gather the cards up and hold the deck in your two hands while thinking about the Sangreal. Shuffle the cards slowly and thoughtfully for a little while, then put them back in their box. Do this exercise for several days, not more than once a day, until the deck feels "tuned in." Again, it is impossible to describe this process any more than a specific color can be described in words. It either "feels right" or it doesn't. You can hold the deck against your forehead so that the long edges of the cards come against your skin. Thus the whole deck comes in simultaneously close contact to you.

After you feel tuned in to your own deck, go through it face up and select the cards that spell SANGREAL. (See Table 2.) Lay them out and look at them. They will be the Chariot, followed by the Ace of Shields, then the Empress, Emperor, Lovers, Ace of Swords, two of Shields, and finally, Justice. This spread is interesting because it speaks specifically of earthlife and our need for establishing the rule of justice here if the work of the chariot is to be done. Now go back to figure 2 on page 30. Note that most of the letters come from the second quadrant of the cycle, with only one from the first and one from the third. The vowels oppose each other, being those of the Shield and the Sword, and there is nothing from the last difficult quadrant at all. The nature of this spread has a strange down-to-earth significance, with virtually none of the mystical and esoteric qualities that one might expect the Sangreal to show.

Right away this should indicate that the business of the Sangreal *is* mainly with this world. Man is supposed to make himself an Emperor, and woman an Empress in their own natures, rulers of themselves and all their realm by the power of two principles of Love and Justice. That is what the work of the Chariot is all about. There the message stands for anyone with insight to read. Could anything be clearer? Christians and Jews alike might note that this message seems straight out of the Bible. Both Old and New Testaments are involved. The message of the Old Testament summed up in one word was Justice, while that of the New is Love. Justice and Love combined are the principles which the Sangreal is trying to instill into humanity. What a message from a deck which was once called the Devil's picture book!

Next you might try spelling out your own name. There is not much need to lay out the cards for this venture, and the more the cards are laid out in the mind instead of on a table top, the greater will grow your understanding. Every name is bound to have its own meaning. Every single word in our language will. You could try taking any word whatever and "Sangrealizing" it.

Some surprising combinations will appear. In case you are tempted to try all the "dirty words" for an experiment, these have quite magnificent meanings in "Sangrealese," and why shouldn't they? The dirt is only in the minds of those intending it. As a king once said: "On y soit qui mal y pense."

The next logical thing is to pick out a "message for the day." This is best done early in the morning so you will have a subject to think about at odd moments during the day. The best tarot to use for this is the "travelers" size because the cards can so easily be held in one hand while being dealt with the other. First shuffle the deck a few times in your left hand, and then begin moving your left thumb and push a few cards at a time into the fingers of your right hand. As the cards pass from one hand to the other, stop and select one on impulse, laying it face down immediately. Continue this action until eight cards have been chosen, then put the rest of the deck away and turn the cards up for reading. First look at the spread as a whole to note if any particular suit predominates, then note the numbers of each card and associate them with their concepts, lastly considering the relationship with that principle through the suit concerned. An eight-card spread is chosen because that is the same number as the letters of the word *Sangreal*.

Make a written note of the cards with their letter-values underneath. This will form a "Word of the Day," or for those who love long words, *Logohemera*. The word may be used for invocation of inner contacts during the day only. A kind of "Sangreal Password" for mental intonation, something similar to a mantra used for transcendental meditation but a great deal more sophisticated than that. Each letter should be given its full sonic and rhythmic value. For example, a spread of 3 of Swords, Ace of Swords, Knight of Rods, 10 of Shields, 7 of Rods, 7 of Shields and 7 of Cups would produce the "word" EEIAIIAO. This should be pronounced Ee Ee I Yay I Yi Yay Oh. Of course, you should feel free to select as many or as few cards as may be convenient. The principle is a lot more important than the practice.

There is a specific way of handling the tarot which will help very considerably. When the cards are slid from the left hand into the right, the fingertips of the right hand should actually contact the face of the cards as the sliding action is taking place. The movement of the pack is therefore controlled by the pressure of your left thumb on the back of the cards, and the fingers of your right hand on their faces. Although your physical eyes cannot possibly identify any of the cards from their backs, your fingertips traversing their faces make an adequate agency for the inner self to use so that a subconscious message can be sent to the brain in time to stop the process and select a card. "Seeing with fingertips" is a faculty known to parapsychologists as a relatively rare gift, and has been noted in physically blind people. The probability is that the ability is more widespread than might be supposed, but has not yet been studied at sufficient depth to remark any relevant factors. Human tactile capabilities are a much neglected branch of practical psychology.

A lot of experiments can be carried out with the magic passwords of the day or special symbols selected under the aegis of the Sangreal. They can be taped and played back for appreciation in a variety of styles to discover what response is forthcoming from the hearer. Differing chants and rhythms can be invented for applying them to various circumstances. On the surface, of course, these may sound like nonsense words. Most of our modern miscalled music is nothing but a combination of three sonic elements—a screech or a whine from a vocalist, a twang from an electric guitar, and a heavy thump or bang from a drum or percussion instrument. If commercialized combinations of just three types of sound connected by relatively senseless words can produce demonstrable effects on young undisciplined minds, how much more significant should reactions with Sangrealized values be on minds prepared to accept spiritual disciplines on encounter levels? Another point to bear in mind is the availability of the human psyche to inner influences. How is the constructive consciousness of God to reach us except through whatever our minds can comprehend? We are mainly connected with commonplace conditions of physical life such as sex, food, self-protection, and the like. How else is it possible to contact the consciousness of an ordinary human being except through such channels?

• • •

Once the tarot has opened up its inner channels of communication, the actual physical cards become less and less necessary as their inner equivalents continue working on their own in the consciousness of whoever has absorbed them deeply enough. They are, after all, only a means of making links between the two different conditions of ordinary worldly awareness, and the instinctual state of deep intuitional subconsciousness. It is even possible to be selective as to the levels of such states by setting the sequence of the Major and Minor Arcana. In other words, just as you have to dial the correct numbers of a telephone to contact a required individual, so is it necessary to activate the ideas of the tarot in the right order before you come in contact with the specific area of consciousness you seek. If the Qabbalistic code is used, the Tree of Life inner intelligences will be signaled, and if the Sangreal circuit is operated, then its appropriate agencies will respond. There are, of course, many other combinations, and not all of them are favorable. At least the Tree or Sangreal system puts you on safe ground.

Let us be absolutely definite that the Sangreal is not God, but an evolutionizing influence as it were emitted from that God, Supreme Being, or whatever else the Life Force of our Universe may be. There is certainly nothing to prevent you from seeking the Sangreal within yourself if you sincerely and honestly intend to commence the quest and continue it to a Grail conclusion. It must be borne in mind that the Quest is not just a "one incarnation" affair, but continues indefinitely until an individuation takes place which may be described as "Gaining the Grail." It is not enough just to *want* the Grail, that is totally insufficient. Such an objective must be loved and *needed* to the point of a desperation which exceeds the need of life. There is an old story told of a disciple who implored his Master to tell him how Truth could be found. The Master told the pupil to fetch a bucket of water. Thinking he was to be shown a vision in the water, the lad brought a bucketful and set it down. He was then instructed to sit and gaze deeply into the water. When the pupil complied, his Master seized him by the back hair and forced his head under the surface until he nearly drowned. At the psychological moment, the Master pulled the lad's head clear and announced, "When you need Truth as desperately as you needed air, it will reveal itself to you." The same story could be applied to the Sangreal.

When the Sangreal is needed with the same intensity that instigates the human life-drive on its most potent and primal levels, it will make conscious contact with the human sender of such a summons because it *must*. It has to be called with *all* the heart, *all* the mind, and *all* the soul. Nothing less will serve. If it should ever be asked how any human could possibly love an abstract idea to such a degree, the answer is that it is no more abstract than Life itself, and only considered abstract because we have not yet come close enough to it. None would deny that love is possible between two ordinary human beings, and yet do we really love that other person, or simply our idea of that person in our own mind? That is how close the Sangreal comes to anyone. Only if and when we ever learn the true value of what we hold within ourselves will we be fit to gain the Grail. Meanwhile if such a simple and easily obtained object as a deck of tarot cards can help us calculate even a fraction of that value, why should any thinking human hesitate to try them?

Why indeed?

That could easily have been the fatal question of the Sangreal. Just, "Why?"